Older People and Their Needs
A Multidisciplinary Perspective

Dedication

This book has been created in appreciative memory of parents, older friends and relatives, and to thank those who accompany them.

Older People and Their Needs

A Multidisciplinary Perspective

Edited by
GIANETTA CORLEY PHD

Chartered Educational Psychologist

W

WHURR PUBLISHERS

LONDON

© 2000 Whurr Publishers
First published 2000 by
Whurr Publishers Ltd
19b Compton Terrace, London N1 2UN, England

British Library Cataloguing in Publication Data
A catalogue record for this book is available from the
British Library.

ISBN: 1 86156 083 4

Printed and bound in the UK by Athenaeum Press Ltd,
Gateshead, Tyne & Wear

Contents

Contributors

Rita Beaumont is a Registered Nurse who is Head of Department: Primary and Continuing Care at the University of Luton. Previously she held posts in the Health Service managing Elderly Care Services.

Dawn Brooker is a Consultant Clinical Psychologist working in the NHS. She is also a freelance trainer and has published widely in the sphere of dementia care. She is an Honorary Lecturer at Birmingham, Coventry and Warwickshire Universities.

Rodger Charlton is a general medical practitioner and a Senior Lecturer in Primary Health Care at Keele University. He was Visiting Fellow, Otago University, New Zealand 1991–1992.

June Copeman is Senior Lecturer at Leeds Metropolitan University and from 1991–1998 was Chair of the Nutrition Advisory Group for Elderly People of the British Dietetic Association.

Gianetta Corley has carried out research, provided postgraduate psychologist training and published on visual impairment and the visual processing of words and pictures, and in this sphere she was an Honorary Consultant Educational Psychologist.

Alison Culverwell is a Consultant Clinical Psychologist in East Kent, having moved from Leeds Community and Mental Health Trust where she worked with older adults and in psychotherapy research.

Mary Gilhooly is Professor of Health Studies and Director of the Centre of Gerontology and Health Studies, University of Paisley. A psychologist by training, Professor Gilhooly's research spans the disciplines of psychology, sociology, law, ethics and gerontology.

Liz Glasgow is the Continence Physiotherapist at the Peter James Centre, Melbourne, Australia. She has postgraduate training in Continence and Pelvic Floor Rehabilitation.

Wendy Gnich is a doctoral candidate at the Centre of Gerontology and Health Studies, University of Paisley, and research associate at the Research Unit in Health and Behavioural Change, Edinburgh University.

Paul Harris is Head of the Psychology Service at Cefn Coed Hospital, Swansea. His published research includes work on identity and self concept. He was formerly Senior Tutor in Psychology, University of Papua New Guinea.

Peter Huxham is Coordinating Chaplain for the Taunton and Somerset NHS Trust since 1992, following thirty years in parish ministry in the Dioceses of Ripon and Salisbury and as a Canon in the Diocese of Salisbury.

Karen Hyland is Dietitian for the Elderly in Barnet Healthcare Trust and Chair of the Nutrition Advisory Group for Elderly People of the British Dietetic Association. Her clinical specialism in dietetics is the care of older people.

Ritchard Ledgerd is Student Officer at the College of Occupational Therapists, London. He has worked as an occupational therapist with older people with mental health problems and physical disabilities in the community, in hospital wards and day hospitals.

Mary Lightfoot is a social worker who has worked mainly in psychiatric settings. Her last post was as Principal Clinical Social Worker in a specialist team at the Portman Clinic, London.

Carol Martin is a Consultant Clinical Psychologist with older people in Leeds Community and Mental Health Trust and lectures at the University of Leeds. She is a UKCP registered psychotherapist.

Liz Randall is Deputy Chief Physiotherapist at the Peter James Centre, Melbourne. She is also a successful sportswoman, representing Australia many times in Masters Orienteering.

Gwilym Wyn Roberts is Group Head, Education and Practice, at the College of Occupational Therapists. He was formerly Course Leader, St Bartholomews and The Royal London School of Occupational Therapy, Queen Mary and Westfield College, University of London.

Lis Schild is Principal Lecturer in the Department of Applied Social Studies in the University of Luton. She was formerly team leader of a hospital social work team for elderly people.

Mary Tilki is Principal Lecturer at Middlesex University. Her particular interests are old age in minority ethnic groups and she is currently researching old age in the Irish community in Britain.

Barbara Wall is a Senior Tutor at the London Foot Hospital and School of Podiatric Medicine. She was previously Senior Lecturer at the University of Westminster – Division of Podiatric Medicine (Chelsea School of Chiropody).

Preface

The final decades of the human lifespan are undeniably complex and challenging, both for individuals themselves and for those who accompany them, and much remains to be illuminated and transmitted about how to prepare well for dignity and quality of life during those years.

This book is presented primarily as a resource for the young postgraduate reader, in professional training, or just trained, or for the older person undertaking further professional development and updating. There is also much which will be of value to those countless informal and family carers who are seeking information and support for their demanding, undervalued and often solitary task. It is not intended to cover basic knowledge nor is the focus on service delivery or policy, though these are inevitably in the background. Each chapter author writes firstly for the reader in his or her own profession. Successful multidisciplinary working demands sound confidence in the value of one's own professional contribution but also an appreciation of the skills of other professionals. The chapters allow many glimpses into the way in which different professional people conceptualize their work and put their unique training into practice. The authors demonstrate a rich resource of practical ideas for wider dissemination and professional use.

This book is being written as the new millennium approaches and as the matter of welfare reform is still a prominent part of the political agenda. The public debates, however, are invariably a question of where responsibility should lie for the provision and cost of a basic level of care at the end of life. Responsibility has been thrust away from the state and back to the individual, family and the community. The intention here is to look beyond the debates on funding and resources, crucial as these debates are, and to uncover and pass on innovative ideas. Many of these ideas demand action early in life – action to preserve health including dental care, action to make adequate financial plans, action to maintain family or community networks, action to render housing, public transport and public buildings accessible for older, less mobile people. It is a matter for regret that there has not been space to include every discipline involved in working to make improvements for older people – those in the sphere of communication and in the leisure, hotel and holiday industry, for example. It should ultimately no longer be possible or necessary to deny the inevitability of ageing nor to be marginalized by the media ideal-ization of youth.

Many professions are now training young personnel for life cycle work, breaking down former barriers between training to work only with children, or only with older people. There is an attempt to look for the common principles which will enable a professional person to apply common skills across the human age span, given appropriate continued professional training and development. Viewing the life cycle as a continuum, the damaging ghetto-ization of older people and those who accompany them could be gradually diminished. A feeling of well-being in older age could become a matter for admiration, emulation and opportu-nity, planned and worked for from the outset.

The chapters each stand alone and do not necessarily demand sequen-tial reading. There are nonetheless themes which permeate the whole structure. The most powerful of these are firstly the presence of rampant ageism in our society, reflected by the undervaluing of the place of older people in it and those who accompany them, and secondly the need for a recognition of the skills required in this sphere, supported by appropri-ately specialized training.

The first and last chapters, by a medical practitioner and by a priest, both encompass this life cycle – both have a meaningful role as a human life begins and ends. Chapter 2 concerns the dynamics of financial security and well-being in the context of the ageing process. Chapters 3 and 4 address issues of nutrition and podiatry vital to lifelong health. Chapters 5 and 6 look at roles and identity as an older person begins to require nursing or care. Comparisons between ethnic communities allow increased aware-ness of different perceptions of roles and support systems. Chapters 7, 8 and 9 concern relationships and communication with older people in their negotiation of tranquillity of mind and in the telling of their unique story. The position of people belonging to minority ethnic communities is considered by attending to the situation of older Irish people in the UK. Chapters 10 and 11 turn to matters of physical independence, mobility and continence and to ways of sustaining quality of life. Chapter 12 is written not from the professional's angle but from the perspective of family carers. Current examples are provided which illuminate the struggles for indepen-dence of older people today. Chapter 13 presents an account of the new quality of dementia care achievable in residential settings.

Multidisciplinary working is difficult to achieve in a culture accustomed to hierarchy, but no one profession has all the skills: each has much to gain from working with others. Older people benefit well in sustaining their desired independence where the professions have been able to accord them a seamless service.

In conclusion, the editor desires to thank all those who have assisted most generously in the creation of this book and in particular Dr Ved Varma in London for his constant professional advice and support, so warmly and unstintingly offered.

Gianetta Corley
Chester and London 1999

Chapter 1
Bereavement – a Natural Part of the Life Cycle

RODGER CHARLTON

It could be disputed whether or not bereavement is a medical problem (Charlton, 1997, 1998), but in terms of the lay person,

> 'Grief is like a raging river.' (Wrobleski, 1994)

It is a significant life event within the life cycle and it is inevitable that all health care professionals will encounter patients who have experienced or are presently experiencing bereavement. Shakespeare in his play, *Much Ado About Nothing* (Act 3, Sc. 2), states,

> 'Everyone can master a grief but he that has it.'

It is a severe loss, something which we cannot conceive, as Freud (1915) suggests,

> 'Our own death is indeed unimaginable and whenever we make the attempt to imagine it we can perceive that we really survive as spectators ... at bottom no one believes in his own death, or to put the same thing in another way, in the unconscious every one of us is convinced of his own immortality.'

Similarly, bereavement in a client or a patient may make a health care professional uncomfortable as he or she is also reminded of his or her own mortality.

Bereavement can take many forms: death, stillbirth, miscarriage, broken relationships such as divorce or loss of employment. In the case of an elderly person, it is likely to be a spouse and possibly a pet or even a child. Health care professionals are trained to treat people who suffer with illness. It must therefore be asked if it is appropriate for them to become involved with the care of the bereaved and thus whether or not bereavement is a health care problem and so one that may lead to illness.

Definition of health

The World Health Organization (WHO) definition of health is:

'The state of complete physical, mental and social well-being, not merely the absence of disease.'

Health is impaired when one or more of these factors that contribute to well-being are compromised and so an illness results. Bereavement is no exception and, as will be discussed later, bereavement has associated morbidity and mortality (Charlton, 1996).

The life cycle

'To die is as natural as to be born.' (Sir Francis Bacon, *Essays*, 'Of Death')

Death and birth are fundamental events which are diametrically opposed in relation to the life cycle. Birth is the providing of new life and hence a new member into the family, whereas bereavement is the taking away of life and the loss of a family member (Charlton and Dolman, 1995). Both events create emotions and reactions of considerable depth and intensity. However, it is of interest that until very recently, medical school training devoted 10 weeks or more to training a doctor how to deliver a baby safely into the world, but only half a day at a hospice showing how to ensure that a dying patient does not leave the world in pain, and with little or no mention of the phenomenon of bereavement.

A reduction in the mortality rate of the Western world has taken place during the present century, with cures being made available for once fatal diseases, such as tuberculosis. Thus, it has been suggested that death has been transformed from being an accepted everyday occurrence and natural part of the life cycle, into a 'taboo subject' (Emerson, 1983). It is rare for the majority of the public to see a dead body (Earnshaw-Smith, 1981) and so death anxieties of the general public may inevitably be enhanced as death more frequently occurs out of sight in hospitals and hospices. Dying has been described as being 'medicalized' (Field, 1994) in institutions where 71% of people die (Thorpe, 1993) and has been reflected upon in a newspaper article as follows:

'We belong to a generation unique in human history; a generation for whom the sight of death and the experience of dealing with it have become alien even to those of advanced years.' (Turner, 1989)

It is therefore probable that the majority of the public have little experi-ence of death and when suddenly faced with it in themselves, or their close relatives, turn to doctors as the initial contact and regard doctors as experts. A questionnaire survey at Birmingham University revealed that only 30.5% ($n = 36$) of clinical introductory students and 52.4% ($n = 75$) of final year students had talked with someone who knew that they were dying (Hull, 1991).

It could be suggested (Charlton and Dolman, 1995) that death is no longer accepted as the natural conclusion to the life cycle. In addition, opportunistic grieving is reduced with the quick and efficient disposal of the corpse by cremation. Reminders of the deceased are discouraged within society as people now feel uncomfortable with them and so instead the bereaved are advised to 'keep busy'. The institutionalization of death, its deritualization, the pressure of society to limit mourning, the decline of the extended family, the breakdown of the community and the drift from religion and cultural traditions has had the effect of oppressing grief and so isolating the bereaved.

Yet, people need to be given time and space to experience their grief surrounded by those they love, know and trust. Whereas purposeful activity can be a very therapeutic part of the healing process for the bereaved, it should not be used to compromise the gentle encouragement that is needed to support the bereaved in the exploration and expression of their grief within each individual's life cycle.

Definitions of bereavement

Bereavement has been defined as 'being robbed of anything we value' (Dening, 1994). It is a loss, particularly the loss through death, but also the loss of a limb, partner, strength, health, independence and many other things. Grief can be defined as the psychological reactions to that loss and mourning is the particular form of grief which is experienced when the bereavement is the death of a personal intimate such as spouse, family member or friend (Field, 1993). An understanding of these concepts is of singular importance to practising health care professionals if they are to offer clients and their families appropriate 'whole person' care (Raphael, 1975).

It has been said that, 'There is no human experience so universal as grief after a bereavement. It is the aching sense of loss, the anger of unjustified hurt, the struggle to adapt to an unwanted newness of circumstances and the absence of relationship' (Davidson, 1988). The trauma which the patient and those involved will experience, can be summarized as the loss which affects the spirit, emotions and psychological make-up of a being, and in turn the physical.

Anticipatory grief

In the case of any serious illness, it has been shown that the cycle of grief, for the patient and their intimates, begins with the breaking of the bad news to them (Kübler-Ross, 1969). Alternatively, it begins when the relatives permit themselves to recognize that the death is imminent or the patient permits himself or herself to anticipate his or her own death (Aldrich, 1963) and thus the anticipatory grief process of the cycle is embarked upon (Evans, 1994). The anticipatory grief process accelerates as the expected time of death draws closer, whereas conventional grief, whilst carrying on indefinitely, is considered to diminish in degree as time passes (Evans, 1994).

Bereavement as a 'medical' problem – impact of bereavement on health

McAvoy (1986) suggests that bereavement is a problem in the strict scientific sense and this has implications for the health of an individual through its associated morbidity and mortality.

Morbidity associated with bereavement

Surtees (1995) in a Scottish study surveyed the psychiatric morbidity patterns experienced by three groups of women six months before (pre) and four months after (post) the following events: (1) bereavement from their spouse, (2) spouse suffering a myocardial infarction and (3) women entering a women's refuge. The results shown in Table 1.1 were obtained using the Research Diagnostic Criteria of Spitzer, Endicott and Robins (1978), where a p value for statistical significance is given and NS where the result was not significant.

Table 1.1. Psychiatric morbidity patterns among three groups of women

	Pre (%)	Post (%)	p value
Any depressive disorder			
(1) Bereaved	9.4	42.6	0.0018
(2) Coronary carers	11.9	19.9	NS
(3) Refuge seekers	40.6	32.3	NS
Major depressive disorder			
(1) Bereaved	3.1	27.1	0.0039
(2) Coronary carers	6.3	8.1	NS
(3) Refuge seekers	28.1	9.2	0.06

This study was used to estimate the prevalence of depressive disorder and the measured effect of bereavement is striking. A similar study in the USA, which specifically looked at the spectrum of depressive phenomena after spousal bereavement, demonstrated that depressive phenomena are more prevalent, persistent and disabling in the first two years following bereavement. This study involved 350 widows and widowers in comparison with a matched control group of 126 demographically similar men and women (Zisook et al, 1994). A personally conducted observational study through carefully recorded case histories postulated a possible association between bereavement and the onset and rapid deterioration of Alzheimer's type dementia (Charlton, 1995).

Mortality associated with bereavement

Bereavement is also associated with increased mortality and this has been known about for a long time. In 1967, Rees published a paper in which he demonstrated a seven-fold increase in mortality among bereaved spouses within the first year of their bereavement when compared with a control group (Rees and Lutkins, 1967).

Considering the recorded effects of bereavement on both morbidity and mortality, it could be suggested that according to the 'Health of the Nation' targets recommended by the Department of Health this is a neglected area of health promotion. However, it should be asked how a health care professional might attempt to provide the necessary care for patients who are bereaved to prevent this associated morbidity and mortality. It should also be borne in mind that some of the evidence for associated mortality and morbidity is conflicting and care should be taken not to over-medicalize grief (Woof and Carter, 1995, 1997).

Management and facilitation of bereavement in the community

It is important to be clear that bereavement is a normal process. However, like birth, death has to a large extent been medicalized. It often occurs in institutions and is swiftly dealt with through disposal of the corpse in the efficient fifteen minute service and clinical atmosphere of the crematorium. Grieving is limited. In addition, with the breakdown of the extended family and decline in religious belief and lack of access to clergy, problems may arise.

Reactions to death are variable, do not necessarily follow a set pattern and cannot always be resolved. There are, however, certain identifiable stages and points of time when events happen more frequently than others and these stages of bereavement have been well described by many psychiatrists including Kübler-Ross et al (1972) and Murray Parkes (1993). Most people progress through these stages, but not necessarily all of them nor in any particular order (Silver, 1980) and a health care professional involved may be able to facilitate this process. If normal stages of bereavement were to be isolated they might be: distress and shock, denial, anger, feeling 'low in spirits', resolution and acceptance.

The grief reaction may on occasions and after a period of time be deemed to be 'abnormal'. A person may get 'stuck' in one of the stages of bereavement and the onset of 'pathological grief' may be witnessed and sometimes clinical depression diagnosed. In this circumstance bereavement has a profound effect on physical and emotional health with enduring functional impairments (Brown and Stoudemire, 1983) or as Burton (1981) defines it,

'Grief concealed strangles the soul.'

It is difficult to define when the grieving pattern is no longer normal and thus the onset of abnormal or 'pathological' grief. Two primary indicators are delayed acceptance or a person appearing to be unaffected by what has happened. Factors that predict a poor outcome and the development of pathological grief include low socioeconomic status, short terminal illness with little warning of impending death, multiple life crises and severe reactions to bereavement (Murray Parkes, 1964; Murray Parkes and Birtchnell, 1971).

One of the most difficult problems that has to be faced is that acquaintances often avoid the bereaved person, because of a feeling of inadequacy over what to say. The result is isolation, thus compounding the problem, and it has been observed that the pain remains with the bereaved and that they inadvertently develop a behavioural disguise that they use in public.

It can be argued whether or not bereavement, which is a natural process and part of the life cycle, is a 'medical' problem. However, in the circumstance of 'pathological' grief, it may be important to obtain a medical assessment. In the management of the grieving process some useful guidelines may be provided for both the lay carer and the professional carer and the following sections outline these.

Sudden death

When death is expected in the case of a loved one who has a terminal illness, there is time to come terms with what is to happen. However, death is always unexpected, even for those who are seemingly prepared. It is particularly difficult when a person dies suddenly without warning and there is then the unenviable task of having to inform a relative or family. Death may occur in the street, the casualty department or during an operation whilst under anaesthetic and it is something that is seldom addressed during health care professional training. It is a time that the relatives will always remember and, if handled badly, may leave lasting scars (McLauchlan, 1990).

Ways of conducting this difficult situation have been suggested, such as seeing the relatives in a private room with another member of staff, being empathetic, avoiding technical information, providing time, being aware of the need for moments of silence, dispelling any self-recrimination and encouraging any reactions such as crying (Bacon, 1989). It is important to review the situation after say half an hour and give the family time to be alone together and to facilitate private viewing of the deceased which will confirm the reality of the situation, initiate grieving and allow a chance to say goodbye. This is described below in a young person, but could easily apply to an older person.

A personal account is given by a doctor (Awooner-Renner, 1991), who after the death of her 17 year old son in a road traffic accident, describes how the natural reaction of the health care professionals is to constrain the griever and when they are in contact with the corpse they are advised 'not to do anything silly'. She recalled how she 'desperately needed to hold' her son, 'to look at him' and 'to find out where he was hurting'. She gives the impression that further training is required in this area concerning communication and sudden death. There is a need for the relatives to have time alone with the deceased person without restrictions, a situation where verbal communication is perhaps not required.

Sudden death and autopsy

In the situation of sudden death, training of health care professionals is needed in requesting consent from relatives for an autopsy (Waldron and Vickerstaff, 1975). In addition, doctors are poor at explaining to relatives the usefulness of autopsy as an examination and hence are hesitant about requesting consent. Relatives have reservations about its usefulness as most would prefer to maintain the physical dignity of a loved one, in preference to knowing the exact cause of death, and so often decline consent. The requesting doctor must display sensitivity and provide adequate time to counsel distressed relatives. In addition, it is important to arrange for follow-up and explanation of events if the relatives wish, for they will remember little, and a structured arrangement for bereavement counselling may be appropriate and to facilitate support for staff who are also grieving (Quill and Townsend, 1991).

The autopsy is a traumatic and intimate examination, especially in the eyes of the deceased's relatives. The useful information which it provides for professionals should not merely remain on file, but rather be disseminated to relatives who wish to learn the circumstances and cause of death (Turner and Raphael, 1997). Such information may aid the grieving process by dispelling feelings of doubt and guilt (Charlton, 1994). Thus a purpose to the autopsy emerges for the lay public in addition to satisfying medical inquiry. This may be further facilitated by the use of a post-autopsy conference with the clinician present so that the cause of death may be explained to the family and discussed (Valdes-Dapena, 1984).

Bereavement support (family, charity and professional)

It has been identified that the best primary support for the bereaved is for a health care professional 'to understand and be available' (Stott and Finlay, 1986). In general practice, an ideal situation exists to help and support the bereaved and provide preventive care where problems are likely to occur. In today's health care provision, this is a fundamental primary health care team responsibility. A leaflet containing explicit written information concerning the necessary arrangements should be available at the time of death. It should contain all local contact points, reflect the ethnicity of the location and be reviewed on a regular basis (North, 1993).

When a bereavement has occurred, a key worker should be allocated from the primary health care team (North, 1993). Allocation will share the responsibility within the team for the continuation of bereavement care and it will also provide a focal care point for the bereaved person. The allocation should take into account the relationships that may already exist, as bereavement support often begins before a patient dies, through good care for the patient and their family. Perhaps the first useful rule is not to put off seeing the bereaved person. It is important to go as soon after the patient has died as is practicable. Second, care should be taken not to go on the day of the funeral ceremony. Third, the person should be given time and periods of silence may be used for non-verbal communication to indicate empathy. The visit should largely be cathartic, with the health care professional spending most of the time listening and thus reflecting the following thought:

> 'I will not insult you by trying to tell you that one day you will forget. I know that you will not. But at least in time you will not remember as fiercely as you do now, and I pray that time may be soon.' (Rattigan, 1953)

It is perhaps one of the most difficult situations for a health care professional and yet it is one which intimates will remember with gratitude if that person is sensitive. In many circumstances that professional may be the family doctor. The initial meeting is often conducted as a home visit and is rarely interpreted as an intrusion on private grief, but should reinforce that the person is a caring individual who may be approached and trusted with problems. To be effective, one has to have examined one's own feelings and fears about death and one's own responses to loss or possible loss. Our own sadness and despair and so empathy will greatly enhance the care we can give (Raphael, 1975). If contact is not established, an alternative might be to post an appropriate, personalized letter as follows:

Dear   ,

We were very sorry to hear that you have recently lost a loved one and would like to offer our sincere sympathy. This letter is to let you know that if I or one of my colleagues can be of any help to you during this very distressing time, please do not hesitate to contact us.

When someone we love dies, particularly someone on whom we have depended, one of our strongest emotions is likely to be sheer panic, a feeling of helplessness and not knowing what to do. Unfortunately during this time of personal distress, decisions and arrangements have to be made. To help you through this time we have made available a local information leaflet.

If you would like to discuss your situation, please let me know and I will organize for us to meet.

With our sincere condolences.

Yours sincerely

A series of reviews is required to assist intimates with progressing through the recognized stages of grieving and thus to prevent pathological grief arising through lack of follow-up or appropriate referral. It is advisable to make entries in the practice visits record to schedule a bereavement review but obviously consultations can be used for opportunistic review if more appropriate.

The initiation of the reviews is integral to the initial meeting when the practitioner can ask if there is anything practical he or she can do to help and make him- or herself available for follow-up. For example, the bereaved may like to come at a later stage to discuss the cause of death and the terminology used in the death certificate (Murtagh, 1983). Following the initial review, those thought to require social support and specialized counselling should be closely monitored and introduced to the local contacts for groups such as CRUSE, Sands or Compassionate Friends. In addition, one should be aware that the first anniversary of a bereavement is a time when someone may feel particularly low in spirits and may even develop inexplicable physical symptoms.

Bereavement counselling

Care and support can be provided by both simple befriending and organized counselling. They are not, however, the same thing but both can be of benefit to the bereaved. Befriending is offering friendship, a listening ear and companionship. In other words, a sharing of grief, where what is required is a good listener and someone with whom tears can be shared. It is seldom seen as an intrusion, for the bereaved are often grateful for a listening ear. This type of psychosocial support can be made available in a structured manner through a network of trained volunteers offering an unselfish, motivated and sympathetic service (Fusco-Karmann and Tamburini, 1994).

Counselling is the offering of a structured programme, identifying the physical, psychological, emotional and social needs of the bereaved person. Working through them in an organized manner is often referred to as 'grief resolution'. It requires the establishment of a working relationship built on trust in which the person is encouraged to express their feelings. This relationship alone should be of benefit. However, given the current situation, where time is a constraint and there is minimal provision made for counselling, an evaluation of a pilot scheme of bereavement counselling could be used to determine the actual benefit (Murray Parkes, 1980).

Befriending and counselling should take place in the situation that is most appropriate to the circumstances. However, they are best done in the home environment where more associations with the person who has died can readily be made. They should be conducted by appropriately trained members of the primary health care team although many different people may be able to help the bereaved, from a neighbour, to a counsellor, the clergyman and the doctor. In New Zealand the undertaker or funeral director continues to provide counselling and support for 12 months following the funeral as part of the contract with the bereaved.

Ideally the counsellor should help the person first to admit their loss and then to identify and ventilate feelings (Jones, 1989). To answer that oft posed question, 'Why?', it is important that they are given the opportunity to explore their feelings for life without their loved one, thus 'letting go'. Regular and available reassurance that their feelings are normal, and that grieving is a normal reaction, is vital. Finally, the most important thing is time, remembering that it often takes longer than the traditional year (Emerson, 1983) and the period is often regarded by the bereaved as a 'limbo of meaningless activity' which passes very quickly (Murray Parkes, 1975).

The process of grief

The process of grief is likened to that of healing, a process which allows the restoration of functioning to take place. Grief work is exhausting, for both the bereaved person and counsellor. Pain is inevitable and cannot be avoided. It stems from an awareness by both parties that neither can give the other what he or she wants. The helper cannot bring back the person who is dead, and the bereaved person cannot gratify the helper by appearing helped (Jones, 1989).

A model of grief which was initially proposed by Sigmund Freud in his work, *Mourning and Melancholia*, suggested that the process might be time limited and that the process should be completed or resolved after a year or two. He proposed that grief is a normal reaction to the loss of a loved one and that grieving is a painful process involving the withdrawal of ties to the deceased, a process called 'decathexis'. According to Freud, grief is 'like an open wound' and mourning should involve a gradual healing process; one of the main tasks of grieving is to achieve decathexis and so detach oneself from the emotional ties to the deceased so as to be able to form new relationships (Freud, 1917).

Death causes a disequilibrium within a person's social world and it might be suggested that four tasks should be undertaken when working with the bereaved (Horacek, 1991).

1. To accept the reality of the loss
2. The griever must experience the pain of grief.
3. To adjust to an environment that no longer includes the deceased
4. The mourner must withdraw emotional energy invested in the dead person and begin to reinvest this energy in other relationships.

Some people may get 'stuck' with the last task and two or more years may be required to complete the tasks. There is evidence that for many individuals mourning may be 'time-unlimited' and that life may always involve despair and associated psychological sequelae or that some people may continue to function normally with everyday living and yet continue to grieve. One study by Gorer (1965) that Horacek (1991) quotes suggests that 38% of people experience time-unlimited grieving of whom half continue to function normally. The assumption may be challenged therefore that grieving can ever be completed, as Freud suggests, within a period of two years. Perhaps redefining of grieving tasks is required so that the bereaved somehow find a way of continuing the relationship with their dead spouse that allows both an appropriate experience of grief and continuing involvement with the living. There have been many 'grief theorists' and it should be stated that it is not the length of time, by itself, that separates normal from abnormal grief reactions, but the reactions experienced over time (Horacek, 1991).

Bereavement, education and the health care team

Bereavement care is a vital area which is often neglected in both health promotion and medical education. In addition, a common theme that appears in the literature is the need for training to recognize the different stages of grieving, both in relatives and in members of the health care team (Taylor, 1989). The teaching of communication skills in this area is important and has many aspects. Communication skills in the area of bereavement should be extended not just to the close family and other intimates of the patient, but to the members of the health care team who should also be given an opportunity to grieve, as they too may also feel a sense of loss (Devassy, 1989).

Meeting the needs of the older person who is grieving

The life cycle is such that with increasing age, adaptation to a new situation becomes more difficult. There are several major life events. One study recorded 43 of these events and was repeated in 1965, 1977 and 1995 and the findings demonstrate that the death of a spouse was the most significant life event (Miller and Rahe, 1997). Old age can be seen as a succession of losses, gradual or sudden, and in addition to the death of a spouse, close friends and family, these may include sensory loss (vision, hearing), memory, employment through retirement, physical fitness and mobility, and worst of all, the loss of independence. There is also a loss of life expectancy and this replaces the perception through life of immortality. This gives rise to the shocking awareness of inevitable and even imminent death, which rapidly replaces the feeling that it is a long time off (Pitt, 1998).

In addition to these problems, there may be anhedonia, the loss of enjoyment in activities that normally bring pleasure, which is one of the biological symptoms of depression. Furthermore, depression in old age is often undiagnosed and untreated. An editorial in the *British Medical Journal* in 1988 states that severe depression affects about 3% of elderly people, but no mention of bereavement is made, although it is stated that elderly patients often minimize feelings of sadness and may become physically preoccupied (Baldwin, 1988). Depressive illness in late life often follows a major adverse life event, like bereavement or acute life-threatening illness, but the association may not always be that the loss precedes the depression: depression may cause loss. Depressed people do not take care to take care of themselves and may become ill, have accidents, and die from self-neglect as well as deliberate self-harm. For others it is a bitter struggle against overwhelming odds where grief becomes abnormal or pathological.

'Do not go gentle into that good night.
Rage, rage against the dying of the light.' (Dylan Thomas, 1914–1953)

It is perhaps true to say that with the advent of counselling there is a growing awareness of the many psychological reactions that may follow the death of a loved one. The elderly are particularly at risk of problems as there may not be a supportive network. Some individuals may present to their GP with symptoms that may initially appear unrelated to grief, presenting as anxiety or depression or in some cases completely somatized (Jones, 1989).

In elderly people the grieving process is lengthier than might be expected and grief-related reactions may include confusion, depression and preoccupation with thoughts of the deceased. Such reactions may be confused with illnesses such as dementia. Another problem that may affect the elderly is 'bereavement overload', caused by multiple losses, not just the death of a spouse (Horacek, 1991).

Conclusion

Bereavement has serious potential consequences for the 'Health of the Nation'. Professionals need to appreciate the unpredictability of the duration of grief and to gain a healthy respect for its natural course in each individual family (Chesler, 1993). It is important to see families after death and if possible several months later to answer questions and help to alleviate their inner turmoil of grief.

Input of care has to be sensitive and carefully planned, remembering that support services can be difficult to 'implement without intruding on people's emotions at a time when they cannot think beyond their pain' (Gorman, 1995). In the case of normal grief, the primary health care team may be in the most ideal situation to help; in the case of pathological grief, referral to a bereavement counsellor or a psychiatrist may be appropriate.

Bereavement is a healing process in which adjustments are made by relatives to their loss in an attempt to come to terms with it (Preston, 1989). The death of a patient is not the end of care, but continues with bereavement care for those who grieve. As we are not easily able to 'calibrate suffering' (Wilkes, 1965) and thus identify grief in a quantifiable manner, it is important for professionals to avoid the notion that people should 'pull themselves together' or that they 'will get over it'.

The support of those who grieve will enable the grief process to proceed smoothly, albeit painfully and help to prevent pathological grief and so psychiatric sequelae. This type of care is a 'healing' therapy for restoring a person to renewed function, a changed person but nevertheless a survivor (Townsend, 1991).

'Grief is itself a medicine.' (William Cooper)

Acknowledgement

The author acknowledges The Claire Wand Fund of the British Medical Association which has funded a research project in bereavement and its sequelae.

References

Aldrich CK (1963) The dying patient's grief. Journal of the American Medical Association, 184(5), 329–31.

Awooner-Renner S (1991) I desperately needed to see my son. British Medical Journal, 302, 356.

Bacon AK (1989) Death on the table. Some thoughts on how to handle an anaesthetic-related death. Anaesthesia, 44(3), 245–8.

Baldwin B (1988) Editorial: Late life depression – undertreated? British Medical Journal, 296, 519.

Brown J and Stoudemire A (1983) Normal and pathological grief. Journal of the American Medical Association, 250(3), 378–82.

Burton R (1981) In: F Dell and P Jordan-Smith (eds) The Anatomy of Melancholy, vol. 2, p. 107. London: JM Dent & Sons.

Charlton R (1994) The post mortem [Letter]. New Zealand Medical Journal, 107, 516.

Charlton R (1995) The onset of dementia following bereavement. Australian Family Physician, 24(7), 1233–6.

Charlton R (1996) Support for widowers. British Journal of General Practice, 46, 113.

Charlton R (1997) Seminar to the Department of Psychiatry, The Medical Institute, Keele University. 20 November 1996.

Charlton R (1998) Bereavement – a medical problem? Parapraxis, 3(2), 31–4.

Charlton R and Dolman E (1995) Bereavement: A Protocol in Primary Care. British Journal of General Practice 45, 427–30.

Chesler MA (1993) Introduction to psychosocial issues. Cancer, 71, 3245–50.

Cooper W (1968) Charity 159. In: B Spiller (ed) Cowper: Verse and Letters. London: Hart Davis.

Davidson P (1988) Grief: a literary guide to psychological realities. New Zealand Family Physician, 15(4), 146.

Dening F (1994) The good of grief. Healthcare, Spring, 31–33.

Devassy KS (1989) A piece of my mind: the empty times. Journal of the American Medical Association, 261, 2699.

Earnshaw-Smith E (1981) Dealing with dying patients and their relatives. British Medical Journal, 282, 1779.

Emerson J (1983) Living through grief. Nursing Mirror, 79 (Issue: 9 Nov), 2–7.

Evans AJ (1994) Anticipatory grief: a theoretical challenge. Palliative Medicine, 8(2), 159–65.

Field D (1993) Education for terminal care in the undergraduate medical curriculum. Critical Public Health, 4(3), 11–19.

Field D (1994) Palliative medicine and the medicalisation of death. European Journal of Cancer Care, 3, 58–62.

Freud S (1915/1959) Thoughts for the times on war and death. In: Collected Papers, Volume IV. New York: Basic Books.

Freud S (1917/1957) Mourning and Melancholia. London: Hogarth Press and Institute for Psychoanalysis.

Fusco-Karmann C and Tamburini M (1994) Training volunteer trainers. European Journal of Palliative Care, 1, 50–1.

Gorer G (1965) Death, Grief and Mourning. Garden City, NY: Doubleday.

Gorman A (1995) An evaluation of a bereavement support service. Palliative Care Today, 4(3), 38–9.

Horacek BJ (1991) Toward a more viable model of grieving and consequences for older persons. Death Studies, 15, 459–72.

Hull FM (1991) Death, dying and the medical student. Medical Education, 25, 491–6.

Jones A (1989) Bereavement counselling: applying ten principles. Geriatric Medicine, 9, 55.

Kübler-Ross E (1969) On Death and Dying. New York: Macmillan Press.

Kübler-Ross E, Wessler S and Avioli LV (1972) On death and dying. Journal of the American Medical Association, 221, 174–9.

McAvoy BR (1986) Editorial: Death after bereavement. British Medical Journal, 293, 835–6.

McLauchlan CAJ (1990) Handling distressed relatives and breaking bad news. British Medical Journal, 301, 1145–9.

Miller MA and Rahe RH (1997) Life changes scaling for the 1990s. Journal of Psychosomatic Research, 43(3), 279–92.

Murray Parkes C (1964) Recent bereavement as a cause of mental illness. British Journal of Psychiatry, 110, 198–204.

Murray Parkes C (1975) Bereavement: Studies of Grief in Adult Life. Harmondsworth: Pelican Books.

Murray Parkes C (1980) Bereavement counselling: does it work? British Medical Journal, 281, 3.

Murray Parkes C (1993) Bereavement. Chapter 14. In: D Doyle, GW Hanks, N MacDonald (eds) Oxford Textbook of Palliative Medicine, pp 665-678. Oxford: Oxford University Press.

Murray Parkes C and Birtchnell J (1971) Bereavement. Proceedings of the Royal Society of Medicine, 64, 279–82.

Murtagh J (1983) Picking up the pieces: the aftermaths of three deaths. Australian Family Physician, 12(4), 280.

North GN (1993) Audit: counselling of the bereaved. Shiregreen Medical Centre, Sheffield (Unpublished).

Pitt B (1998) Coping with loss series: Loss in late life. British Medical Journal, 316, 1452–4.

Preston J (1989) The consequences of bereavement. The Practitioner, 233, 137–9.

Quill TE and Townsend P (1991) Bad news: delivery, dialogue and dilemmas. Archives of Internal Medicine, 151, 463–8.

Raphael B (1975) The presentation and management of bereavement. Medical Journal of Australia, ii, 909–11.

Rattigan T (1953) Collected Works. London: Hamilton.

Rees W and Lutkins S (1967) Mortality of Bereavement. British Medical Journal, iv, 13–16.

Shakespeare W (1907 edition) Much Ado About Nothing. London: The University Press.

Silver RT (1980) The dying patient: a clinician's view. American Journal of Medicine, 68, 473–5.

Spitzer RL, Endicott J and Robins E (1978) Research diagnostic criteria: rationale and reliability. Archives of General Psychiatry, 35, 773–82.

Stott NCH and Finlay IG (1986) Care of the Dying. Edinburgh: Churchill-Livingstone.

Surtees P (1995) In the shadow of adversity: The evolution and resolution of anxiety and depressive disorder. British Journal of Psychiatry, 166, 583–94.

Taylor AJW (1989) Viewpoint: Grief counselling from the mortuary. New Zealand Medical Journal, 102, 562–4.

Thomas D (1951) 'Do not go gentle into that good night'. In H Gardner (ed) The New Oxford Book of English Verse, 1250–1950, p 942. Oxford: Oxford University Press.

Thorpe G (1993) Enabling more dying people to remain at home. British Medical Journal, 307, 915–18.

Townsend S (1991) Understanding grieving. New Zealand Family Physician, 18, 19–20.

Turner G (1989) The lost art of dying. Sunday Telegraph, 26 Feb, 14–15.

Turner J and Raphael B (1997) Editorial: Requesting necropsies. British Medical Journal, 314, 1499–500.

Valdes-Dapena M (1984) The post-autopsy conference with families. Archives of Pathology and Laboratory Medicine, 108, 497–8.

Waldron HA and Vickerstaff L (1975) Necropsy rates in the United Birmingham Hospitals. British Medical Journal, ii, 326–8.

Wilkes E (1965) Terminal cancer at home. Lancet, i, 799.

Woof R and Carter Y (1995) Bereavement care [Letter]. British Journal of General Practice, 45, 689–90.

Woof WR and Carter Y (1997) Review: The grieving adult and the general practitioner: a literature review in two parts (part 1). British Journal of General Practice, 47, 443–8.

Wrobleski A (1994) Suicide: Survivors: A Guide for Those Left Behind. Minneapolis: Minneapolis Publications.

Zisook S, Schuchter SR, Sledge PA, Paulus M and Judd LJ (1994) The spectrum of depressive phenomena after spousal bereavement. Journal of Clinical Psychiatry, 55 (supplement 4), 29–36.

Chapter 2
Health, Wealth and Happiness: Studies in Financial Gerontology

WENDY GNICH and MARY GILHOOLY

This chapter provides a review of the research literature in the field of financial gerontology. The main aim is to highlight the primary areas of interest in the field, focusing on the extent to which, and the reasons why, the financial needs of older individuals impact on quality of life. Inherent weaknesses in the literature will also be presented, with the aim of guiding future research.

The chapter is divided into five main sections which address the following questions: (1) What is financial gerontology? Many of the themes presented in the first section will be emphasized later in the chapter. (2) What factors have led to the emergence of the new discipline of financial gerontology? This section includes a discussion of the 'timeliness' of financial gerontology. The purpose of this section is to set the research literature in context by providing an overview of the current economic and political climate in developed countries. (3) What constitutes financial well-being? (4) Does financial well-being determine quality of life? Section 4 provides an overview of the research literature relating to the relationships between financial status, physical health and psychological well-being. (5) What are the problems and gaps in financial gerontology research? The fifth section draws attention to gaps and problems in developing research in this new field.

What is financial gerontology?

Neal Cutler, Director of the Boettner Institute of Financial Gerontology in Pennsylvania, USA, coined the phrase 'financial gerontology' in 1990 to describe the relatively new field of study concerned with the dynamics of financial security, well-being and quality of life, particularly in middle and old age (Cutler, 1997; Gregg, 1992). Financial gerontologists maintain that money is an empowering resource. They strive to understand what constitutes financial well-being and are concerned with the impact that financial well-being has on well-being and life satisfaction.

A key aim for those working in this field is to link academic study to professional practice with a view to increasing financial knowledge, financial security and, thus, quality of life. The diligent reader may have noticed that the focus of financial gerontology is on middle as well as later years of life. As Gregg (1992) states,

> 'Gerontology is not the study of old people ... Gerontology is the study of the process of ageing.'

Why study financial gerontology now?

Words like 'new' and 'emerging' are inherent in the definition of financial gerontology. Due to the changing structure and lifestyle of people in industrialized nations, the financial well-being of elderly people is becoming an increasingly important area for research. This section explains why financial gerontology is particularly timely in relation to the current political and economic climate in most developed countries. Three main factors are discussed: (1) concern over increasing dependency ratios, (2) the widening divide between rich and poor, and (3) changing lifestyles.

Concern over increasing dependency ratios

Elderly individuals are often portrayed as dependent on the working population. Increases in the proportion of non-working to working people, known as dependency ratios, are viewed as a major cause for concern.

Throughout the twentieth century the proportion of people aged 60 or over has increased in all countries of the world. Moreover, this has been coupled with a decrease in the birth rates of most industrialized nations. The consequence of these demographic shifts is that there will be fewer people of working age paying taxes to support the growing number of pensioners. In fact, the worker to pensioner ratio is projected to decrease dramatically during the first three decades of the next century in most industrialized countries (Ermisch, 1990). To illustrate, Europe as a whole will see a projected fall in the ratio of persons aged 15–64 to persons aged 65 and over from 6.62 in 1960 to 3.15 in 2025. Similar patterns are predicted for the USA from 6.45 in 1960 to 3.17 in 2025, with the largest deficit in Japan from 11.11 in 1960 to 3.17 in 2025 (United Nations, 1989).

The rising burden imposed on a declining working population by the growing number of retired individuals with increasing pension demands is making decreased reliance on the government an increasing explicit aim of social security policy (Falkingham and Victor, 1991). Walker (1992) notes that in the states of northern Europe 'pensions are the largest single item of welfare spending: 42 per cent in France, 47 per cent in Germany and Italy and 34 per cent in the UK'. For Britain alone this amounted to £21,000 million in 1989/90 (Cmnd 1014, 1990). Retirement pensions are, therefore, potentially a prime target for government cuts. In fact, Ermisch (1990) predicts that 'after the turn of the century, if not before, periodic political strife over pensions is likely to be in store for most if not all industrialized countries'. In light of population increases within the generally 'less able' sectors of the population, the over 75 age group, concern is also apparent over potential increases in bills for health and care services (Parker and Clarke, 1997).

Although there have been calls for a less pessimistic approach (e.g. Thane, 1988; Gillion, 1991) the British government is already looking to reduce spending. In a recent Green Paper, New Ambitions for our Country: A New Contract for Welfare, emphasis was put on the need for individuals to provide for secondary pensions and start saving towards retirement (Cmnd 3805, 1998).

The widening gap between rich and poor

In Britain, proposed government cuts to the social security budget are often justified by reports of the 'greening of the aged'. It is argued that the elderly are retiring with higher incomes and larger occupational pensions and more than ever before are likely to own their own home (Johnson and Falkingham, 1992). The reported affluence of those over retirement age gives credence to the idea of reducing pensions and other benefits to the older population and the increasing privatization of health care. As Johnson and Falkingham (1992) state, 'Ability to pay has already become the catch phrase of the nineties'.

It is rarely disputed that improvements in the absolute standard of living of British pensioners have occurred over the past few decades. The average income of those over 65 rose by 51% more than the rate of inflation between 1979 and 1992. However, there is increasing evidence to suggest that not all sectors of the population have benefited equally from economic improvements. Although the 'average' economic status of the elderly may be improving relative to other societal groups, those who are financially least well off have benefited less than the wealthier sections of the population. Thus a growing divide between rich and poor is evident. On average, a single pensioner was £37 a week better off in 1993 than in 1979. However, the poorest fifth of single pensioners gained just £12 a week (Hills, 1995). Quoting averages masks the variety of experiences within the pensioner population.

This expansive divide between rich and poor sectors of the population is by no means an exclusively British phenomenon. Although income may be more equally divided between older individuals in Sweden and Norway, the USA, Israel and Germany all face greater inequalities in income distribution than the United Kingdom (Walker, 1993).

Changing lifestyles

In addition to increased longevity and the pressure being placed on individuals by the state to be responsible for their own economic future, two fundamental changes have occurred with regard to work patterns during the twentieth century (Gregg, 1992). Firstly, people are spending longer periods within the education system and, tend to enter the workforce at a later age than past generations and secondly, society is moving towards earlier retirement. As Askham, Hancock and Hills (1995) point out, 'retirement can no longer be seen as a short period of rest before death'. In terms of an individual's 'wealth span' (Gregg, 1992), the 'Accumulation Stage' has been reduced, while the 'Expenditure Stage' is lengthened. Thus, financial resources have to be acquired in a shorter time and last a longer time. Askham et al also suggest that pensioners may have higher expenditure needs than in the past; a higher proportion of older people are now home owners and thus have the added costs of maintaining their own property. In addition, people may have to travel further afield to access shops and amenities, making a car a necessity. Moreover, it seems future generations of elderly individuals will not only have to strive to provide an adequate income and reasonable savings in retirement but will also have to provide for the potentially substantial costs of health and residential care in later life.

In conclusion, changes at both the individual and population level ensure that older individuals are going to be placed under increasing financial strain, unless they can ensure their own economic self-sufficiency in later years.

What constitutes financial well-being?

The term 'financial well-being' is fundamental to the study of financial gerontology but there is considerable controversy over how it should it be defined and measured. This section will begin with a very brief discussion of the important distinction between objective and subjective indicators of economic well-being. This is followed by a review of research, firstly, documenting the interesting relationship between objective and subjective financial well-being and, secondly, suggesting possible explanations for the unanticipated findings.

Financial well-being and measurement

There is considerable controversy surrounding how to measure financial well-being. While most would agree that income, savings and net worth are important components of financial well-being, others suggest that less concrete factors like satisfaction with material standard of living may be important. Providing a definition of financial well-being is not as straight-forward as it may appear. Economic well-being is a complex multi-faceted concept, and as yet the research literature does not provide a definitive guide to its make-up. However, an important distinction has been made between objective and subjective financial well-being. The importance of both objective and subjective measures is advocated in the literature.

Objective measures of financial well-being refer to factual conditions; household income or the total value of savings held by an individual provide an indication of objective economic well-being. By contrast, subjective measures refer to an individual's own evaluation of their life experiences. The extent to which people feel restricted by their financial state, or how satisfied they are with their current income, both provide subjective indicators of economic well-being.

The relationship between objective and subjective indicators of financial well-being

Common sense suggests that there should be a strong correlation between objective and subjective financial measures. In other words, those with higher incomes and savings would be more satisfied with their economic situation than those on low incomes with little or no savings. Surprisingly, the relationship between objective economic resources and financial satisfaction is often low, particularly in samples of older adults. Campbell, Converse and Rodgers (1976) found the correlation to be only 0.23 in a national sample of American adults. Moreover, George (1992) suggests that in quantitative terms, satisfaction with financial resources explains only half of the variance in satisfaction with financial resources for the adult population. This figure falls to approximately 25% if older adults' perceptions of financial well-being are compared with objective status.

Research consistently shows that older adults are often satisfied with substantially lower levels of income than their younger peers. For example, Fletcher and Lorenz (1985) examined various influences on the relationship between objective and subjective indicators of economic well-being. Results showed that the relationship between family income and financial satisfaction was weaker for those over 54 years of age.

Fletcher and Lorenz (1985) explain their findings in terms of 'accommodation theory'. They propose that those who experience fixed economic conditions, like the majority of older individuals, accommodate to them over a period of time. Thus, the standard to which they compare their current and future situations is lowered and satisfaction rises without a commensurate improvement in economic well-being. When little can be done to alter an undesirable situation, lowering the standards to which comparisons are made may provide an alternative, cognitive means of coping.

More recently, Goetting et al (1996) found, in a study of community-dwelling centenarians, that the overwhelming majority (95%) indicated that compared with others of the same age, they were doing the same or better in financial terms, when by objective standards the opposite would have been expected. It is suggested that older individuals tend to compare themselves with those who are worse off and that this process of downward comparison results in a more positive evaluation of the adequacy of their financial resources than their actual incomes would reveal. Furthermore, longitudinal research on a probability sample of older adults uncovered a strong bias towards positive assessments of financial adequacy even under conditions of poverty. The authors conclude that 'as older adults age they discount needs relative to available income' (Hazelrigg and Hardy, 1997). These and similar findings demonstrating positive assessments of life satisfaction in poverty have been termed the 'satisfaction paradox' (e.g. Olson and Schober, 1993).

The failure of economic status as a predictor of financial satisfaction amongst older people

Various social psychological processes are hypothesized as mediating the relationship between objective and subjective financial well-being (e.g. Liang and Fairchild, 1979; Liang, Kahana and Doherty, 1980). Most theories are based around the postulate that the degree of satisfaction experienced by a person at any one time is a direct function of a cognitive comparison between some standard and actual conditions (Diener, 1984). For example, 'relative deprivation theory' suggests that various subjective judgements of how one is doing in comparison with one's social circle may influence the relationship between objective reality and individual subjective assessments of that reality.

Support for the mediating role of various psychological comparisons was found by Usui, Keil and Durig (1985) in a community sample asking people aged 60 and over to compare their financial situation with that of their closest relative, friend and neighbour. The findings revealed that the better off the respondents perceived themselves to be financially, in relation to these 'significant others', the greater their life satisfaction. This relationship was independent of numerous indicators including objective income.

There is also evidence to suggest that comparison with one's own expectations and desires, or even how fair one's own financial situation is perceived to be, may help to explain the lack of correspondence between objective and subjective indicators of economic well-being, particularly for older people. These propositions are based on 'aspiration' and 'equity' theory respectively. Campbell et al (1976) tested the hypothesis that satisfaction levels were a function of the discrepancy between people's aspirations and achievements. Results indicated that this explanation only operated significantly for young and middle-aged adults.

Carp and Carp (1982) conducted a similar investigation with one important distinction; they included a measure of perceived equity. Once again, results showed that aspiration theory helped explain variance in financial satisfaction for younger adults but not older individuals. However, perceptions of equity were significant mediators of satisfaction for the older respondents. Thus, older adults who viewed their financial situation as fair were satisfied with their financial resources even if they did not meet up to their personal aspirations.

George (1992) suggests that, not only do people tend to lower their aspirations as they get older, but older individuals actually view the world as more equitable than their younger peers. Whereas younger adults are concerned with status attainment, and achievement, older adults are more concerned with maintaining their current economic position. Thus it appears that various social judgements or comparisons may help explain why older individuals are seemingly satisfied with lower levels of objective wealth than their younger peers. However, longitudinal research is needed before cohort differences can be ruled out and any firm conclusions drawn.

Does financial well-being determine quality of life?

Most people would agree that financial well-being is an important component of quality of life. Despite the often weak relationship between objective economic resources and financial satisfaction documented above, both objective and subjective financial indicators have been found to be important predictors of life quality.

Bild and Havinghurst (1976) consider adequate financial resources to be 'the single most important determinant of well-being of persons at any stage in the life cycle'. Although not an end in itself for many elderly people, research consistently documents that whether objectively or subjectively measured, financial well-being has a significant and direct impact on life satisfaction, psychological well-being and physical health, in addition to its indirect impact on well-being via access to resources and services in other highly valued life domains.

This section will present an overview of the literature pertaining to the relationships between financial well-being, physical health and psychological well-being. It begins by giving a brief overview of the relationship between economic status and physical health. However, the main body of the review concentrates on the relationship between financial well-being and subjective or psychological well-being. In order to elucidate the relationship between financial satisfaction and psychological health the focus is on potential mediators or intervening variables. The role of activity and the environment will be considered before discussing important findings from the literature on financial strain. The section will end on a positive note by discussing ways of avoiding the negative impact of financial strain in later life.

Economic status and health

A vast, well-established body of literature documents the relationship between socioeconomic status and physical health, with a higher prevalence of illness among persons of lower socioeconomic status (e.g. Palmore, 1981; Marmot et al, 1991). Moreover, there is evidence to suggest that the relationship between socioeconomic status and health does not only hold under conditions of poverty. Adler et al (1994) report evidence that the association occurs at every level of the socioeconomic hierarchy. In other words, those regarded as being at the top of the class distribution will also tend to have better health status than those in the middle of the distribution, although these groups are unlikely to be experiencing conditions of poverty. House et al (1990) concluded that people with higher socioeconomic status are able to delay not only mortality, but also significant morbidity and disability until comparatively late in life, whereas those in lower socioeconomic groups experience significant levels of mortality, morbidity and disability starting relatively early in mid life. As Smith (1994) notes, 'increased wealth can improve health and lengthen longevity for a number of reasons – better access to medical care, reduced risk behaviours and a better diet and nutrition to name just a few'.

Economic status, life satisfaction and psychological well-being

A similar pattern of results is apparent when one considers the relationship between socioeconomic status, subjective well-being and psychological well-being. Numerous studies suggest that there is a positive relationship between socioeconomic status and psychological well-being (e.g. Langer, 1963; Dohrenwerd and Dohrenwerd, 1969; Kessler and Cleary, 1980; Ying, 1992). Moreover, income is often reported to be the most influential component of socioeconomic status in relation to subjective well-being (Larson, 1978). Family income is repeatedly found to be an important determinant of life satisfaction (e.g. Edwards and Klemnack, 1973; Doyle and Forehand, 1984; Gitmez and Morcol, 1994).

Although less well investigated, subjective measures of financial well-being such as financial satisfaction and perceptions of financial adequacy are also repeatedly found to correlate with subjective well-being. Subjective financial well-being appears partly to mediate the effects of income on subjective well-being. George (1992) reviewed three studies that included measures of objective financial well-being, financial satisfaction and life satisfaction; all three documented that subjective financial well-being mediated the effects of income on subjective well-being.

Furthermore, subjective financial well-being is often found to explain more of the variance in quality of life measures than objective economic status. Medley (1976) suggests that satisfaction with standard of living may be of greater importance to outlook on life than actual financial conditions. A number of studies have found that perceived financial adequacy is a substantially stronger predictor of life satisfaction than objective indicators of socioeconomic position (Spreitzer and Snyder, 1974; Ackerman and Paolucci, 1983). More recently Nevenka's (1997) study of a representative sample of the adult population in Slovenia confirmed that 'a perceived lack of money to cover everyday expenses has greater influence on satisfaction with life than average income per capita in the household'. Thus, it seems that satisfaction with one's financial condition may partially mediate the relationship between economic status and overall well-being.

The role of activity and the environment

A number of other possible mediating factors, which may help reveal the causal processes by which economic status may generate differing levels of subjective well-being, are also suggested in the literature. The role of income in increasing activity level is thought to be particularly important. George (1992) identified six studies of older people that found factors other than financial satisfaction which mediate the relationship. Five out of the six concluded that the effects of income on subjective well-being were mediated by measures of activities. Self-rated health was found to be the mediator in the other study. However, the effects of health on subjective well-being were mediated largely by a measure of activities.

Neighbourhood quality may be another important mediator (e.g. Danigelis, Fengler and Cutler, 1986). Rohe and Stegman (1994) conducted a longitudinal study aimed at investigating the relationship between home ownership and subjective well-being. Their findings indicated that home ownership impacted positively on life satisfaction. However, they also found that irrespective of tenure, housing condition influenced self-esteem and life satisfaction.

Studies of financial strain: self-esteem and perceptions of control

Further evidence of variables that mediate the relationship between economic and psychological well-being can be found if we look at research focusing on the effects of financial strain. Some studies suggest that the relationship between financial status and subjective well-being is non-linear, with the relationship substantially stronger at the lower end of the income distribution (e.g. Vaughan and Lancaster, 1980). Income is thought to have a higher impact on quality of life when basic needs or levels of sustenance are not being met (Larson, 1978; Palmore and Luikart, 1972; Spreitzer and Snyder, 1974). Financial satisfaction may also be a stronger correlate of life satisfaction in less well off countries (Diener and Diener, 1995). These findings, coupled with the realization that continuous and ongoing stressors, often known as chronic strains, may have an especially deleterious effect on elderly persons, have led to numerous investigations on the effects of financial strain.

An important discovery is that economic strain appears to affect psychological well-being adversely, firstly by lowering sense of control or mastery over the environment and secondly by lowering feelings of self-efficacy, or self-esteem. Pearlin et al (1981), using longitudinal data to study the process of stress in relation to life events, found that involuntary job loss inevitably led to an increase in experiences of financial strain. Furthermore, financial strain led to a reduction in perceptions of control and feelings of self-esteem. These changes were related to depressive symptoms.

Krause, Jay and Liang (1991) found a similar pattern of results in a nation-wide survey of both American and Japanese elderly. Once again, results indicated that, as financial problems increased, respondents experienced a diminished sense of self-efficacy and a significant decline in feelings of control. Despite cultural differences and values, similar results were found for both American and Japanese samples.

More recently, Keith (1993) conducted an examination of the differential effects of gender on the experience of financial strain. Although her results suggested that women were more likely than men to experience a diminished sense of control, this was explained by differential exposure to the stress itself. Keith suggests that financial problems may have especially deleterious effects on the control perceptions of older people because many of them rely on fixed sources of income and, therefore, may have less opportunity to alter their economic position. Thus, lowered self-esteem and perceptions of control may be important pathways through which financial strain adversely affects psychological well-being.

Avoiding the negative impact of financial strain in later life: social support and retirement planning

On a more positive note, a number of factors appear to reduce or 'buffer' the effects of financial strain. Social support is one means of coping. People with good supportive networks are found to display fewer symptoms of psychological distress (e.g. Mendes de Leon et al, 1994; Chung, 1995). Informational and reciprocal support have been shown to be particularly beneficial (Krause, 1987).

However, a cautionary note should be made in that there may be a fine line between the positive and negative effects of support. Krause (1995) found that, although emotional support may originally reduce the effects of chronic financial strain, further increments in emotional assistance are associated with increased psychological distress. More recent research by Krause (1997, 1998) has revealed that an important distinction may be between 'anticipated' and 'received' support. For example, a large probability study of older adults living in the People's Republic of China found that individuals who received economic assistance in times of need showed more negative effects of financial strain than those who received no support. However, having the knowledge that help was at hand if necessary was found to be negatively correlated with psychological distress (Krause, 1998).

It appears that financial help from family and friends may actually foster feelings of dependency and, thus, further diminish feelings of control. Hennon and Burton (1986) found that control and financial independence were powerful predictors of life satisfaction. The more that elderly people were dependent on kin and others, the less satisfied they were financially. As Soldo (1981) highlights, older individuals want to be financially independent and only turn to family for financial assistance when they have no other options available to them.

Financial planning may be another important factor. Krause (1993) found that older adults who plan ahead financially are less likely to encounter financial problems, in turn leading to decreased dependence on family and friends. He suggests that the best way to ensure financial independence may be to plan ahead and take action while still in the labour force to ensure adequate resources in later years. Numerous studies, mainly from the retirement literature, document that financial planning is significantly related to satisfaction in late life.

Anderson and Weber (1993) tested the hypothesis that planning for retirement is a necessary, or at least desirable, activity if one's goal is to achieve a sense of satisfaction in retirement. Their sample was divided into three distinct groups: (1) those who participated in formal pre-retirement programmes; (2) those who undertook their own planning; and (3) those who failed to make any preparations. Results indicated that the self-planners were significantly more satisfied with their retirement lifestyles than those who had not planned. Those who took part in structured programmes were also more satisfied than those who did not plan. However, this finding was not significant. Moreover, Anderson and Weber (1993) identified financial independence as one of four factors having the greatest impact on life satisfaction during retirement. They conclude that 'individuals may enhance their likelihood of achieving satisfaction during retirement by taking an active role in planning'.

Dorfman (1989) arrived at a similar conclusion in her study of two rural communities. She found that the extent to which participants had planned for retirement, read about retirement, and been exposed to television and radio programmes about retirement were all positively related to their perceptions of retirement. However, Knesek (1992) found that only 5% of the variance in retirees' financial satisfaction was attributable to planning behaviour.

There is some evidence that the timing of retirement preparation may be particularly important to subsequent life satisfaction in retirement. Hornstein and Wapner (1985) found that pre-retirement programmes were of little value when they were provided just a few months prior to the transition itself. In fact, a negative effect was apparent, as the employees involved seemed to experience a strong sense of frustration. Gregg (1992) emphasizes the need to plan throughout the life span if financial well-being in old age is to be secured.

A growing body of research has investigated the correlates of retirement preparation. These include proximity to retirement, educational status, occupational status, race and health. Gender is also related to preparation, with women generally planning less than men (e.g. Kilty and Behling, 1986; Atchley, 1991; Julia, Kilty and Richardson, 1995). Numerous authors have also noted the importance of income and financial resources to the retirement preparation process (e.g. Beck, 1984; Turner, Bailey and Scott, 1994). However, attitudinal factors, which may be more amenable to change, have also been shown to play an important role in the decision to plan. Those with higher levels of life satisfaction and more positive attitudes to retirement are more likely to undertake preparatory activities (Goudy, Powers and Keith, 1975; Atchley, 1991).

What are the problems and gaps in financial gerontology research?

This section highlights a number of weaknesses in the research literature and provides suggestions for future research. The main criticism of previous research is that few studies have included well-developed measures of financial well-being. This criticism has been firmly levelled at the measurement of objective financial well-being. However, it also pertains to previous measurement of the subjective side of financial well-being.

Epenshade and Braun (1983) suggest that measurement of objective 'economic status' has been handicapped by equating it with household income, ignoring other important economic resources, for example, savings and home equity. This may be particularly true in relation to elderly people, since older individuals tend to have lower incomes, but more resources available in the form of assets such as savings and property. In fact, home ownership constitutes the main form of wealth held by elderly people (Gibbs and Oldman, 1993). For example, 50% of the population aged 65 and over in Britain are presently home owners and, in the vast majority of cases, own their property without outstanding mortgages (OPCS, 1992). Thus, although money income remains the simplest measure of economic status, it clearly undervalues the true ability of retired people to maintain their economic position (Burkhauser and Wilkinson, 1983).

Additionally, the division and flow of wealth between members of the household is rarely taken into consideration. Overall, a household may appear quite affluent, but there may be situations where not all individuals have equal access to or control of the family resources. Moreover, surveys rarely question respondents' specific sources of income. A wage gained through employment may have a very different impact on subjective perceptions and measures of well-being than an equivalent income gained through entitlement to benefits.

Krause (1996) conducted a nation-wide panel study to investigate the effects of welfare participation on self-esteem in later life. Although the relationship between state provision and self-esteem was not significant for the elderly population as a whole, older male recipients experienced a significant reduction in feelings of self-efficacy when in receipt of state benefits.

George (1992) notes that one of the most often debated methodological issues on research on economic status in general, and the relationship between economic status and well-being in particular, is the extent to which the use of overall income measures distorts findings. There is now empirical evidence to suggest that better specification of economic variables increases the explained variance of perceived well-being in both economic and non-economic domains of life (Douthitt, MacDonald and Mullis, 1992). Mullis (1992) also concludes that a comprehensive measure of objective economic well-being, based on permanent income, annuitized net worth and household economic demands, performs better as a predictor of psychological well-being than current reported income.

Turning to the subjective measurement of financial well-being, most research has focused on the objective economic conditions of the elderly, ignoring the importance of subjective perceptions of economic status. Moreover, those that do measure subjective financial status often rely on single item indicators, despite research evidence suggesting that questions measuring, for example, overall financial satisfaction, satisfaction with one's level of income, and satisfaction with one's standard of living, may all measure separate aspects of financial satisfaction (Herzog and Rodgers, 1981).

Finally, another important methodological point is that the great majority of research on financial well-being has been carried out in America. Conclusions may be very different when research examines the relationship between financial well-being and quality of life in countries with very different cultural values, norms and welfare systems.

There is as yet no way of knowing how far findings conducted overwhelmingly on American samples will mirror realities in other countries, including Britain, or how findings will hold up to examination when more comprehensive measures of economic well-being are used. Future research needs to include broader, more comprehensive measures of objective economic well-being in addition to extensive measures of subjective financial well-being. Furthermore, in order to examine the generalizability of present findings, future studies need to be based on geographically and culturally diverse samples.

The authors are currently conducting an examination of the relationship between financial well-being and quality of life among middle-aged and elderly individuals residing in Renfrewshire in Scotland. The study has two main aims: (1) to examine the complex relationship between objective economic status, financial satisfaction, psychological well-being and physical health, and (2) to examine the extent to which people living in the West of Scotland are able and willing to meet the increasing financial demands of later life. However, this is only one small step towards addressing these timely and far reaching issues. Research still has a long way to go in deciphering the complex causal pathways through which economic well-being influences both the quality and quantity of life.

Concluding comment

There is little doubt that financial well-being is a primary need of elderly individuals if they are to maintain their pre-retirement quality of life and live independently and happily in the community. Current research has gone some way to increasing our understanding of what constitutes financial well-being and has partially illuminated its relationship with physical and psychological functioning. On the positive side, it seems that material resources not only fulfil basic needs but also enable individuals to lead fuller, more active lives. In contrast, financial strain impacts negatively on well-being, by reducing perceptions of control and self-esteem. The extent to which social support may alleviate these negative effects is still equivocal and may depend on the type of support received. Economic problems can also trigger a series of secondary stressors such as housing problems and poor nutrition.

Matilda White Riley in the 1990 Boettner Lecture concluded that a critical challenge to the well-being of future society is to find and implement the answer to the question: 'How can the quality of the added years be optimized in the twenty-first century?' Gregg (1992) proposes that one important response to this question is to ensure 'the maintenance of full financial function as nearly as possible to the end of life'. The field of financial gerontology undoubtedly has an important role to play.

References

Ackerman N and Paolucci B (1983) Objective and subjective income adequacy: Their relationship to perceived life quality measures. Social Indicators Research, 12, 25–8.

Adler NE, Boyce T, Chesney MA, Cohen S, Folkman S, Kahn R and Syme SL (1994) Socioeconomic status and health: The challenge of the gradient. American Psychologist, 1, 15–24.

Anderson CE and Weber JA (1993) Pre-retirement planning and perceptions of satisfaction among retirees. Educational Gerontology, 19, 397–406.

Askham J, Hancock R and Hills J (1995) Opinions on Pensions. London: Age Concern Institute Of Gerontology, King's College London.

Atchley RC (1991) Social Forces and Ageing, 6th edn. Belmont, CA: Wadsworth.

Beck SH (1984) Retirement preparation programs: Differentials in opportunity and use. Journal of Gerontology, 39, 596–602.

Bild B and Havinghurst RJ (1976) Senior citizens in great cities: The case of Chicago. Gerontologist, 16, 3–88.

Burkhauser RV and Wilkinson JT (1983) The effects of retirement on income distribution: A comprehensive income approach. Review of Economics and Statistics, 65, 653–8.

Campbell A, Converse PE and Rodgers WL (1976) The Quality of American Life. New York: Russell Sage Foundation.

Carp FM and Carp A (1982) Test of a model of domain satisfactions and well-being: Equity considerations. Research on Aging, 4, 503–22.

Chung E (1995) Social support and self-efficacy as mediators between stress and depressive symptoms in older adults. Doctoral Dissertation. Michigan: University of Michigan.

Cmnd 1014 (1990) The Government's Expenditure Plans 1990–1991 to 1992–1993. London: HMSO.

Cmnd 3805 (1998) New Ambitions for our Country: A New Contract for Welfare. London: The Stationary Office.

Cutler N (1997) Encyclopedic knowledge about financial gerontology. Journal of the American Society of CLU and ChFC.

Danigelis NL, Fengler AP and Cutler SJ (1986) Predicting perceived financial well-being of the aged. Paper presented at the 38th Annual Scientific Meeting of the Gerontological Society of America.

Diener E (1984) Subjective well-being. Psychological Bulletin, 9, 542–75.

Diener ED and Diener M (1995) Cross-cultural correlates of life satisfaction and self-esteem. Journal of Personality and Social Psychology, 68, 653–63.

Dohrenwerd BP and Dohrenwerd BS (1969) Social Status and Psychological Disorder: a Causal Inquiry. New York: Wiley.

Dorfman LT (1989) Retirement preparation and retirement satisfaction in the rural elderly. Journal of Applied Gerontology, 8, 432–50.

Douthitt RA, MacDonald M and Mullis R (1992) The relationship between measures of subjective economic well-being: A new look. Social Indicators Research, 26, 407–22.

Doyle D and Forehand MJ (1984) Life satisfaction and old age: A re-examination. Research on Aging, 6, 432–48.

Edwards J and Klemnack D (1973) Correlates of Life Satisfaction: A re-examination. Journal of Gerontology, 28, 497–502.

Ermisch J (1990) Fewer Babies, Longer Lives: Policy Implications of Current Demographic Trends. York: Joseph Rowntree Foundation.

Espenshade TJ and Braun RE (1983) Economic aspects of an aging population and the material well-being of older persons. In: MW Riley (ed.), Aging In Society: Selected Reviews Of Recent Research, pp. 25–51. London: Laurence Erlbaum Associates.

Falkingham JA and Victor C (1991) The myth of the woopie?: Incomes, the elderly, and targeting welfare. Ageing and Society, 11, 471–93.

Fletcher CN and Lorenz F (1985) Structural influences on the relationship between objective and subjective indicators of economic well-being. Social Indicators Research, 16, 335–45.

George LK (1992) Economic status and subjective well-being: A review of the literature and an agenda for future research. In: NE Cutler, DW Gregg and M Powell Lawton (eds), Aging, Money And Life Satisfaction: Aspects Of Financial Gerontology, pp. 69–100. New York: Springer.

Gibbs I and Oldman C (1993) Housing wealth in later life: A mixed blessing? Discussion Paper No.5. York: Centre for Housing Policy, University of York.

Gillion C (1991) Ageing populations: spreading the costs. Journal of European Social Policy, 1, 107–28.

Gitmez AS and Morcol G (1994) Socioeconomic status and life satisfaction in Turkey. Social Indicators Research, 31, 77–98.

Goetting MA, Martin P, Poon LW and Johnston MA (1996) The economic well-being of community dwelling centenarians. Journal of Ageing Studies, 10, 43–55.

Goudy WJ, Powers EA and Keith P (1975) The work-satisfaction, retirement attitude typology: A profile examination. Experimental Ageing Research, 1, 267–79.

Gregg DW (1992) Human wealth span: The financial dimensions of successful ageing. In: NE Cutler, DW Gregg and M Powell Lawton (eds), Aging, Money And Life Satisfaction: Aspects Of Financial Gerontology, pp. 169–89. New York: Springer.

Hazelrigg LE and Hardy MA (1997) Perceived income adequacy among older adults: Issues of conceptualization and measurement, with an analysis of data. Research on Ageing, 19, 69–107.

Hennon C and Burton JR (1986) Financial satisfaction as a developmental task among the elderly. American Behavioural Scientist, 29, 439–52.

Herzog AR and Rodgers WL (1981) Age and satisfaction: Data from several large surveys. Research on Aging, 3, 142–65.

Hills J (1995) Inquiry Into Income And Wealth, vols 1 and 2. York: Joseph Rowntree Foundation.

Hornstein G and Wapner S (1985) Modes of experiencing and adapting to retirement. International Journal of Aging and Human Development, 21, 299-314.

House JS, Kessler RC, Herzog AR, Mero RP, Kinney AM and Breslow MJ (1990) Age, socioeconomic status, and health. Milbank Quarterly, 68, 383–411.

Johnson P and Falkingham JA (1992) Income, wealth and health in later life. In: P Johnson and JA Falkingham (eds), Aging and Economic Welfare, pp 49–83. London: Sage.

Julia M, Kilty KM and Richardson V (1995) Social worker preparedness for retirement: gender and ethnic considerations. Social Work, 40, 610–20.

Keith VM (1993) Gender, financial strain, and psychological distress among older adults. Research on Aging, 15, 123–47.

Kessler RC and Cleary PD (1980) Social class and psychological distress. American Sociological Review, 45, 463–78.

Kilty KM and Behling JH (1986) Retirement financial planning among professional workers. Gerontologist, 26, 525–30.

Knesek GE (1992) Early versus regular retirement: Differences in measures of life satisfaction. Journal of Gerontological Social Work, 19, 3–34.

Krause N (1987) Chronic financial strain, social support and depressive symptoms among older adults. Psychology and Aging, 2, 185–92.

Krause N (1993) Race differences in life satisfaction among aged men and women. Journal of Gerontology, 48, S235–44.

Krause N (1995) Assessing stress-buffering effects: a cautionary note. Psychology and Aging, 10, 518–26.

Krause N (1996) Welfare participation and self-esteem in later life. Gerontologist, 36, 665–73.

Krause N (1997) Anticipated support, received support and economic stress among older adults. Journal of Gerontology, 52, 284–93.

Krause N (1998) Financial strain, received support, anticipated support, and depressive symptoms in the People's Republic of China. Psychology and Aging, 13, 58–68.

Krause N, Jay G and Liang J (1991) Financial strain and psychological well-being among the American and Japanese elderly. Psychology and Aging, 6, 170–81.

Langer M (1963) Life Stress and Mental Health. New York: The Free Press.

Larson R (1978) Thirty years of research on the subjective well-being of older Americans. Journal of Gerontology, 33, 109–25.

Liang J and Fairchild TJ (1979) Relative deprivation and perception of financial adequacy among the aged. Journal of Gerontology, 34, 746–59.

Liang J, Kahana E and Doherty E (1980) Financial well-being among the aged: A further elaboration. Journal of Gerontology, 35, 409–20.

Marmot MG, Smith GD, Stansfield S, Patel C, North F, Head J, White I, Brunner E and Feeney A (1991) Health inequalities among British civil servants: The Whitehall II study. Lancet, 377, 1387–93.

Medley ML (1976) Satisfaction with life among persons sixty-five years and older. Journal of Gerontology, 31, 448–55.

Mendes de Leon CF, Rapp SS and Kasl SV (1994) Financial strain and symptoms of depression in a community sample of elderly men and women. Journal of Ageing and Health, 6, 448–68.

Mullis RJ (1992) Measures of economic well-being as predictors of subjective well-being. Health Behaviours And Life Quality, 26, 119–36.

Nevenka CS (1997) Socio-economic determinants of well-being. Paper presented at the 5th European Congress of Psychology, Dublin, Ireland.

Olson GI and Schober BI (1993) The satisfied poor: Development of an intervention oriented theoretical framework to explain satisfaction with a life of poverty. Social Indicators Research, 28, 173–93.

OPCS. 1992-Based Population Projections, Series PP2, No 19, Microfiche.

OPCS (1992) General Household Survey 1990. London: HMSO.

Palmore E (1981) Social patterns in normal ageing: Findings from the Duke longitudinal study. Durham: Duke University Press.

Palmore E and Luikart C (1972) Health and social factors related to life satisfaction. Journal of Health and Social Behaviour, 13, 68–80.

Parker G and Clarke C (1997) Will you still need me, will you still feed me? Paying for care in old age. Social Policy and Administration, 31, 119–35.

Pearlin LI, Lieberman MA, Menaghan EG and Mullan JT (1981) The stress process. Journal of Health and Social Behaviour, 22, 337–56.

Riley MW (1990) Aging in the Twenty-first Century. Boettner Lecture. Boettner Research Institute: Bryn Mawr, Pennsylvania.

Rohe WM and Stegman MA (1994) The effects of home ownership on the self-esteem, perceived control and life satisfaction of low-income people. Journal of the American Planning Association, 60, 173–84.

Smith P (1994) New directions in socioeconomic research on ageing. In: RP Abeles, HC Gift and MC Ory (eds), Aging and Quality of Life, pp. 275–94. New York: Springer.

Soldo BJ (1981) The living arrangements of the elderly in the near future. In: SB Kiesler, JN Morgan and VK Oppenheimer (eds), Ageing: Social Change. New York: Academic Press.

Spreitzer E and Snyder EE (1974) Correlates of life satisfaction among the aged. Journal of Gerontology, 29, 454–8.

Thane P (1988) The growing burden of an ageing population? Journal of Public Policy, 7, 373–87.

Turner MJ, Bailey WC and Scott JP (1994) Factors influencing attitude toward retirement and retirement planning among mid-life university employees. Journal of Applied Gerontology, 13, 143–56.

United Nations (1989) World Population Prospects. UN: New York.

Usui WM, Keil TJ and Durig RK (1985) Socioeconomic comparisons and life satisfaction of elderly adults. Journal of Gerontology, 40, 110–14.

Vaughan DR and Lancaster CG (1980) Income levels and their impact on two subjective measures of well-being: Some early speculations from work in progress. The 1979 Proceedings of the American Statistical Association. Washington, DC: American Statistical Association.

Walker A (1992) Age and attitudes: Main results from a eurobarometer survey. Brussels: Commission of the European Communities.

Walker A (1993) Poverty and inequality in old age. In: J Bond, P Coleman and S Peace (eds), Ageing in Society: An Introduction to Social Gerontology, pp. 280–303. London: Sage.

Ying Y (1992) Life satisfaction among San Francisco Chinese Americans. Social Indicators Research, 26, 1–22.

Chapter 3
Nutrition Issues in Older People

JUNE COPEMAN and KAREN HYLAND

Introduction

'Good nutrition contributes to the health of older people, and to their ability to recover from illness.' (DoH, 1992 p. 6)

The variety of nutrition issues that can affect older people is enormous. Initially this chapter considers the age-related changes in the body that can impact on nutrition. The subsequent sections examine significant issues, following a natural progression from health to death. Adequate appropriate nutrition is essential in all phases, affecting the maintenance of health, likelihood of recovery and quality of life. The increasing focus on nutrition may enable older people to remain independent longer besides improving their quality of life.

The chapter takes a symptomatic rather than disease-specific focus. For example, swallowing difficulties will be discussed rather than Parkinson's disease, motor neurone disease or stroke.

Defining terms – who is old?

As ageing is a continuous process, deciding when someone is old is arbitrary. The World Health Organization uses chronological age in the following classification: 45–59 middle-aged; 60–74 elderly, 75–89 old; 90+ very old. In the UK it is customary to consider 65 years, the retirement age for men, as the start of old age. As the elderly population is so diverse, covering over thirty years, it is useful to subdivide it into ten-year divisions.

65–74 – fit, younger older person
75–85 – elderly person
over 85 – frail, elderly person

In the UK and throughout Western Europe the proportion of older people over 85 years is likely to increase dramatically in the next century so that reducing dependency in later life will be increasingly important.

Age-related changes that impact on nutrition

Ageing is a normal process which involves biochemical and physiological changes throughout the body. The rate of these changes differs between body systems and between individuals. Illness and chronic medical conditions may increase the rate of degeneration.

The composition of the whole body changes, with a greater proportion of body fat and less lean tissue and bone. The basal metabolic rate declines with age, probably as a result of the reduction in lean body mass. There is a reduction in height caused by the degeneration and compression of the vertebral discs.

The mechanism governing homeostatic regulation is less efficient so that it takes longer for an old person to respond to cold or heat. That is, they start shivering later in response to cold and initiate sweating at a higher room temperature. This means that the older person is more susceptible to hypothermia.

Webb and Copeman (1996) identified four issues of particular relevance to nutrition and older people: skeleton changes, the effects of ageing upon physical fitness and strength, fluid balance and renal function, and the impact of ageing on the immune system. Sensory function changes, such as a decreased number of taste buds and decreased visual acuity, and gastrointestinal deterioration, with reduced muscle function and muscle tone in the large intestine, also impact on nutrition and absorption.

Physical activity improves muscle strength, increases flexibility and enhances psychological well-being. These factors are important for older people as they will improve mobility and help maintain cardiac function. Increased regular activity, even of low intensity, can reduce morbidity and mortality.

After the menopause the rate of calcium reabsorption is greater than the amount being absorbed; hence the bones become weaker and more likely to fracture. Weight-bearing physical activity, such as walking, may slow down this process. As fractured neck of femur is a major cause of hospital admission and mortality, this has financial and health implications.

The risk of dehydration is greater in older people for a variety of reasons. With ageing, the skin becomes thinner and therefore more water is lost via this route. The kidneys are not able to concentrate urine to the same degree, as the renal plasma flow and glomerular filtration rate decline with age. Additionally, the thirst mechanism is not as sensitive so that older people may not feel thirsty.

Improving the nutritional status of older people

It is well documented that as dependence increases, so the nutritional status of older people in the UK declines (Caughey et al, 1994; McCaffery, 1994; McWhirter and Pennington, 1994; Mowe, Bohmer and Kindt, 1994). Undernutrition can complicate illness, delay recovery, potentiate infection, enhance the risk of pressure sores, decrease the rate of wound healing, prolong any hospital stay, and increase mortality rates (Table 3.1).

Table 3.1. Undernutrition leads to health problems

Reduced psychological well-being (increased anxiety, depression, apathy and loss of concentration)
Depressed immune function
Reduced muscle function
Loss of cardiac muscle and reduced cardiac function
Wasting of respiratory muscles and reduced respiratory response to oxygen deficit
Increased risk of hypothermia
Increased incapacity and risk of falls and injury

The high burden of disease and undernutrition (Chandra, 1993) seen in old age decreases immunological vigour in older people, so there is an increased incidence of infections, auto-immune and immune complex diseases, and cancers. Immune competence declines with age and responses are markedly depressed in malnutrition (Table 3.2).

Table 3.2. Physiological changes in malnutrition

Gastric acidity may be reduced (achlorhydria), predisposing to gastrointestinal infections
The effectiveness of mucosal surfaces as barriers to infection may be reduced
Wounds heal more slowly
The ability of phagocytes to kill ingested bacteria is reduced

Older people are vulnerable to nutritional depletion due to the effects of ageing and, therefore, emphasis should be put on the nutritional care provided for older people at home, in hospital and in residential care.

The factors affecting the nutritional status of older people can be broadly categorized into three areas:

1. Intrinsic factors – naturally occurring ageing processes which affect nutritional status.
2. Pathological factors – disease status that may directly or indirectly affect nutritional status.
3. Extrinsic factors – environment, alcohol, dependency, social isolation, drugs.

Ideally every older person should be considered individually to ensure their nutrition is optimal and any specific factors recognized and tackled. Davies and Knutson (1991) have developed a useful grid system to help with the identification of elderly people 'at risk' of poor nutritional intake.

Screening is the process of identifying older people who are already malnourished, or at risk of becoming so. Appropriate 'screening tools' are used in hospitals and institutions, but are not yet sufficiently available in the community.

Nutrition assessment is a more detailed process using a range of methods to identify and quantify nutritional status. Although usually carried out by a dietitian, much of the information can be gathered and assessed against specific criteria. Most assessment tools can include these elements:

- Eating patterns and habits including ethnic and cultural behaviour.
- Food likes and dislikes, with any known digestive problems, and current appetite.
- Height, weight and trends in weight loss and/or gain.
- Activity and rest patterns.
- Medical and physical condition.
- Mental state.
- Dental and oral health.
- Swallowing and chewing difficulties and mouth condition.
- Other risk factors – socioeconomic circumstances.

With the identification of any problems affecting the nutritional intake and nutritional status, early intervention can be initiated to resolve some of the difficulties and limit their impact.

Eating to maintain health

Factors affecting food choice

Food is an essential part of living, having many functions besides relieving hunger. It is an important vehicle for social relationships, communication and control. It conveys friendship, integration and acceptance and demonstrates differences in social standing. It fulfils social, emotional and psychological needs. For healthy living everyone should have adequate access to food to meet their various needs, including religious, cultural and dietary.

Factors affecting food choice are complex. Webb (1995) constructed a model for food selection based on the concept of a hierarchy of constraints upon availability. The progression from what is physically available through to what is personally eaten shows clearly how food choice is restricted (Table 3.3).

Table 3.3. What food is really available

Constraints to availability	Example
Physical	Shops only stock what they expect to sell
Economic	Is the food item affordable on a restricted income?
Cultural	Is the item considered food, is it familiar?
Gatekeeper	Who does the shopping, what do they purchase?
Personal	Personal likes, dislikes and food habits

After Webb (1995).

For older people access to food – being able to reach the supermarket, or being able to carry heavy purchases – are important initial constraints. A limited income further reduces choice, and having to rely on other people to undertake food purchases, even with a shopping list, is an additional restriction.

Other factors affect food choice such as:

- cooking facilities,
- cooking ability,
- knowledge of budgeting,
- interest in food,
- cooking for one,
- state of health,
- physical ability,
- bereavement.

Older people often live in inadequate housing with poor cooking facilities and may not be able to purchase newer equipment such as a microwave. Often widowers have great difficulties as their previous shopping and cooking experience may be limited. Cookery classes which meet social and culinary needs are valuable.

Current nutritional guidelines for healthy eating

Fit older people

The nutritional needs of the younger, older person (65–74 years) are very similar to those of people aged between 20 and 65. To stereotype, these individuals are often fit, free-living older people who play an active role in society. It is important that they are encouraged to remain physically active and mentally alert.

The current guidelines for healthier eating are to:

- Increase the amount of cereals and bread, preferably wholegrain, pasta and potatoes eaten, with additional fluid. Many older people suffer from constipation which is exacerbated by a low fibre intake and reduced mobility.

- Increase the quantity of fruit and vegetables eaten. The current recommendation is for five portions of fruit or vegetables a day. This could consist of, for example, fruit juice at breakfast, cabbage and tinned fruit at lunch, a salad for the evening meal and a banana during the day. Besides providing soluble dietary fibre (non-starch polysaccharide (NSP)) fruit and vegetables are valuable sources of vitamins, especially vitamin C and folic acid.
- Reduce sugar consumption (found in sweets, cakes, biscuits as well as that added to drinks). Although containing energy, foods high in refined carbohydrates are not nutrient rich; that is they do not contain many vitamins, minerals and other essential nutrients.
- Reduce the quantity of fat eaten (found in biscuits, cakes, pastries besides butter and margarine). Cooking methods should be modified to encourage grilling, boiling, baking and roasting without fat, instead of frying.

These guidelines are summarized pictorially in the Food Guide Plate in the UK (HEA, 1994) and in the Food Guide Pyramid for the USA (USDA,1992).

In 1992 the Department of Health working party on the Nutrition of Elderly People confirmed that for fit older people these general principles of healthy eating were applicable (DoH, 1991, 1992).

Frail elderly people

Special consideration must be given to frail elderly people. These individuals will be living in the community or sheltered housing with some support services. They may have some sensory impairment, restricted mobility, and will be experiencing the signs of ageing. Typically they will be over 80 years old. In this situation, encouraging the consumption of sufficient nutrient-rich food is important. The individual must be:

- provided with a diet that is generous in energy;
- offered a wide range of nutrient rich foods, i.e. foods that will provide adequate vitamins, minerals and protein;
- encouraged to increase their intake of vitamin C; for example, fortified fruit drinks and citrus fruit should be included in the diet daily;
- encouraged to expose some skin to sunlight regularly during the months May to September. The recommended requirement for vitamin D cannot be met from food alone. Ultraviolet (UV) rays from the sun act on the exposed skin to produce vitamin D; therefore housebound individuals must be considered for prescribed supplementation.

The Caroline Walker Trust expert working party (1995) produced guidelines for the nutritional content of community meals and advice about catering in residential settings. Community meals are delivered to an individual in their own home, they may be ready cooked hot meals or prepacked frozen meals which the individual cooks later. The term can also include meals served at luncheon clubs or day centres.

Meal times and the service of meals

The total environment for the service of meals is important as it affects the quantity of food consumed. Therefore, in residential settings and at luncheon clubs or day centres, the dining room should be attractive, warm and clean, with easy access and suitable furniture. The physical and social environments besides the actual meal influence food wastage. Social factors include selecting dining companions and allowing sufficient time for the meal to be an enjoyable occasion. If assistance is required with feeding it should be offered discreetly with the helper seated by the client. Table 3.4 lists some of the factors to consider.

Table 3.4. Factors to consider in the service of meals

Environment	Issue
Physical environment	Seating arrangement
	Chairs of appropriate height and type
	Appropriate cutlery
	Reduce the noise level
	Limit distractions
	Avoid offensive odours
Social environment	Sufficient time for eating
	Compatibility of dining companions
	Personal preferences, e.g. resident who wishes to eat alone
	Pleasant and non-patronizing staff
	Appropriate and discreet assistance
The meal	Portion size
	Appearance
	Taste, smell, colour and texture
	Individual likes and dislikes
	Familiarity and cultural acceptability
	Temperature
	Second helping available
	Sufficient fluid (tea, water, coffee, fruit juice)

Reproduced from Webb and Copeman (1996) *The Nutrition of Older Adults*.

When helping people with a poor appetite, small attractive meals should be offered, with snacks in between the main meals. As every mouthful must count in nutrient and energy terms, the food must be nutrient rich.

Feeding someone with dementia

It is estimated that about 2% of 65–75 year olds and 20% of over 80 year olds have some form of dementia, with progressive neurological changes. As people with dementia have difficulties with reasoning and memory and experience mood and behaviour changes, this disease has a marked impact on daily life and the ability to eat well.

The nutritional needs of older people with dementia are similar to other older people, although the constant pacing up and down may require additional energy and the side effects of prescribed drugs should be considered.

Enabling the individual to maintain eating independence for as long as possible requires consideration of the eating environment and the supply of finger foods. A messy independent eater is better than a clean dependent person.

Key strategies include:

- a quiet calm dining area;
- keeping to familiar foods, drinks and routines;
- allowing enough time for people to eat;
- giving encouragement and help to eat;
- using salt/pepper pots rather than individual wrapped items;
- offering finger foods;
- providing snacks between meals;
- altering food textures;
- having adequate number of carers (formal and non-formal);
- enabling regular contact between client and carer;
- ensuring consistency of staff care;
- staff training;
- treating other medical conditions, e.g. depression, anxiety, paranoia.

In an institutional setting, an eating policy should address planning and organization, residents' choice and practical issues. The latter should include how the food is served; for example, does the food need to be cut into bite size pieces before it is given; are the clients capable of serving themselves or does the food need to be on individual plates. Crockery should be familiar, serviceable and of an acceptable design. Where possible, people should be able to choose whether they prefer a cup and saucer or a mug, for example. The use of 'baby plastic dishes' should be discouraged. Underpinning this policy must be the belief that staff involvement and commitment are critical factors and that the person with dementia needs to be treated with respect and given choice within each individual's capability and dignity.

Skilled help may be needed to offer suggestions for dealing with particular mealtime behaviours. These can be grouped around the style of eating and pattern of intake, resistive or disruptive behaviours and oral behaviour. In response to someone eating desserts first, the meal could be served in courses, or if someone interrupts or wants to help they should be given a meal service related task, perhaps setting the tables. A plastic spoon will be helpful if someone bites on a spoon, and the practice of holding food in the mouth can be tackled with verbal cues and gentle massage of the cheek (Expert Working Group, 1998).

Food hygiene

It is important to consider the basic rules of good hygiene when feeding older people, particularly those who have reduced immunity, and increased susceptibility to infection. Older people are more prone to foodborne infections and large institutions have the potential to cause food poisoning. The three general aims crucial to ensuring the microbiological safety of food prepared for older people are:

1. To minimize the risks of bacterial contamination; i.e. buy fresh, keep food covered, wash hands thoroughly, use clean utensils, surfaces, separate chopping boards, separate raw from cooked foods.
2. To maximize the killing of bacteria during food preparation; i.e. avoid raw and undercooked eggs; defrost thoroughly before cooking, cook all parts of meat, poultry to 70°C.
3. To minimize the time that food is stored under conditions that permit bacterial growth; i.e. prepare as close to consumption as possible, discard past sell-by date food. Store leftovers appropriately, keep food cool below 5°C, and not at 65°C or above.

In chronic illness – maintaining function

In many cases of chronic illness the food intake is changed either because the appetite is suppressed or because the nutrient and energy requirements are altered. This section identifies the problems, and their possible causes. These problems can be caused by physical/practical, physiological/medical or emotional factors (Table 3.5).

Practical difficulties include not being able to use a tin opener, lift a saucepan or grip ordinary cutlery. Specially adapted cutlery and other aids to assist in food preparation are available. Arthritic hands may not be able to open the food packaging.

Whenever an individual is experiencing symptoms such as nausea, an interaction between the various medications or a side reaction of a specific prescribed drug should be considered. The interplay between drugs can have a marked impact on the vitamin and mineral status in the individual.

Depression, anxiety and other psychological problems are common among older people. They should be identified and treated promptly as they can dramatically affect the individual, including the inclination to prepare and consume food.

Table 3.5. Nutrition-related problems and their possible causes

Problem	Possible causes
No interest in food	No appetite Anorexia Nausea Depression Altered or no sense of taste and smell Side effect of radiotherapy Side effect of chemotherapy Cachexia
Inability to place food in mouth, reduced manual dexterity	Unable to use cutlery Unable to unwrap food Poor hand–mouth coordination Stroke, rheumatoid arthritis, osteoarthritis
Problems in mouth	Sore mouth Dry mouth Mouth infection Ill fitting dentures Inability to chew Inability to move food round mouth No saliva produced
Swallowing difficulties	Delayed swallow Poor posture Oesophageal stricture Physical abnormality Parkinson's disease, stroke
Indigestion (stomach)	Hiatus hernia Poor posture Gastric ulcer Rapid ingestion of food, achlorhydria
Malabsorption (small/large bowel)	Drug interaction Bacterial overgrowth Coeliac disease Pancreatic insufficiency Food intolerance
Constipation (large intestine)	Low fibre intake Reduced mobility Low fluid intake Reduced peristaltic action
Incontinence	Bladder dysfunction Infection

If someone has a sore or dry mouth they will not be inclined to eat. Very hot food or sour fruits will aggravate any pain and should be avoided until the mouth infection is treated. A dry mouth can be a side reaction to drugs or radiotherapy. In some situations saliva production is diminished, making it difficult to manipulate food round the mouth. Artificial saliva is prescribed which will help lubricate the food.

In rehabilitation – food encourages recovery

The informal carer

In all aspects of nutrition for older people it is necessary to note that the informal carer, a relative or friend will give most of the practical care. It is important that the health care professional provides adequate, appropriate information and support to enable the carer to provide the correct type, level and duration of care, with confidence, and know how, when and where to refer to 'the professional'.

Deciding the appropriate intervention

Early identification of nutritional vulnerability implies the need for a systematic approach to deciding what action is required.

'Taking Steps to Tackle Eating Problems', a handbook and poster for those who care for older people, is published by NAGE (1994) and provides practical suggestions for tackling the key nutritional issues for older people. It poses the question 'do you have reason to be concerned about your client's nutritional status?' and leads the reader to find appropriate solutions.

Wood has produced a chart which indicates 'The Pathway, for Providing Nutritional Support' appropriate to all individuals including older people (Wood, 1998).

Both these excellent flow charts endorse the view that effective interdisciplinary working can improve outcome; that is, the dietitian, speech and language therapist, physiotherapist, occupational therapist, psychologist, medical practitioner and nurse, working in partnership.

Nutrition supplementation

The simplest way of providing nutritional support is to encourage the older person to eat more. The provision of and access to small snacks and frequent meals is not always easy. Some tips include:

• Eat little and often – try to have some food every two to three hours.
• Have snacks between meals: nibbles, cheese and crackers, milky drinks.
• Make everything as nutritious as possible.
• Enrich an ordinary food with another energy and/or nutrient dense food that does not increase the volume of the meal, e.g.
  – milk powder added to ordinary milk and then used for drinks, breakfast cereals, puddings or soups;

–   cream added to soup, puddings, potatoes;
–   grated cheese added to soup, potatoes, vegetables;
–   butter/margarine added to potatoes and vegetables.

A nutritional supplement is any item that is given in addition to the ordinary diet to increase the energy and/or nutrient intake of an inadequately nourished person.

These include:

• Dietary supplements – well known commercial products like Complan and Build-up are concentrated energy/nutrient sources that are usually consumed in liquid form, readily digested and absorbed.
• Protein and energy meal supplements – based on skimmed milk powder and milk protein or fruit juice and amino acids and fortified with minerals, vitamins and sometimes fibre.
• Carbohydrate supplements – based on glucose polymers – they are much less sweet than sugar and add energy (4 kcal/g) without bulk, e.g. Polycose, Maxijul, Caloreen.

In the short term, food supplements, usually consisting of energy powders, milk or fruit juice based, flavoured, energy-dense beverages and desserts can be prescribed. The range of nutrition support products is extensive. The local dietitian will know what is usually available in hospital and the community (hospital and GP prescribed). The manufacturers will provide recipes and tips on use to add variety.

The use of nutritional supplements needs to be monitored and subjected to regular review, particularly their impact on other food and fluid consumption, and haematological changes.

In the longer term, using other food such as butter, cheese and milk powder to enrich the diet is preferable. Multivitamins may be useful if there is long-term limited dietary intake.

Enteral feeding

Whenever possible, nutritional needs should be met by eating and drinking normal food (often more acceptable); but, if the individual is unable to take adequate food or fluid orally (identified by assessment and observation), for example because of dysphagia, there is an immediate requirement to consider 'artificial feeding'. This may be required either as a supplement to the oral intake or as a total replacement for it. In enteral feeding the nutrients are passed directly into the stomach by the use of a tube that is introduced through the nose and into the stomach – the nasogastric tube.

The King's Fund (KFC, 1992) estimated that around 2% of hospitalized patients in Great Britain received some form of artificial feeding, emphasizing that the procedure is usually carried out in health institutions by trained health care professionals. Strict hygiene practices must be maintained whenever artificial feeding is used. Generally a prescribed quantity of appropriate sterile feed is delivered into the individual from a reservoir assisted by a 'pump'.

For long-term artificial feeding of older people in the community (home or residential care), gastrostomy feeding, where the tube has been inserted directly into the stomach by surgical means, has become widely used. It has a number of advantages over nasogastric feeding:

* It is more discreet.
* There is no irritation of the nose and oesophagus.
* It does not interfere with rehabilitation of normal swallowing or speech.
* It can be left in place for several months.

All older people will have an individual feeding regime prescribed and instructed by the dietitian and nutrition nurse, which requires carer training/education, monitoring and regular review.

Changes in the texture of food

The texture of food is very important to its palatability, and generally meals should consist of a variety of different textures. In some medical conditions the texture of food needs to be modified:

* problems in the mouth, e.g. ill fitting dentures, candida, cancer of the mouth;
* problems with swallowing reflex;
* physical obstruction, e.g. oesophageal stricture;
* some psychiatric disorders;
* neurological changes, e.g. after a stroke.

Textures of food have been classified by dietitians and speech and language therapists, depending on their ease of consumption. One such classification is shown in Table 3.6.

An individual with progressively worsening levels of dysphagia might be offered:

* a soft diet, e.g. using minced meat; flaked fish; soft fruit, vegetables and mashed potato (with food enrichment, e.g. butter/margarine, milk powder);
* a soft smooth diet where food is soft and mashed, e.g. pureed meat with gravy, fish in sauce, mashed soft vegetables, soft mashed potatoes, milk pudding, fruit yoghurts (with food enrichment);

• a pureed diet (homogenized) where food is pureed using a blender and additional fluid is added, e.g. pureed meat, potato, vegetables and fruit, smooth yoghurt, mousse, ground rice pudding.

Table 3.6. A classification of food textures with food examples

Texture classification	Example of food
Hard	Apple
Chewy	Cooked meat
Soft	Cake, bread and butter (no crust)
Liquid hard lump	Muesli
Liquid soft lump	Cornflakes and milk
Thickened soft lump	Plain yoghurt and banana
Thickened hard lump	Stew with chewy meat
Liquid	Milk, water and orange juice
Slide down easily	Butter, smooth peanut butter, mousse

Reproduced from Webb and Copeman (1996), The Nutrition of Older Adults.

As the degree of restriction increases so is the likelihood of an inadequate intake. Pureed food becomes more dilute with added fluid, and often has a watery taste, and unacceptable appearance. If a whole meal is liquidized together, the resulting mixture is often revolting, and bears little resemblance in appearance or taste to the original. This is not recommended – but one can use commercial food moulds, to serve pureed vegetables separately from potatoes and meat/fish. Some pureed foods benefit from being prepared with a little thickening agent, e.g. cornflour, arrowroot. As the pureed diet is generally inadequate in energy (even if consumed), food and nutrition supplements are required to prevent malnutrition, e.g. milk powder, butter/margarine, glucose polymer, ascorbic acid (vitamin C).

Liquids can present particular problems to some dysphagic people, because they may reach the back of the mouth too quickly, before the airway is blocked, resulting in choking or aspiration. A number of thickening agents have been commercially produced, e.g. Thick and Easy, Thixo D. These products can be stirred into hot or cold liquids (in recommended quantities) to make them thicker, and easier to swallow. The speech and language therapist, dietitian and nurse can give guidance on the amount to use to effect the best/most appropriate result. Ready-made fruit juice versions are also available. The manufacturer will supply recipe ideas if asked.

Impact of supplementation

There is a considerable body of evidence that nutritional supplementation has substantial beneficial effects upon nutritional status, reduces mortality and morbidity and increases quality of life.

How can these be measured?

1. Better nutrition knowledge and heightened awareness amongst older people, their carers and health care professionals.
2. Improved training to increase awareness and recognition of the signs of malnutrition.
3. Provision of adequate amounts of appetizing, acceptable and nutritious food.
4. Nutritional assessment of older people and initiation of corrective measures with realistic targets that can be measured.
5. Routine monitoring of intake:
   - quantity of meals eaten 1/4, 1/2, 3/4: all;
   - number of meals and snacks eaten;
   - number of drinks consumed;
   - consumption of nutrition supplement products;
   - note plate waste; refusal;
   - anthropometric indicators, e.g. weight and weight change;
   - haematology, if appropriate.
6. Observation:
   - physical appearance;
   - mental alertness.

End of life issues – 'dying with dignity'

Good nutrition decreases morbidity and mortality – and increases the quality of life, but no-one lives for ever! The rate of disability increases roughly exponentially throughout adult life. This means that unless there are improvements in the health and general well-being of older people, then increased life expectancy could be accompanied by increasing numbers of older people suffering from chronic mental and physical diseases and disabilities, e.g. Alzheimer's disease, osteoporotic fractures.

It is the duty of the carers of older people to preserve life – but not necessarily at all costs. Enabling an incurably ill person to die peacefully and with dignity is also part of the carer's role. Treatment should be designed to relieve the person's suffering, even if it results in the person dying earlier than anticipated. The rapid growth in the proportion of the population over retirement age affects everyone. This has led to many ethical questions, and the introduction of laws related to the problems of older people and those with responsibilities towards them, i.e. 'capacity' – competence to do certain things, 'living wills'.

Most people would agree that if possible, home is the best place to die, but for many this is not practicable. The health care team should share common values and aims for their older patients, and presume that they have 'capacity' unless proven otherwise. Good communication between the older person and carers and relatives is essential so that their values and end of life decisions are known. An effective case conference can establish the agreed course of action, to facilitate dying with dignity.

Dehydration

One important issue related to the end of life is dehydration. This is a serious but preventable condition in older people, most relevant to the demise of an older person.

Dehydration is partly a consequence of the normal process of ageing, but there are also factors resulting from multi-pathology and institutional factors which contribute to dehydration (Table 3.7).

Table 3.7. Causes of dehydration in older people

Pathological	Ageing process	Iatrogenic
Pyrexia	Reduced total body water	Drugs, e.g. diuretics
Renal failure	Reduced renal function	Institutionalization
Immobility	Altered thirst perception	Fluid restriction
Confusion		Urinary incontinence
Drowsiness		
Depression		

A daily intake of about 1,500ml to 2,000 ml is required to ensure that chronic dehydration does not occur. About 1% of older people admitted to community hospitals suffer from clinical dehydration, and as many as 25% of immobile elderly patients suffer from mild chronic dehydration (Rolls and Phillips, 1990).

The effects of dehydration on older people are:

* loss of skin elasticity;
* increasing risk of pressure sore development;
* bad tasting mouth;
* confusion which interferes with the recognition of thirst;
* drowsiness which interferes with the recognition of thirst;
* altered cardiac function;
* constipation;
* urinary tract infection;
* electrolyte imbalance.

These problems are more severe in older people who are disabled or mentally impaired.

The provision of adequate fluids must be made a priority in the care of older people (a fluid loss of 20% can be fatal), and the most appropriate drinking vessel used. A suggested 1,500 ml, i.e. 6–8 cups, per day fluid intake regimen for an older person is outlined in Table 3.8. The restoration of normal hydration, even if it means using a nasogastric tube regimen or peripheral/subcutaneous fluids, will increase the sense of well-being and comfort.

Table 3.8. A suggested 1,500 ml fluid intake regimen for an older person

Beverage	Volume (ml)
Early morning tea	150
Fruit juice	100
Tea/coffee with breakfast	150
Morning tea/coffee/milk/ supplement	150–200
Soup/water	200
Tea/coffee after lunch	150
Afternoon tea/coffee/milk/supplement	150–200
Drink with dinner	150
Tea/coffee after dinner	150
Evening drink*	150
Night drink	150
Total	1,600–1,700 ml

*Often omitted due to risk of night-time micturition.

Therapeutic diets

Therapeutic diets for diabetes mellitus, chronic renal failure, diverticular disease, constipation, and other chronic diseases such as anaemia, when first adopted, can give rapid symptomatic relief and act as a powerful, positive reinforcement to encourage the individual to continue with the restriction; but, at the end of life, dietary advice should be directed towards the restoration of nutritional adequacy, and prevention of malnutrition. The benefits of changing dietary intake to reduce the risk of chronic disease or reducing symptoms of a known disease become less important.

It is the role of the carer and responsibility of the health care professional to agree priorities – it may be appropriate to increase the insulin or drug therapy to accommodate some refined carbohydrate in a person with diabetes, if they want chocolate puddings, and to permit glasses of cold milk to the person with end-stage renal failure. If there is doubt, a medical practitioner should be consulted, but strict adherence to a limiting therapeutic diet at the end of life is unnecessary.

Palliative care

The relief of symptoms without curing the disease is significant in the nutritional care of older people. 'A little of what you fancy' is a good maxim to use in the care of the dying. This is easier to achieve at home than in an institution due to the increased access and/or availability of food. But it may be neglected or uneaten due to a change in mental capacity, taste changes, or appearance. The carer must not be put off or disappointed. As with fluid intake, a record of the likes and dislikes and quantity eaten should be kept. If not accepted at once, a further try is recommended a few days later. This is an opportunity to be imaginative and unconventional – cornflakes and milk can be eaten any time of the day or night, the hot main meal can be served at 9 a.m. if it is eaten. Different combinations of food, or ordering of the menu, or dessert before dinner may be more acceptable!

References

Caroline Walker Trust Expert Working Party (1995) Eating Well for Older People. London: Caroline Walker Trust.

Caughey P, Seaman C, Parry D, Farquhart D and MacLannan WJ (1994). Nutrition of old people in sheltered housing. Journal of Human Nutrition and Dietetics, 7, 263–8.

Chandra RK (1993) Nutrition and the immune system. Proceedings of the Nutrition Society, 55, 77–84.

Copeman JP (1999) Nutritional Care for Older People – A Practical Handbook. London: Age Concern.

Davies L and Knutson KC (1991) Warning signals for malnutrition in the elderly. Journal of the American Dietetic Association, 91(ii), 1413–17.

Department of Health (1991) Dietary References Values for Food Energy and Nutrients for the UK. Report of the Panel on Dietary References Values of the Committee on Medical Aspects of Food Policy, Report on Health and Social Subjects Number 41. London: HMSO.

Department of Health (1992) The Nutrition of Elderly People. Report of the Working Group on the Nutrition of Elderly People of the Committee on Medical Aspects of Food Policy, Report on Health and Social Subjects Number 43, p. 6. London: HMSO.

Expert Working Group (1998) Eating well for older people with dementia. Potters Bar: Voluntary Organisations Involved in Caring in the Elderly Sector (VOICES).

HEA (1994) Health Education Authority. The Balance of Good Health – the national food guide. London: Health Education Authority.

KFC (1992) King's Fund Centre. A Positive Approach to Nutrition as Treatment. London: King's Fund Centre.

McCaffery P (1994) Department of the Environment. Living Independently. A Study of the Home Needs of Elderly and Disabled People. London: HMSO.

McWhirter JP and Pennington CR (1994) Incidence and recognition of malnutrition in hospital. British Medical Journal, 308, 945–8.

Mowe M, Bohmer T and Kindt E (1994) Reduced nutritional status in elderly people is probable before disease and probably contributes to the development of disease. American Journal of Clinical Nutrition, 59, 317–24.

NAGE (1994) Taking steps to tackle eating problems. Skipton: Nutrition Advisory Group for Elderly People (NAGE). Available from NAGE, The British Dietetic Association, Unit 21, Goldthorpe Industrial Estate, Goldthorpe, Rotherham, South Yorkshire S63 9BL.

Rolls BJ and Phillips PA (1990) Aging and disturbances of thirst and fluid balance. Nutrition Reviews, 48, 137–44.

USDA (1992) United States Department of Agriculture. The Food Guide Pyramid. Home and Garden Bulletin number 252. Washington, DC: United States Department of Agriculture.

Webb G (1995) Nutrition. A Health Promotion Approach. London: Edward Arnold.
Webb G and Copeman JP (1996) The Nutrition of Older Adults. London: Arnold.
Wood S (1998) Nutritional support. Professional Nurse Study Supplement 13(6), s15.

Further reading

Beales D. Denham M and Tullock A (1998) Community Care of Older People. Abingdon: Radcliffe Medical Press.
Pender F (ed) (1994) Nutrition and Dietetics – A Practical Guide to Normal and Therapeutic Nutrition. Edinburgh: Campion Press.
Thomas B (ed.) (1994) Manual of Dietetic Practice, 2nd edn. Oxford: Blackwell Scientific Publications.

Chapter 4
Podiatric Problems in the Older Person

BARBARA WALL

It is projected that by the year 2000 there will be 12 million people of pensionable age living in the United Kingdom, each of whom will have walked an average of 70,000 miles during their lifetime. With each step taken the various mechanical forces acting on the feet are equivalent to five times the body weight; so it is not surprising that results from a recent survey indicate that in the United Kingdom a third of all people of a pensionable age receive treatment for foot problems (Elton and Sanderson, 1987). However, this survey and other studies indicate that a fifth of people over 60 years of age assessed by the authors as needing podiatric care did not receive it (Kemp and Winkler, 1983). Females live longer than males and this is important when considering the provision of podiatric care, as females tend to have more foot pathologies than their male counterparts. For example, in a large study of 3,201 people with foot problems, as many as two thirds, as expected, were over 65 years of age, but surprisingly, from the age of 55 years and onwards, already more than half were women (Dobby, 1993).

Feet are complex structures; each foot comprises 26 bones and 30 synovial articulations. It takes approximately 18 years for these structures to complete growth; therefore abnormal stresses applied to developing feet may cause problems later in life. The key to healthy feet in the elderly lies in preventing problems in youth. Feet should not be considered in isolation from the rest of the body. Abnormalities at the spine, hip, knee or ankle will be reflected in altered foot function during the gait cycle and often result in abnormal movement at the subtalar and midtarsal joints. These complex synovial articulations are crucial in allowing the foot to adapt to different surfaces, and to allow energy efficient gait. Abnormal motion at these joints can lead to either excessive or inadequate movement in the forefoot, in turn leading to toe deformities and altered pressure loading. Resultant abnormal stresses acting on the epidermis can lead to the production of corns, callosities and ulceration. In addition, soft tissues such as tendons, muscles and ligaments can become damaged as a result of altered foot function.

Many systemic diseases have direct effects on foot health and a person's mobility. Not only does rheumatoid arthritis produce deformed and painful joints which are subjected to excessive mechanical stresses and damage, but the disease can adversely affect tissue viability and wound healing. Drugs, such as corticosteroids, taken to modify this particular disease, can affect wound healing and may cause osteoporosis.

In the older person many tissues are altered by the physiological ageing process. Contemporary work in the field of molecular genetics is arguably the most important contribution to understanding this process. For example, age-associated defects in mitochondrial DNA produce reactive oxygen species (free radicals) that damage many types of tissue.

Anatomical structures, important in allowing normal foot function, are affected by ageing. Some of these will be discussed below. The stratum corneum is the outermost layer of the epidermis. It normally provides a protection for the underlying structures. However, in the older person the lipids found within this epidermal layer become altered and reduce its protective barrier action (Rogers et al, 1996). In the elderly the skin is often described as being atrophic, with loss of elasticity and a reduced metabolic rate (Gilchrest, 1996). In the older person the dermis has large amounts of abnormal elastic fibres deposited within it. This change is accompanied by collagen degeneration (Quaglino et al, 1996). With these alterations the normal protective functions of the epidermis and dermis are compromised and these structures will be rendered liable to damage.

The association of osteoporosis with the ageing process is well documented. In the foot, osteoporotic bones subjected to abnormal stresses – particularly when there is deformity (e.g. hallux abducto valgus) – can become fractured (pathological stress fractures).

Systemic diseases associated with advancing age may have a direct impact on foot health and function.

Ischaemia

Reduced arterial blood supply will adversely affect tissue viability and increase the likelihood of infection. The causes of ischaemia are numerous. However, the commonest cause of chronic ischaemia in the elderly is atherosclerosis that affects the tunica intima of medium and large diameter arteries.

It is important to recognize the signs and symptoms associated with lower leg and foot ischaemia so that problems can be anticipated and hopefully prevented.

The major signs are absent foot pulses (dorsalis pedis and posterior tibial pulses); a useful quantitative method of assessing perfusion is by calculating the ankle brachial systolic pressure index for each of these vessels. The systolic blood pressure at the ankle vessels is measured using a handheld Doppler and this figure is divided by the systolic pressure measured at the brachial artery. A ratio of <0.8 indicates ischaemia and ratio of <0.5 is considered to represent critical ischaemia. In ischaemia the foot is cool, and the skin appears atrophic and cyanotic in colour; however, pallor will develop when the leg is elevated. Patients may complain of intermittent claudication and/or rest pain, both of these symptoms being associated with the metabolic demands of tissues (in particular muscle) failing to be met by the reduced blood supply to that tissue. These symptoms, particularly that of rest pain, when accompanied by an ankle brachial systolic pressure index of 0.5 or less, patches of gangrene or ulceration, indicate that the foot is critically ischaemic and requires referral for a specialist opinion.

Rheumatoid arthritis

This multisystem disorder affects approximately 2% of the adult population in the United Kingdom. It predominantly affects females and can occur in relatively young people. However, many people with rheumatoid arthritis have a relatively normal life expectancy and survive to old age.

The disease not only causes pain and excess pressure loading over prominent joints, but can result in peripheral neuropathy and vascular changes. With the development of bioengineering technology, routine provision of prosthetic hips and knees is commonplace, and it is not uncommon for people with this disease to be wheelchair bound purely because of foot pathologies.

Rheumatoid arthritis also affects the hands and impairs an elderly person's ability to perform tasks such as cutting toenails.

Diabetes mellitus

Diabetes mellitus affects 2% of the population, and for every person diagnosed with diabetes there is another undiagnosed diabetic. There are two main categories of diabetes, Type 1 and Type 2. The latter type appears in older people and can be a major cause of morbidity and mortality. There are several complications of diabetes that directly or indirectly affect the feet; these are shown in Table 4.1.

Atherosclerosis will produce chronic ischaemic changes similar to those described earlier. However, the distal and patchy distribution of the atherosclerotic plaques in the person with diabetes has implications for its surgical management.

Peripheral neuropathy found as a complication of diabetes can result in motor, sensory and autonomic fibre dysfunction; neuropathic changes are found in more than 50% of patients over 60 years of age.

Table 4.1. Complications associated with diabetes mellitus that can affect the feet and lower limbs

---

1. Vascular:
Accelerated onset of atherosclerosis, affecting distal arteries and with patchy distribution of plaques
Abnormally functioning vascular endothelium with associated changes in the microvasculature

2. Altered components of blood:
Abnormal white blood cells that are less effective in destroying microorganisms
Abnormal platelet function

3. Neurological:
Peripheral neuropathy, affecting motor, sensory and autonomic modalities
Sensory impairment reduces warning symptoms of pain
Motor dysfunction may produce deformity of the toes
Autonomic dysfunction leads to reduced sweating and to abnormalities in blood flow

4. Increased predisposition to infection:
As a result of ischaemia, neurological changes and abnormal white blood cells (see above)

5. Impaired vision:
Diabetic retinopathy and cataract formation limit the patient's ability to examine their feet for signs of infection and damage

6. Renal disease:
Oedema can result from renal complications. In renal transplant patients there is an increased risk of vessel calcification and digital gangrene

7. Effects of abnormal glycosylation of protein:
Collagen and keratin are affected by non-enzymatic glycosylation; this interferes with normal wound healing and tissue viability

---

Motor fibre involvement can affect the small intrinsic muscles of the foot. This causes clawing and retraction of the toes, which in turn will increase the angulation at the metatarsophalangeal joints and lead to trauma of the skin and underlying tissues from ground reaction forces.

Sensory neuropathy will impair the person's ability to perceive protective pain and temperature stimuli, both of which are protective warning signs of impending damage. When damage is not detected, the damaging agent will continue until tissues are traumatized.

Autonomic neuropathy leads to specific changes in the feet. Arteriovenous shunting occurs, which allows diversion of blood through the deeper thermoregulatory arteriovenous shunts at the expense of perfusing superficial nutritive capillaries, thus compromising skin viability (Edmonds, 1986). A foot affected by autonomic neuropathy appears warm with bounding pulses and distended veins; however, the skin will appear atrophic. The condition of the skin is exacerbated by reduced sweating as a consequence of autonomic dysfunction.

Over the past ten years evidence has demonstrated that autonomic, as well as sensory, neuropathy is implicated in Charcot joint formation in the diabetic foot. In the early stages the affected joint is swollen, and the surrounding and overlying tissues are hot and erythematous; the signs and symptoms can mimic deep infection, However, on further investigation the patient is generally afebrile, with an unremarkable white blood cell count, and on surgical exploration of the foot infection will not be found. It is thought that abnormal blood flow causes osteopenia; this together with loss of protective pain sensation and proprioception causes excess mechanical force to act on abnormal bone, which leads to microfractures. Unless treated by immobilization, the deformity progresses, resulting in severe joint deformity. The relentless destruction of joints in the midtarsal region of the foot can result in the classic 'rocker bottom' foot, which is extremely difficult to accommodate in footwear, and the prominent joint is very susceptible to ulceration.

Stroke

Stroke is common in the elderly, and again its aftermath can have specific effects on the feet. Abnormal gait patterns develop and these can lead to pressure areas developing which ulcerate and become secondarily infected. Conversely, people who have had a stroke may become immobile and develop pressure lesions over prominent areas, for example the heels. One cause of stroke is atherosclerotic changes in the cerebral vessels. The same disease process can involve the arteries supplying the lower limbs and the complications of ischaemia (discussed earlier) may affect the foot. Balance can be affected, leading to falls which contribute directly, and indirectly, to morbidity and mortality rates in the elderly.

Specific foot problems

Toenails

Toenail problems in the elderly have been highlighted in two studies of foot pathologies affecting the older person (Vetter et al, 1985; Cartwright and Henderson, 1986). Onychogryphosis, where the nail plate becomes thickened and distorted, is a particular problem. Changes in the structure of the nail are to be expected with increasing age: mechanical forces over the years alter the nail matrix and the nail bed. Both these structures contribute cells to the growing nail plate. Developmentally and histologically the nail plate is closely related to skin; therefore changes in the latter, associated with ageing, will be reflected in the nail plate.

Although the nail plate may be thickened and distorted, it is important that toe nails are cut straight across, avoiding cutting down the sides, which can cause splinters of nail to penetrate the soft tissues of the nail sulcus and allow infection to develop (onychocryptosis). When an individual, or her family or carers, cannot manage to cut the nails, a State Registered Podiatrist should be consulted. The State Registered Podiatrist can use specialist skills and equipment to reduce the thickness of nails and to remove corns and callosities that can develop around and under the nail (onychophosis). Not only are hypertrophic nails painful, due to the sheer bulk of nail tissue, there is also the possibility of ulceration developing on the nail bed (subungual ulceration).

Fungal infections of the nail (onychomycosis) are common. The nail plate appears dystrophic, friable, discoloured and accompanied by a characteristic musty odour. Diagnosis is confirmed by mycological examination of toe nail clippings. Treatment is not always necessary; however, with the advent of effective systemic preparations management is far more successful today than it was several years ago. Topical treatment often requires exceptional patient compliance, with the affected nails being painted daily for several months before infection is eradicated.

Skin conditions

Corns and callosities should be managed by a State Registered Podiatrist. The use of corn 'cures' is not recommended; these 'cures' often contain acids which macerate the epidermis and can allow the ingress of microorganisms, with resultant infection and possible ulceration of the skin. It is also worth noting that these preparations cannot 'cure' corns; corns and callosities build up in response to abnormal mechanical stresses acting on the epidermis and underlying tissues. Until these stresses, for example exerted by tight shoes, are eradicated the corns and callosities will continue to develop.

The skin in elderly people tends to be dry (anhidrotic), and it is important that affected areas, for example around the periphery of the heel, do not become fissured as breaches in the epithelium will allow the entry of pathogens. An emollient cream, preferably unscented to avoid sensitivity reactions, should be used after bathing to help rehydrate the skin. Some elderly people, particularly those with hallux abducto valgus and associated lesser toe deformities, develop maceration and fissuring of skin between the toes. Again, these 'wet' fissures can allow the entry of pathogenic microorganisms. It is important to ensure that the feet are dried carefully after bathing. The application of surgical spirit to the interdigital spaces can help in reducing maceration.

It is worth noting that if any of the signs of spreading infection occur on the dorsal aspect of the foot (for example, cellulitis or lymphangitis), it is imperative that the interdigital spaces and toe webbing are examined as they are frequently the primary site of the infection.

Fungal infection of the skin is relatively common, and is often accompanied by onychomycosis (see above). The affected area is dry, erythematous, pruritic and scaly, although some fungal infections may present with small vesicles. Topical treatment with antifungal creams such as itraconazole preparations are often effective; as with fungal nail infection, the diagnosis is made by mycological examination of skin scrapings.

With increasing age there is an associated increase in malignant and premalignant skin lesions. Moles and pigmented areas should be monitored for signs of change (e.g. increase in size, uneven pigmentation, ulceration, bleeding or pain). If the health care worker is concerned, immediate referral to a specialist is mandatory. It should be noted that amelanotic melanomas can occur (often around and under toenails); these often present as atypical nodules that ulcerate and increase in size. Again urgent referral is indicated.

Toe deformities

Common toe deformities that are found in the older person include hallux abducto valgus, hammer, clawed and retracted toes. The prominent joints are subjected to excess mechanical forces and the overlying skin develops corns and callosities. With increasing age osteoarthrosis causes the joints to become fixed. There are adaptive changes in the joint capsule and associated tendons and ligaments; thus the deformities are not amenable to non-surgical correction. However, surgery may be contraindicated because of reduced healing potential, or problems associated with the administration of general or local anaesthesia. Therefore a conservative and palliative approach is indicated in managing many cases. Protective padding (felts, foams and silicones) can be used to deflect stresses away from the prominent areas, and to 'replace' the fibro fatty tissue that is normally found on the plantar aspect of the foot acting as a shock-absorbing structure, but which atrophies with age. In many cases, these devices are converted into permanent orthoses that can be worn in the patient's shoes. Currently, there are a multitude of materials available. This allows manufacture of very specific orthoses with very different properties.

Footwear

Regardless of a person's age, and whatever structural changes have occurred in their feet, it is important that shoes fit properly. The main points of advice that should be offered to people when buying shoes are shown in Table 4.2.

In the older person there are occasions when specialist footwear is required to accommodate the deformed joints, or to prevent trauma to anaesthetic feet. There are two main types of specialist footwear available: bespoke footwear, which is made on a last unique to a specific patient, or semi-bespoke footwear, which is constructed on a common last, but has

Table 4.2. Points to look for when buying shoes and hosiery

- Have your feet measured for *length* and *width* before you buy shoes
- Buy your shoes in the afternoon – to allow for any swelling that can occur during the day
- Whenever you have new shoes *check your feet regularly* (every one or two hours) for signs of rubbing of your feet
- Your shoes should, ideally, be made of soft leather and be free of seams that may rub your foot (particularly over the tops of your toes)
- Your shoes should have laces or buckles to hold the shoe in close contact with the foot and prevent movement of the foot within the shoe. If laces or buckles are difficult Velcro straps can be used instead
- Check the inside of your shoe for ridges or uneven surfaces that could rub
- Make sure that the toe box of your shoe is deep enough
- Check that your shoe fits snugly around the heel and that your heel does not slip out when you walk
- Although you should have your feet measured, check that there is approximately a thumb's width gap between the end of your longest toe and the end of the shoe.
- The soling material should be cushioning, be light in weight and be non-slip (leather is not a good idea)
- Socks, tights and stockings should be free of seams and contain some natural fibres (cotton or wool) whenever possible. Hosiery that is too tight or 'rucks' up can be as damaging as ill fitting shoes

individual adaptations (e.g. extra width at a specific point, or extra depth in the toe area to accommodate hammer toes).

In some cases modifications can be made to 'off the shelf' shoes by a State Registered Podiatrist; these modifications include balloon patching and the addition of rocker soles.

Slippers are not encouraged; they are often ill fitting and encourage falls as the wearer adopts a shuffling gait in order to keep them in contact with the feet. The nature of the material that slippers are constructed of appears soft, but in fact is often inelastic and can cause abnormal mechanical stress on the toes.

Although research is sparse it would appear that ill fitting footwear, other than slippers, contributes to falls sustained by the elderly.

Ulceration

An ulcer can be considered as a wound that does not heal and becomes chronic. Foot ulcers impair mobility, and can decrease quality of life to a major extent in the elderly.

In order to make an accurate diagnosis, and therefore provide effective management, it is important to be familiar with the aetiology and pathogenesis of different types of ulcers that affect the feet.

If ulcers are thought of as chronic wounds it is reasonable to assume that any adverse alterations in normal wound healing will predispose to chronicity and ulceration. Some of these adverse alterations in the wound healing process are shown in Table 4.3.

Table 4.3. Factors that may lead to impaired wound healing

Vascular disease:
Arterial, venous and lymphatic disease

Neurological disease:
Peripheral and central nervous system disease leading to motor, sensory and autonomic signs and symptoms

Diseases that compromise the immune system:
Primary disorders of neutrophils or macrophages
Secondary to drug therapy, e.g. corticosteroids or antimetabolites

Arthropathies:
e.g. Rheumatoid arthritis, leading to deformity, and possibly reduced sensation and vasculitis

Metabolic and endocrine disease:
e.g. Disorders of the adrenal glands. Diabetes mellitus

Oedema:
Oedema is associated with many pathologies. Oedema will adversely affect tissue viability because it increases the diffusion distance between blood vessels and tissues. In addition, the excess fluid will compress microvessels

Haematological disorders:
Anaemia, which reduces oxygen carriage; leucocyte dysfunction, which can impair immunity

Nutritional deficits:
Malabsorption or reduced intake of essential nutrients, e.g. proteins, vitamins and minerals

Psychosocial problems:
Depression, and other states where the person is unable to care for himself or herself

---

At a cellular level the process of wound healing can be inhibited with advancing age. Wound healing is conveniently described as having three phases, which are summarized in Table 4.4.

In the older person there are quantitative and qualitative alterations at all three stages of the normal healing process that can adversely affect wound healing. The process will be further compromised if there is accompanying systemic disease, or if there is a lack of certain nutrients, for example zinc and vitamin C. When nutritional deficiencies are suspected, referral to a dietitian is indicated. Drug therapies such as corticosteroids will also impair the healing process.

Table 4.4. Stages in wound healing

Stage 1: stage of DEMOLITION
Clotting occurs on the wound surface (platelets have a growth factor effect as well as a haemostatic action – platelet-derived growth factor (PDGF) and transforming growth factor beta (TGF ß)
Exudate accumulates on the wound surface
Inflammation occurs in surrounding tissues
Neutrophils migrate into the wound followed by macrophages. These cells are important in removing debris
Epithelial cells begin to move over the wound surface within 24 hours. Epidermal growth factor (EGF), somatomedins (IGF I and IGF II insulin like growth factors I and II) promote basal epidermal cells to mitose
Fibronectins (from fibroblasts) form a 'scaffold' for cell movement

Stage 2: stage of GRANULATION
'Buds' from surviving surrounding vasculature grow into the wound (neo-angiogenesis). For this to be efficient debris must be cleared by macrophages and other cells
Low oxygen tension within the wound and resultant acid (low) pH also encourage vessel growth (via growth factors)
After about five days fibroblasts produce Type III collagen and matrix in response to TGF ß and basic fibroblastic growth factor (bFGF)
Myofibroblasts (modified fibroblasts which possess contractile protein within their cytoplasm) stimulated by TGF ß and PDGF cause 'shrinkage' of the wound
Collagen is produced in large quantities
Capillaries within the wound atrophy and are obliterated by collagen
Fibroblasts, which during activity are plump and large, become smaller

Stage 3: stage of REMODELLING
This can last for months
There is continual rebuilding and breaking down of collagen, in order to make the wound as strong as possible with Type I replacing Type III collagen

If an ulcer is considered as a 'chronic wound', the *reason* for the chronicity can be used to describe the type of ulcer. It is important before making a diagnosis that a full history of the ulcer is taken. The main points that should be considered are shown in Table 4.5.

Ischaemic ulceration

Ischaemic ulcers are associated with feet and legs that display signs and symptoms of chronic arterial insufficiency. These have been discussed earlier. The commonest cause of chronic ischaemia in the older person is atherosclerosis. However, ischaemia may be caused by vasospastic disorders such as Raynaud's disease, or inflammatory disorders of blood vessels associated with connective tissue disorders such as rheumatoid arthritis. Small vessel disease is associated with diabetes mellitus.

The ischaemic ulcer is typically found on the sides of the foot, the dorsal aspects and apices of digits, over the malleoli or under toenails. Its typical appearance is described in Table 4.6.

Table 4.5. History of the ulcer

1. How long has the ulcer been present?
2. Are there any changes in the *size or appearance* of the ulcer?
3. Has the *number* of lesions/ulcers changed?
4. Have there been any *previous incidents* of similar lesions?
5. Is there any *pain or abnormal sensation* associated with the lesion?
6. Are there any other *signs and/or symptoms* that may be related to the ulcer, e.g. ischaemic changes
7. Does the patient know the *cause* of the ulcer?

Table 4.6. Features of ischaemic and neuropathic ulcers

Type of ulcer	Ischaemic	Neuropathic
Size	Relatively small	Can be very large
Surrounding tissue	Little inflammation, little or no hyperkeratosis	Often heavy hyperkeratotic build up
Sides	Straight, ulcer often appears 'punched out'	Often undermining and tracking
Base	Adherent yellow slough, with little granulation tissue	Slough is often present, but there is frequently copious granulation tissue
Other	Painful, associated with other signs and symptoms of chronic ischaemia	Relatively painless. There may be associated deformity from motor nerve involvement, and signs of autonomic nerve involvement

Treatment is aimed at reducing stress over the ulcer and preventing infection. In order to prevent infection full aseptic techniques must be employed when treating the ulcer. Slough should be removed with extreme caution in order not to damage the sparse and delicate granulation tissue that is associated with ischaemic ulceration; additionally, these ulcers are often very painful and must be handled with care to prevent further distress to the patient. Shoes must be examined to ascertain that there are no rough areas or prominent seams that could cause further damage. They must not be tight or blood supply will be compromised further. The same comments apply to hosiery.

Neuropathic ulceration

These ulcers are associated with damage to the sensory nervous system. Although there is often a reduction in the amount of pain associated with neuropathic ulcers, they are not necessarily totally painless. The typical appearance of a neuropathic ulcer is shown in Table 4.6.

Neuropathic ulcers often support healthy granulation tissue, as the blood supply to the ulcer is not necessarily compromised. Epidermis surrounding neuropathic ulcers becomes hyperkeratotic and it is important that this is removed, using an aseptic technique, by a State Registered Podiatrist. Removal of hyperkeratotic tissue is important in order to allow drainage of the ulcer and to allow full examination of the extent of the ulcer. Neuropathic ulcers can be very deep and can track to joint spaces or result in osteomyelitis. In many cases, providing that any infection is treated adequately, and pressure reduced from the ulcer site using techniques such as total contact casts, healing will occur. However, if pressure is not permanently reduced, ulceration will return. Therefore once the ulcer has healed, attention must be given to providing suitable shoes and pressure relieving insoles. It is vital that callosities that build up over prominent sites are reduced by a State Registered Podiatrist to prevent breakdown of the tissues under the toughened stratum corneum.

Deciding on the most appropriate wound dressings can be a complex matter. As biotechnology progresses the type and number of dressings available have rocketed. Many specialist texts and journals are available to help the health carer decide on which one is most appropriate for each individual case. However, it is vital that each ulcer is treated and managed on its own merits, and that the wound dressing is used in strict accordance with the manufacturer's instructions.

It should be reiterated that when treating all ulcers a full aseptic technique must be employed and notes must be written in full in order to monitor the ulcer's progress. The points that should be noted are shown in Table 4.7. Deterioration of any ulcer warrants prompt referral for a specialist opinion.

Table 4.7. Points to observe when examining an ulcer

---

1. The precise *position* of the ulcer on the foot
2. The *size* of the ulcer. This should be measured accurately by tracing the outline of the ulcer onto special grid marked paper
3. The *general appearance* of the ulcer and the surrounding tissue, e.g. presence of callus or maceration. Note should be made of signs of local or spreading infection (cellulitis, lymphangitis, lymphadenitis)
4. The *sides* of the ulcer. When the walls undermine viable tissue the true extent of the ulcer must be assessed by careful use of a sterile probe
5 The *base* of the ulcer for the presence of slough, granulation tissue or deeper structures such as bone or tendon. Radiographs should be obtained if deeper structures are thought to be involved
6. The ulcer *depth* should be assessed. Chronic ulcers are associated with fibrous tissue tying the base to underlying structures; by gently moving the ulcer, the degree of fibrous involvement may be estimated
7. Any *discharge* should be noted and a specimen sent for microscopy and culture. The colour, consistency and odour of discharge should be noted. The quantity may be assessed by inspecting dressings and finding out how often dressings are changed

---

Conclusion

With an increasing elderly population it is important to recognize the signs of foot problems and to seek help as soon as possible. As discussed earlier, many foot problems encountered in elderly people start in childhood and adolescence. Foot health education in youth is vital in preventing disability and immobility in later years.

Foot problems, especially those perceived as relatively minor, such as thickened toenails and corns, can cause significant pain, immobility and lack of independence. Many foot problems are amenable to straightforward and simple treatment. More complex problems, perhaps related to complications of other disease processes, may not be so easily managed. However, in the majority of cases treatment is available to enable a better quality of life for the elderly person and their family and carers.

The State Registered Podiatrist is able to help with all aspects of foot care, but it is vital that all professionals involved with the elderly work together as a multidisciplinary team. This approach has several benefits: it enables an holistic approach in care, and it can reduce repetition in management plans which can be time-consuming and frustrating for the patient and for the provider. In future years evidence-based care provision will become more important, and this will rely on shared experiences of all health care professionals.

References

Cartwright A and Henderson G (1986). More Troubles with Feet. London: HMSO.

Dobby JL (1993). An evaluation of courses of training and education which lead to State Registration as a Chiropodist. Published by The Chiropodists Board, Council for Professions Supplementary to Medicine, 1993.

Edmonds ME (1986). The diabetic foot: pathophysiology and treatment. Clinics in Endocrinology and Metabolism, 15, 889–916.

Elton PJ and Sanderson SP (1987). A chiropodial survey of elderly persons over 65 years in the community. The Chiropodist, 42, 175–8.

Gilchrest BA (1996). A review of skin ageing and its medical therapy. British Journal of Dermatology, 135, 867–75.

Kemp J and Winkler JT (1983). Problems Afoot: Need and Efficiency in Footcare. London: Disabled Living Foundation.

Rogers J, Harding C, Mayo A, Banks J and Rawlings A (1996). Stratum corneum lipids: the effect of ageing and the seasons. Archives of Dermatological Research, 288, 765–70.

Quaglino D, Bergamini G, Boraldi F and Pasquali Ronchetti I (1996). Ultrastructural and morphometrical evaluation on normal human dermal connective tissue – the influence of age, sex and body region. British Journal of Dermatology, 134, 1013–22.

Vetter NJ, Jones D and Victor C (1985). Chiropody services for the over 70s in two general practices. The Chiropodist, 40, 315–23.

Chapter 5
Nursing the Elderly Person: a Community Perspective

RITA BEAUMONT

The nursing care of dependent elderly people has become a major issue for the 1990s. Current health and social policy has had a significant impact on older people, particularly on their need for continuing care in the community (Department of Health, 1995b). Significant changes have occurred on the boundaries of health provision; accompanying cost-containment measures have profoundly affected older people, many of whom have found themselves means tested for services that were previously provided free. Elderly clients have a clear nursing need that must be provided in a range of care settings; these include own home, nursing home, residential home, supported housing or hospital environment. The Royal College of Nursing (1997b) forcefully argued the role of the nurse as an enabler of health in continuing care settings; they have continued to articulate the restoration and maintenance of optimum health as being the foundation of social well-being.

Intervention in the care of an older person may clearly result in health gain. However, much care cannot be quantified in these ways. Examples of this include increased knowledge and compliance through teaching about medication or individual psychosocial assessment which reduces the need for financial restraint (RCN, 1997b).

The increasing number of older people, especially the very frail elderly, has put an increasing demand on society for high quality care which is both cost efficient and effective in outcome. As the older person's ability for personal care decreases he or she becomes increasingly dependent on both the statutory and voluntary services. The complementary role of the informal carer has become paramount as an underpinning factor in care provision.

The impact of the NHS and Community Care Act (Department of Health, 1990) was considerable, with the transfer of the budget for some nursing and residential care from central to local government. This resulted in a changed role from service supplier to lead agency in assessment of need and coordinator of care. The implementation of the NHS and Community Care Act 1990 in 1993 resulted in increased support for the elderly living at home, and created a financial disincentive for the social services to fund places in residential care. This increased the numbers of frail dependent elderly in the community. The implementation of the Act has led to a conscious effort to explore and clarify the functions of both health and social care sectors in the provision of care. The exact boundaries of health and 'social' care differ nationally (NAHAT, 1993), resulting in a lack of standardization across the country. The need for clear patient assessment to be established, enabling care planning, both long and short term, has become vital. Nurses, as key members of the multidisciplinary care team, have an important role to play in both assessing need and providing hands-on care and support to informal carers.

The assessment of nursing needs

Assessment provides a basic framework for establishing the range of care needs of each elderly client and a tool to aid case management. Effective assessment enables the following to be established:

- a comprehensive overview of health status;
- the level of nursing intervention needed;
- evidence to support decision making and practice, including cost implications;
- evidence to determine goals and objectives to be set;
- responsibilities for care provision to be established.

Sensitive, systematic assessment is an essential requirement in the successful implementation of good practice in caring for the elderly client. It is also a key component in implementing government policy in community care settings. The Centre for Policy on Ageing (1990) and the Department of Health (1990) both recommended the development of local strategies for needs assessment. However, Dickinson and Ebrahim (1990) pointed out that in many cases, the rhetoric of full and comprehensive assessment is rarely fulfilled in practice. The use of a problem-solving framework is the linchpin to successful assessment, enabling the assessment of need to become integral to the care process. It also provides the basis for long-term care (DoH, 1995b).

A range of assessment tools can be found when the literature is explored. These each have an appropriate place in the overall assessment of elderly clients. The tools include: the Barthel Index (Mahoney and Barthel, 1965), the Crighton Royal Behaviour Rating Scale (Wilkin and Jolley, 1979), the Clifton Assessment Procedures for the Elderly (Pattie and Gilleard, 1979), Senior Monitor (Goldstone and Maselino-Okai, 1986) and

Criteria for Care (Ball and Goldstone, 1984). Whilst these tools do not specifically identify nursing needs, they do articulate the need for care within a multidisciplinary arena.

Nolan and Caldock (1996) identify that a framework for assessment should embrace the following criteria:

* flexible, and able to be adapted to a variety of circumstances;
* appropriate to the audience it is intended for;
* capable of balancing and incorporating the views of a number of carers, users and agencies;
* able to provide a mechanism for bringing different views together while recognizing the diversity and variation within individual circumstances.

Assessment is the first phase in the circular process of providing an individual nursing care plan for each client. The process involves problem-solving, critical decision-making, clinical skills and application of theory to practice. Successful assessment of the elderly client requires the nurse to develop well defined history-taking skills, as well as keen skills of observation and interpretation of both verbal and non-verbal communications. A comprehensive collection of information must be gathered. This includes details of biological and physical aspects, psychological, psychosocial and functional aspects, family relationships, social networks, previous occupational pursuits, religious beliefs and social networks (RCN, 1997a). A framework for assessing the nursing needs of the older person is shown in Table 5.1.

Table 5.1. A framework for assessing the nursing needs of older people

Biography	Nursing assessment
Health status	Health care needs
Medical diagnosis	Self-care deficits
Personal circumstances	
Care plan	Identified needs for nursing
Nursing needs	

Source: RCN Assessment Tool for Nursing Older People (RCN, 1997a).

As the nurse becomes more expert, the quicker and more accurate judgements and predictions become (Benner and Wrubel, 1989). Experience and expert skills are vital when caring for elderly clients, if effective and efficient care is to be provided. Whilst the total needs of the elderly can only be met within a multidisciplinary provision, the unique purpose of nursing was defined by the RCN/Age Concern (1997) as:

'A service for older people who have their nursing needs identified by a nurse and receive that care either directly or under the supervision and management of a nurse who is registered by the United Kingdom Central Council for Nurses, Midwives and Health Visitors, UKCC.'

The development of the RCN Assessment Tool (RCN,1997a) provides a comprehensive instrument for use in a range of care settings, as part of the total assessment process, interfacing with a range of other professions. The tool uses as its foundation Seedhouse's (1986) concept of health, along with the domains of the RCN framework for outcome definition in the care of older people, outlined in 'What a Difference a Nurse Makes' (RCN, 1997b). Table 5.2 lists the diverse function of nursing and multiple roles performed by registered nurses (RCN, 1996). For the elderly person needing both nursing and social care, both disciplines should be involved jointly in assessing needs, planning care and commissioning appropriate services. These must be coordinated to provide a seamless service, and regularly evaluated for effectiveness. The need for this collaborative approach was borne out by Hancock (1993) who identified that the effective assessment and delivery of services for the elderly requires close collaboration between local authorities, health authorities and other agencies, including the voluntary sector. She believed, in particular, that the assessment of an elderly person's needs should be a 'multidisciplinary exercise', which recognizes the responsibilities and contribution of each agency in providing the most appropriate services (Hancock, 1993).

Table 5.2. Nursing functions

The role of the nurse includes:

Supportive functions: including psychosocial support; emotional support; assisting with easing transition; enhancing lifestyles and relationships; enabling life review; facilitating self-expression and ensuring cultural sensitivity.

Restorative functions: aimed at maximizing independence and functional ability, preventing further deterioration and/or disability, and enhancing quality of life. This is undertaken through a focus on rehabilitation that maximizes the older person's potential for independence, including assessment skills and undertaking essential care elements (for example, washing and dressing).

Educative functions: the registered nurse teaches self-care activities (e.g. self-medication), health promotion, continence promotion and health screening. With other staff, the registered nurse engages in a variety of teaching activities that are aimed at maximizing confidence in competence and continuously improving the quality of care and service delivery.

Life-enhancing functions: this includes all activities that are aimed at enhancing the daily living experience of older people, including relieving pain and ensuring adequate nutrition.

Managerial functions: the registered nurse undertakes a range of administrative and supervisory responsibilities which call for the exercise of managerial skills. Such responsibilities include the supervision of care delivered by other staff and the overall management of the home environment.

Source: Introduction to the RCN Assessment Tool for Nursing Older People (1997a).

The role of the community nurse

District nurses have for many years provided much of the professional support for elderly people and their carers in community settings. All elderly people over 75 years of age are entitled to a yearly home health screening visit from their GP as part of the 1990 GP contract agreements. These visits include:

- an assessment of the home environment;
- an appraisal of lifestyle and significant relationships, including the presence of a supporting carer;
- mobility assessment;
- mental assessment;
- assessment of hearing and vision;
- assessment of general function;
- review of medication.

Many of the screening procedures are carried out by suitably qualified community nurses on behalf of the GP or, in some cases, by practice nurses. In a few areas, health visitors have a specialist remit with elderly clients. The health surveillance of elderly people was a key priority identified in *Caring for People* (DoH, 1989). It was seen as a strategy for reducing the need for hospital and residential care and prolonging independence. The benefits of community nursing for their practice were articulated to GPs in *Buying Community Nursing* (RCN, 1993). The benefits were seen to include the opportunity to integrate the work of both community nurses and practice nurses. The introduction of GP fundholding in many areas has resulted in a review of the role of the district nurse in relation to providing cost-effective services for elderly patients, with subsequent review of the skill mix available. It remains to be seen how the role will change again with the introduction of Primary Care Groups. District nurses must continue to demonstrate that they provide the best option, clearly supporting positive outcomes to care. The introduction of the Specialist Practitioner: Home Nursing training provides a vehicle for district nursing into the next century. Table 5.3 demonstrates the programme outcomes to be attained by the end of the training period. This adds to the key issues in district nursing practice previously identified by the District Nursing Association.

Changing and developing roles in nursing

Statistical information (DoH, 1992) revealed that 18,000 nurses were employed in the district nursing service in England and Wales. This number covers the full spectrum from qualified district nurse to nursing auxiliaries, with approximately 50% holding a district nursing qualification. The introduction of extensive skill mix analysis in the service has resulted in a realignment of the balance (Value for Money Unit: NHSME, 1992). The knowledge, on qualifying, of the holders of the Diploma of Higher Education (Nursing Studies) has changed the role of the qualified district nurse from an overall hands-on caregiver to a manager of the district nursing team, acting also as a specialist practitioner with overall accountability for patients. The traditional role of the nursing auxiliary has also changed from the 'bath nurse' to a more rounded role as support worker, many holding Vocational Qualifications at levels 2 and 3. Whilst they are unable to provide the same level of trained nurse care to clients, they do provide support within the professional team. The introduction of varying levels of nursing skill within the community nursing team has been accompanied by a drop in the number of district nurses being trained, whilst the number of referrals and the complexity of presenting problems has accelerated.

Table 5.3. Community nursing in the home – district nursing

SPECIFIC LEARNING OUTCOMES
The nurse should achieve the following specific outcomes applied to district nursing:

Specialist clinical practice
- Assess the health-related needs of patients, clients, their families and other carers and identify and initiate appropriate steps for effective care for individual and groups.
- Assess, diagnose and treat specific diseases in accordance with agreed nursing/medical protocols.
- Assess, plan, provide and evaluate specialist clinical nursing care to meet care needs of individual patients in their own homes.

Care and programme management
- Contribute to strategies designed to promote and improve health and prevent disease in individuals and groups.
- Manage programmes of care for patients with chronic disease.
- Play a key role in care management as appropriate.

Source: The Councils Standards for Education leading to the Qualification of Specialist Practitioner (UKCC Registration letter 20.1994).

Support for the carers

The effectiveness of support for informal carers of elderly clients was investigated by Atkin and Twigg (1993). They found that support fell into two broad areas:

1. Community nurses gave practical help such as changing dressings, giving injections and help with personal hygiene. Some carers particu-

larly welcomed this practical help as a relief from tasks which they otherwise might have found difficult or embarrassing to do themselves.

2. Community nurses were also reported to give help to carers in the form of emotional support. Carers valued the opportunity to have someone else with whom to talk and discuss their worries. It was also an opportunity for the community nurse to give information about benefits and services available to the carer and, where required, make the necessary referrals for those services.

As a result of increasing demands for community nursing and changes in the balance of skills within a local team, the time for emotional support for carers has been reduced. The time of the trained nurse is now almost entirely taken up with carrying out the more complex technical tasks. Atkin and Twigg (1993) reported that the problems associated with the actual support available for carers have meant that the potential for their support has yet to be fully realized. In the work by Twigg (1989) a framework for explaining the relationship between professionals and carers was developed. In this work, three types of relationship between the community nurse and informal carers were described:

1. As resource: here needs are viewed as being subordinate to the client.
2. As co-client: here needs are seen to be acknowledged and met, even if this is at a secondary level.
3. As co-worker: here the carer is viewed as working in parallel with the professional.

This framework provides a good starting point on which to build a strong understanding and relationship between carer and nurse.

Victor (1991) identified that many elderly people are supported by their partners, with women more likely to live longer. The consequence of this is that many elderly women have no partner to support them. Carers who are not partners are more likely to be women, particularly daughters and daughters-in-law (Victor, 1991). However, caring is not solely a female domain. In a survey by Walker and Warren (1996) 35% of one sample were male. Some carers are well supported by informal networks of friends and relations, whilst others receive help via external organizations such as Age Concern or the Carers National Association. A number of carers supporting elderly people are still employed, with the added task of balancing the demands of work and the role of a carer (Laczko and Noden, 1993), with possibly less income than non-carers at their disposal. In some areas services such as night sitters and care attendant schemes are available. An example of this is Crossroads, an organization that offers care attendants to give flexible practical help in the home to provide a break for carers (Twigg, 1992).

Support outside the home

Whilst many elderly people are able to live independently in their own homes, increasingly support from outside the home is needed if care in the community is to be successfully maintained. The care required embraces a range of provision from basic primary care to highly technical interventions. There is a higher prevalence of many physical and mental health problems among both the oldest age groups and women. This is a cause for concern for policy-makers in view of the projected increases in the oldest age groups, the predominance of women in these groups and the likely increased need for health care services for these groups (Tester, 1996).

Table 5.4 provides an outline of the health care needs and services outside the home (Tester, 1996).

Table 5.4. Health care needs and services outside the home

Services to meet needs	Examples of services
Physical and mental health care	
Assessment and monitoring	GP, specialist clinic, day hospital
Treatment, medication, surgery	Acute hospital, pharmacy, dentist
Nursing, dressings, injections	Hospital or clinic nurse
Mental health care	Physiotherapy, speech therapy
Therapy, rehabilitation	Health checks by GPs, screening programmes
Prevention and health promotion	Older people's nurse, health adviser
Basic care	
Meals, laundry, bathing	Hospital or day care unit
Counselling, emotional support, social contacts	
Coping with illness, disability, dying	Counsellor, self-help group, hospice,
Arrangements for hospital discharge	Hospital social worker
Company, social activities	Voluntary visitor, day care activities
Support for informal carers	Carer group, respite care in hospital
Transport	
To hospital, GP, clinic, optician	Ambulance, transport/escort service
Information and advice	
On health problems	Health care professionals
On services and benefits available	Leaflet displays in hospital, clinic

Source: Community Care for Older People: A Comparative Perspective (Tester, 1996).

Whilst the main aspects of health care provision are available via nursing, medical and therapeutic sources in either a hospital or domiciliary setting, vital basic support comes from social welfare agencies to aid health care professionals to provide a holistic service to the elderly client and carer. The health services offered to older people are affected by general health policies and systems. These, in practice, place greater priority on acute hospital care and services for younger people than on services to meet long-term care needs of people with disabilities (Tester, 1996). However, with good coordination, maximum outcome can be gained to ensure an effective provision that is efficient and appropriate to meet patient needs.

The introduction of the Patient's Charter (DoH, 1995a) provides a further dimension to patient choice; this has a special significance in providing a choice of where clients wish to be cared for and by whom. Nurses working in the community have been given a unique opportunity to move away from a traditional medical model of care to ones embracing a holistic individualized approach, taking into account the patient's lifestyle and family situation, and taking into account the contribution made by the other members of the multiagency/multiprofessional team. The development of the primary health care team approach to care has helped promote a better understanding of the various roles and skills of multidisciplinary team members to maximize support to elderly clients and their carers. The World Health Organization (1978) noted the importance of primary health care in achieving its strategy of health for all by the year 2000. Effective primary health care needs both primary medical care and the skills of a multidisciplinary team of health care workers, each bringing a discrete area of expertise yet working together to maximize the contribution to the health and welfare of the elderly client.

A mix of available skills is also an integral aspect of efficiently managing health services in the community. The aim of effective skill mix relates to creating a balance of interrelated skills, provided by highly qualified practitioners and unqualified care assistants in such a way as to ensure a quality service at a cost efficient rate – value for money. It is important that grade mixes are responsive to client needs to provide a flexible service delivered at the point of need.

The growth of services in the independent sector, providing home-based services and residential care, has widened the range of choices available to elderly clients and their carers. However, this choice may be narrowed down by cost. Many elderly people continue to live independently in their own homes, or with the support of formal services and informal carers to the end of their lives; however, for some there comes a time when a move to a residential environment proves to be necessary. Often the move is precipitated by the loss of a partner or other carer. The chosen accommodation may be in a residential home, a nursing home or sheltered housing; provision may be in either the public or private sector. The expansion in private care agencies and private residential and nursing homes has increased the need for thorough inspection and monitoring by the statutory services. It remains to be seen if the increase in the private sector as a prime care provider of services for elderly people leads to a reduction in those provided by the statutory services, rather than complementing them in terms of both quality and quantity.

Conclusion

Growing old is inevitable and whilst increasing numbers of the elderly patients are living to extreme old age this can be a time of fulfilment for both the patient and the nurse working in the community setting. The dependency of many of the patients has risen considerably since the recent NHS and community care reforms. The demand, particularly on the district nursing service, has increased at a time when the number of trained district nurses is falling; whilst skilled 'physical tasks' are being performed, the necessary 'emotional support' to the patient and carers is becoming more difficult to provide. The balance between health and social care needs is a fine one, with each supporting the other to provide a total planned programme for each elderly person. Each service has a vital role to play in assessing needs and implementing appropriate 'packages of care'. To provide a good quality service, adequate resources must be allocated; these resources must be managed well to maximize outcomes. Key to good service provision is a well-educated workforce, prepared to meet the challenges of caring for an increasingly elderly population.

David Skidmore (1997), in his closing comment in the book Community Care: Initial Training and Beyond, says the following:

'Being old is something that happens to other people; being chronically ill is something that happens to other people. If you listen you might glean clues regarding how best to address a person and, ultimately, facilitate their return to health, or at least assist them improve the quality of their life.'

References

Atkin K and Twigg J (1993) Nurses' effectiveness in supporting carers. Nursing Standard, 7(42), 38–9.

Ball J and Goldstone L (1984) Criteria for Care. Newcastle upon Tyne: Polytechnic Products.

Benner P and Wrubel J (1989) The Primacy of Caring. Stress and Coping in Health and Illness. Menlo Park, CA: Addison-Wesley.

Centre for Policy on Ageing (1990) Community Life: A Code of Practice for Community Care. London: Centre for Policy on Ageing.

Department of Health (1989) Caring for People. London: HMSO.

Department of Health (1990) NHS and Community Care Act. London: HMSO.

Department of Health (1992) Health and Personal Social Services Statistics for England. London: HMSO.

Department of Health (1995a) Patient's Charter. London: HMSO.

Department of Health (1995b) NHS Responsibilities for Meeting Continuing Health Care Needs, HSG (95) 8, LAC (95) 5. London: HMSO.

Dickinson E and Ebrahim S (1990) Adding life to years: quality and the health care of the elderly. Geriatric Medicine, 112, 12–17.

Goldstone l and Maselino-Okai CV (1986) Senior Monitor: An Index of the Quality of Nursing Care for Senior Citizens on Hospital Wards. Newcastle upon Tyne: Polytechnic Products.

Hancock C (1993) New dimensions in caring. Elderly Care, 3(1), 18–19.

Laczko F and Noden S(1993) Continuing paid work with eldercare: the implications for social policy. In: KA Luker (ed.) Health and Social Care in the Community, 1(2), 81–9.

Mahoney F and Barthel D (1965) Functioning evaluation: the Barthel Index. Maryland State Medical Journal, 14, 61–5.

National Association of Health Authorities and Trusts (NAHAT) (1993) Care in the Community, Definitions of Health and Social Care: Developing an approach: Research paper 5. Birmingham: NAHAT.

NHSME (1992) The Nursing Skill Mix in the District Nursing Service, Value for Money Report. London: HMSO.

Nolan M and Caldock K (1996) Assessment: identifying the barriers to good practice. Health and Social Care in the Community, 4(2), 77–85.

Pattie A and Gilleard C (1979) Manual of the Clifton Assessment Procedures for the Elderly. Sevenoaks: Hodder and Stoughton.

Royal College of Nursing (1993) Buying Community Nursing. London: RCN.

Royal College of Nursing (1996) Nursing Homes: Nursing Values. London: RCN.

Royal College of Nursing (1997a) Assessment Tool for Nursing Older People. London: RCN.

Royal College of Nursing (1997b) What a Difference a Nurse Makes: A Report on the Benefits of Expert Nursing to the Clinical Outcomes for Older People on Continuing Care. London: RCN.

Royal College of Nursing and Age Concern (1997) Funding Nursing in Nursing Homes. London: RCN.

Seedhouse D (1986) Health: Foundations for Achievement. Chichester: Wiley.

Skidmore D (1997) Community Care: Initial Training and Beyond. London: Arnold.

Tester S (1996) Community Care for Older People: A Comparative Perspective. London: Macmillan Press.

Twigg J (1989) Models of carers: how do agencies conceptualize their relation with informal carers? Journal of Social Policy, 18(1), 43–66.

Twigg J (1992) Carers in the service system. In J Twigg (ed.) Carers: Research and Practice. London: HMSO.

United Kingdom Central Council for Nursing, Midwivery and Health Visiting (1994) The Councils Standards for Education – leading to the Qualification of Specialist Practitioner, UKCC Registration letter 20.1994.

Victor C (1991) Health and Health Care in Later Life. Milton Keynes: Open University Press.

Walker A and Warren L (1996) Changing Services for Older People. Milton Keynes: Open University Press.

Wilkin D and Jolley D (1979) Behavioural Problems Among Older People in Geriatric Wards, Psychogeriatric Wards and Residential Homes 1976–1978, Research Paper no.1, Psychogeriatric Unit, University Hospital of South Manchester.

World Health Organization (1978) Report on the Primary Health Care Conference. Alma-Ata: WHO.

Chapter 6
Grandparenting:
Implications of the Role for
Community Carers

LIS SCHILD

Introduction

This chapter focuses upon the significance of the contribution that the life experiences and insights of older people can bring to the implementation of their care in the community by professional social and health care practitioners. All life changes are contextualized for individuals by reference to earlier experiences and interpreted according to cultural and social expectations. This chapter will use a piece of qualitative research, which explored the role of grandparents across a range of cultures and countries, as an illustration of one way in which professionals can learn from and respond to the wealth of life experience which elders bring with them into the arena of assessment for, and delivery of, the care which is the focus of current professional social work practice. The research, reported in two papers, Barrett et al (1996) and Schild and Ali (1997), explored experiences and beliefs about the role of grandmothers and, in the final cohort, the role of grandfathers, in three cohorts of older people: the first in Luton was primarily, though not exclusively, a white population; the second, in St Lucia in the Caribbean, was mainly black; the third consisted of south Asian Muslims in Azad Kashmir, Pakistan during 1995 and 1996.

The implementation of the National Health Service and Community Care Act 1990 provided a significant impetus to review the quality of social care for elderly people and encouraged debate on assessment and care management, which has enhanced professional awareness of the important skills and knowledge required of the qualified worker. However, budgetary constraints and political imperatives have changed the social work task in ways that have challenged the basic assumptions and values of the profession. The vision, first described in the Griffiths Report, Community Care: Agenda for Action (Griffiths, 1988), and affirmed in the White Paper Caring for People (DoH, 1989), of a move away from a resource-led towards a needs-led service, where need is defined by the user, has only partially materialized. Overt service rationing has become the norm. As a recent research report on family carers says: 'The community care policies implemented since April 1993 call for more people to be supported in the community but the extra funds have not kept pace with increasing demand. There is an older and more disabled population, more call for post-hospital community services ... Community care statistics indicate a trend to tighter targeting and more intensive services ... In response to overspent community care budgets, local authority social services departments are urged to restrict eligibility to those most in "need"' (Healy and Yarrow, 1997). Within this context, the importance of listening to the voice of older people and allowing their insights to inform best practice must be a priority.

Two conversations recently highlighted the significance of the changing nature of relationships with the users of community care experienced by social work and social care practitioners. They reveal the cultural shift that social workers have undergone as a result of the NHS and Community Care Act. The first involved a qualified and experienced social worker who had added to her professional qualification a further diploma in working with visually impaired people. She described how her role cut across the 'commissioner/provider split' which followed implementation of the Act and how qualified social work colleagues, whose role was entirely within the commissioning roles of assessment and care management, no longer saw her as a 'proper social worker' since, as well as assessing need, she also provided mobility training and other specific services for visually impaired people. Historically most social workers would acknowledge an element, within their practice, of practical provision of care, counselling and support, as well as assessment for services. Time and structural constraints within the division of roles no longer allow this practice. However, in the 'Rules and Requirements for the DipSW (Diploma in Social Work)' (1996), the Central Council for Education and Training in Social Work (CCETSW) specifies as one of the six core competences required of the qualified social worker, the requirement to 'intervene and provide services to achieve change, through provision or purchase of appropriate levels of support, care, protection and control'. It breaks this competence down further. The first practice requirement is to 'contribute to the management of packages of care, support, protection and control'. The second is to 'contribute to the direct provision of care, support and protection'. It would seem then that the ability both to manage and deliver packages of care remains a core competence to be evidenced within the training of the qualified social worker.

The second conversation was with a group of lecturers reviewing the content of their qualifying nurse training programme around caring for older people. Concern was expressed that students on the Adult Pathway showed little interest in nursing older people and seemed to have some anxiety about relating to them. How could this fear be overcome and a vision of older people with much to give and to share be communicated to student nurses? The need to make a link was explored between the limited sample of older people that nurses, and indeed social workers, see in their professional work and their experience of elders within their families. To do this, voluntary agencies in the area providing clubs and support to people in their latter years were listed. How many offering a service to seventy, eighty, ninety year olds were managed by people of similar age but rather less frailty? Perhaps placements in some of these organizations could balance the experience of ageing by providing, in one place, two models of normal ageing? The Government's Manifesto picks up this theme in a different context, when it talks about the value of 'the positive contribution that older people make to our society, through their families, voluntary activities and work'. However, too often this contribution is obscured by the need for care, which may eventually accompany very old age.

A poem written some twenty years ago still has something to say to practitioners working with older people today. The poem, entitled 'A Crabbit Old Woman', is printed in full at the end of this chapter, since its precise source is not known. The story is that it was found among the belongings of an elderly patient, 'Kate', after her death in hospital, having been without speech but still able to write during the final weeks of her life. Discussion with health care colleagues then reflected its theme, that a lifetime's experience is all too easily obscured by that life's ending. She could no longer speak, but she was still able to experience, reflect upon and write about this final phase of a long and full life. Setting her reflections within the context of a busy and fulfilling life, she challenges her nurses (though it could just as easily have been her social worker or care assistant) to take another look.

> 'What do you see, nurses, what do you see?
> Are you thinking when you are looking at me
> A crabbit old woman, not very wise,
> Uncertain of habit, with faraway eyes,
> Who dribbles her food and makes no reply,
> When you say in a loud voice, "I do wish you'd try!"'

Describing and reflecting upon the stages of her life, Kate shadows Erik Erikson's (1977) Eight Ages of Man, finally reaching the stage he describes as maturity, balancing her despair at the way life is ending with her assurance that she is 'living and loving life over again'. The poem's final lines challenge the professionals' tendency to see older people outside of their life's context, to depersonalize them and so to defend themselves against the anxiety of facing their own mortality as she is facing hers. Kate concludes her reflections thus:

'I'm an old woman now and nature is cruel,
'Tis her jest to make old age look like a fool.
The body it crumbles, grace and vigour depart,
There now is a stone where once I had a heart.
But inside this old carcass a young girl still dwells,
And now and again my battered heart swells;
I remember the joys, I remember the pain,
And I'm living and loving life over again;
I think of the years, all too few, gone too fast,
And accept the stark fact that nothing can last.
So open your eyes, nurses, open and see
Not a crabbit old woman. Look closer – see ME!'

How hard it can be to *see ME*, the totality of the personality, in the setting of illness and dependency. It is within that final phase that professionals are most likely to meet as strangers, people who in their personal lives have had a range of identities, including parent, grandparent and, increasingly, great grandparent. They may well also have a recent significant identity as carers, innovators, students, teachers. The success of the Open University and the more recent University of the Third Age attests to this in enabling older people to continue their personal development into retirement. The research described below is offered as an example of one tool which can be used in bridging this gap in younger professionals' understanding of the life roles by which frail older people perceive their identity.

Listening to grandparents from a range of ethnic communities

(Barrett et al, 1996; Schild and Ali, 1997)

> 'When a child is born, so are grandmothers' (Levy, 1993)

The original impetus for this research came from a group of students working towards the Diploma in Social Work who interviewed and observed elderly women within a family context, as part of their studies. Students would normally be expected to observe a young child in his or her family but this group, who did not plan to work with children, were looking for insights beyond their own experience. Their findings suggested that an exploration of the role of grandmothers would yield some interesting data to help them towards an understanding of the family contexts in which they worked. The spirit behind this piece of research, therefore, was the belief that the researchers could learn from older people, value their perceptions, experience and perspectives and use the knowledge gained to inform practice. To this end, the focus was on grandparents geographically local to the area of practice and distant communities which represented the original social and cultural context of significant local groups. Discussion of some of the research techniques used may be found in Walker (1985). Reflection on the issues raised by this approach to, and interpretation of, the findings can be found in the writings of Fennell (1990) and Gearing and Dant (1990).

During 1995 and 1996 two cohorts of grandmothers were interviewed by staff from the University of Luton, one in the Caribbean island of St Lucia and one in Luton. The opportunity to extend the study to a third group came with another University project in 1996, which explored links between Pakistanis living in Luton and Azad Kashmir and the concept of Kashmiri identity, through a field trip to Pakistan. Research was carried out mainly although not entirely, by interviews with individuals. A total of 85 grandparents, mainly grandmothers, were interviewed in the Caribbean island of St Lucia, in Luton, England and in villages around Mirpur and Kotli, small country towns in Azad Kashmir, from which many families have emigrated to Luton over the past twenty years. The research explored the role of grandparents, particularly grandmothers, and attempted to identify any cultural differences in grandmothering styles between the different cohorts.

The findings

The roles of the grandmother/grandparent

The first phase of the study identified some possible cultural differences between grandmothers interviewed in England and the Caribbean. The main difference identified was that the typical St Lucian family was likely to be an extended one, with the grandmother acting as a surrogate mother (67%), whereas the English family was more likely to be a nuclear one, with none of the English grandmothers playing this role. Grandmothers in St Lucia were also more likely to be seen as stricter matriarchal figures than the mothers, with a significant role as disciplinarian. Both cohorts of grandmothers thought it important to act as an educator to their grand-children, particularly as the custodian of the cultural and family history. The response to questions about the changing role of grandmothers indicated that most of the Luton grandmothers perceived a significant change in their own role compared with their memories of the role, while less than half of the St Lucian grandmothers thought this was so. However, there were indications that culturally the two societies were moving closer together as family structures changed. 'An interesting irony began to emerge. Caribbean families were becoming more nuclear, based on the UK model. And in the UK, families were attempting to return to an extended model, much like the image of the Caribbean families' (Barrett et al, 1996).

The grandmothering roles identified through the early phases of the research included the grandmother as surrogate mother, the grandmother as disciplinarian/educator and the grandmother as a cultural and family historian. These roles were affirmed through the third phase, which also pointed to important cultural differences within the Pakistani community which differentiated between the roles of paternal and maternal grandparents. The extended family in Azad Kashmir and also in Britain focused on the home of the husband's family, so that paternal grandparents (Dada/Dadi), with whom a grandchild lived, had a quite different role from the maternal grandparents (Nana/Nani). Within that difference, the grandmothering roles identified in the first two phases of the study are reflected in the expectations of paternal grandparents. The role of maternal grandparents is more akin to that attributed by the first phase of the study to all grandmothers as 'being there to love the grandchildren and as an extension of support from the parents' (Barrett et al, 1996).

The research has highlighted some commonalities and differences across the cohorts interviewed. Perhaps the most obvious cultural difference lies in the social structure of the Muslim communities explored in Pakistan compared with the Christian base of both the English and Caribbean cohorts. The formal structure of the Muslim community, with a clear role within the family for the paternal grandparents, leads to different expectations and life experiences for paternal and maternal grandparents, not experienced generally in the Caribbean or English cohorts interviewed. There was some evidence that expectations of grandmothering had changed more within the Caribbean and English groups in recent years than in the Pakistani group, in spite of the effects of emigration on family structures.

Changes in the grandparenting roles

The study also asked whether the role of the grandmother (grandparents) had changed over the generations, inviting interviewees to remember their own experiences of grandmothering. Members of the first two cohorts did have memories of their grandmothers and were able to reflect upon some of the differences. These included the fuller education received by younger grandparents and likelihood of paid employment, as well as the increased likelihood of geographical separation which made close, daily contact impossible. In Pakistan most grandparents had no memory of their own grandparents, either because they had died, or because they lived a distance away. However, where they were remembered, it was mainly the paternal grandparents who had played similar roles to grandparents in the West Indies, with grandmothers having a greater and more expansive role than grandfathers.

Differences in the role as surrogate mother were identified, together with the experience of living in extended or nuclear families, with grandmothers in St Lucia taking this role as did the paternal grandmothers in Pakistan. Grandmothers in St Lucia and Pakistan thought the role had changed less than did grandmothers in England. However, the pattern of emigration had had a significant effect on the grandparenting role, particularly for Pakistani families, where education, cultural and religious development and understanding of the complexities of family relationships are all part of the role of paternal grandparents.

The comparative youth of grandmothers and the likelihood that they were in paid work, in both St Lucia and Luton, had affected the practical role of grandmothering in a way not yet experienced in rural Pakistan. A common finding across all three phases of the research was that grandparents continue to have a definite role to play in the lives of their children and grandchildren, even when separated by thousands of miles. While its practical outworking may be different, the focus remained the same. Strategies to ensure the role was fulfilled by maintaining links included phone calls, letters, visits back, tape recordings, visits to England. Many grandparents living in Pakistan were experiencing increasing difficulty in obtaining visas to visit England, which was affecting the nature of the links.

Importantly, a number of issues were raised by this research which have implications for the context in which practitioners assess and deliver a range of services to elderly people.

Issues raised by the study and implications for professional practice

The research identified common experiences of the role of grandmothers across several cultural, religious and geographical divides while also raising questions about the nature of the comparisons and the basic assumptions of the researchers.

'This research was carried out to a common format but with a very varied sample. Those interviewed were people whose ages varied from forty years to ninety four and whose present living circumstances ranged from a small village in rural Pakistan, through a Caribbean island community where wide extremes of wealth existed within the group of respondents, to a large urban environment in the United Kingdom. Individuals were busy managing large extended families, developing their professional careers, enjoying retirement having lived and worked abroad, attending social centres to alleviate loneliness, living alone or with a spouse, in local authority residential homes and various settings in between. Their history as grandparents began a few months before interview and extended to some seventy years.' (Schild and Ali, 1997)

Loss of role for people in residential care 'who need special consideration'

In his useful chapter on 'Research ethics and older people in researching social gerontology', Butler (1990) raises some important issues for the researcher to consider. Butler refers to older people with special needs living in an institutional setting as a 'captive' audience who need special consideration in research. His concern, shared by all social care practitioners, is that these older people may be too readily excluded from a research enterprise because of the rights of individuals to be protected from involvement in an activity which they may not understand. In the research described here, those older people who were themselves being cared for were unlikely to be able to look after their grandchildren. Their responses would be influenced by the fact that they no longer had the capacity to respond currently to the issues raised. Care has to be taken to protect the sensitivities and rights of vulnerable people in their participation in research activity carried out in accordance with nationally accepted codes of ethical practice, but to exclude this group of older people unnecessarily is to lose valuable insights.

Too often an assessment of the *need for residential care* can lead to a disregard of the significance of the individual's personal and cultural history in their *experience of care*. Insight into the differing roles played by grandparents, such as was gained through the research, which may lead to an exploration of the assumptions and values of both giver and recipient of care may improve the appropriateness of the quality and the content of care. In particular, understanding the role of grandparent, which can be seen to be culturally determined, may enhance the professional's understanding of the needs of the individual within the context of residential care.

The story of 'Kate', described earlier, gives an example of how easily professionals may miss opportunities to gain insight into the individual's understanding of their previous life experiences which will be informing their current experience of care. The attention that one person receives as part of a research programme may enable him or her to recover a sense of role which had been lost through the experience of receiving care. The richness of Kate's inner life, as shown in her writing, could perhaps have been accessed before her death by a skilled practitioner taking time to establish, in the absence of speech, alternative ways of communication. Reminiscence therapy offers one way into maintaining the sense of social role and the mental health of frail older people. The type of qualitative research described in the earlier paragraphs, carefully constructed, may offer a use for reminiscence that can be seen to value a role familiar to those interviewed.

In her reflections upon her own experience of being a grandmother, Margot Jefferys offers an autobiographical approach. In the wide-ranging text, *Critical Approaches to Ageing and Later Life* (Jefferys, 1997), she points out that 'recent studies based on empirical data suggest that grandparenthood remains a welcomed status. It helps to compensate for the more disagreeable aspects of ageing. Even if, in current times, contributing to the household and child-rearing tasks may be less important aspects of the role for many grandparents, affectional bonds forged between them and their grandchildren help to sustain the cohesion of the family as a primary socializing unit'. Margot Jefferys goes on to point out that both the experience and the relationships of grandparenthood inevitably change over time. The capacity to explore the meaning of these relationships as a tool in understanding the identity of older people is a skill that professionals should foster.

Assumptions about the roles of grandmothers/grandfathers in different ethnic and cultural groups

The research described above, through comparison of the data gained from the three cohorts, showed significant variations in the socially defined roles of grandparenting within different cultural and ethnic groups. Professionals must be alert to the way in which their own experiences affect their assumptions about the value placed on the roles which older people have played and their meaning for the individual. The first two cohorts were seen as having much in common in spite of some cultural differences, a feeling that 'a grandmother is a grandmother, regardless of colour, money or age' and that the grandmother's role is one of 'being there to love the grandchildren and as an extension of support from the parents' (Barrett et al, 1996). The distinction between the roles of maternal and paternal grandmothers, with the maternal grandmothers having the primary role in the first two groups examined, was not reproduced in the findings from the third cohort. Of the grandparents interviewed in Pakistan, many had two distinct roles. The primary role is that of the paternal grandparent, with whom the sons' children usually live, following the Muslim culture where, on marriage, the daughter-in-law moves into the home of her husband's parents. In this situation, the role of practical caring and 'mothering' requires close contact and involvement with the day-to-day care and upbringing of the grandchildren. This was divided between the two maternal grandparents, with grandmother filling the role of carer and grandfather providing that of educator and cultural historian. Both had a role in interpreting the grandchild's position in the complex and extensive extended family into which he or she had been born. However, many also had a secondary role as maternal grandparents, which was much closer to that identified for all grandparents in the other cohorts of 'being there' for the grandchildren.

Assessment for community care

How then can this approach provide some pointers to ways of using an awareness of different culturally prescribed roles, in this instance the grandparenting role, to inform assessment for care within the community? In the new culture of care management, with the impact of budgetary constraints and the managerial planning rather than interpersonal focus which practitioners are expected to bring to the individual assessment for care, professionals should be alert to the wide range of expectations older people and their families have of appropriate roles and relationships within the giving and receiving of care. In the context of care management which has followed the implementation of the National Health Service and Community Care Act 1990, an expanding range of literature has attempted to offer tools for the assessment of elderly people that have meaning to the social as well as the health care practitioner. Among these, a useful text edited by Ian Philp (1994) offers a range of assessment methods for use in history taking. In his foreword to the book, Shah Ebrahim talks about taking a history as 'the means by which doctors, nurses, therapists and social workers work out what has happened, what caused the problems and how best to solve the problems' and he describes holistic assessment as 'essential to describe and intervene in the many different ways that diseases, social circumstances and individual characteristics interact to cause impairment, disability and handicap'.

Social work practice has gained much from the rigorous approach to assessment and case management that the health service adopted some years earlier. In its Requirements for Qualification, the Central Council for Education and Training in Social Work describes the value base of social work (CCETSW, 1996) and places a high value upon awareness of issues of diversity in the social work task. 'This diversity is reflected through religion, ethnicity, culture, language, social status, family structure and lifestyle', to name but a few variants. It is perhaps, therefore, disappointing for the social worker to note the absence, in 'Social functioning of the elderly' (Challis et al, 1994), of any direct reference to these issues in the various instruments described. The assumption that they will have been addressed as part of the context setting for a more formalized assessment must be questioned. The importance of addressing these areas, to understand better the needs of the individual being assessed, in order to optimize the quality of life of older people receiving care, is illustrated in the findings of the grandparenting research described, which begins to identify the wide range of experiences and expectations of grandparenting to be found in different ethnic and cultural communities.

Comparative youth of grandparents – across the generations

The expectation that grandparents would be working was common to some Caribbean and English grandmothers, though not to the Muslim grandmothers. This raised a dilemma for some, which is reflected in the response of others of a similar generation to the challenge of care for their own elderly parents. 'These younger, working grandmothers reported that they felt they "missed out" on their grandchildren, but, especially in St Lucia, many younger grandmothers were not willing to readily "give up" their lives to look after their grandchildren' (Barrett et al, 1996). Within the sample described above, the ages of grandmothers varied from 40 to 94 years. For those in their forties, some still had children at home to care for, some had just re-established careers, having launched their children into independent adulthood, some continued to care for adult children, and inevitably some had responsibility for their own parents.

A recent research study highlights the tensions and opportunities for grandparents and grandchildren where the grandparent is living in the same household as one or more grandchild, because of a need for care (Healy and Yarrow, 1997). One third of the households studied included children. 'The family carer usually tried to shield her children from disruption and responsibility for the resident grandparent.' In spite of this, some of the children were helpful, taking on a caring role such as providing the occasional meal or undertaking to 'granny sit'. For others, it became a focus of tension within the family, with grandmother telling the grandchild what she or he should be doing.

At a time when the proportion of very old people is rising, the responsibilities of grandparents can extend across three or possibly four generations from grandparents to grandchildren, presenting a challenge of care to which not all are able to respond. The age of first time grandparents has always covered a wide range but, as life expectancy increases, many couples delay having their first child well into their thirties, reconstituted families extend the years over which children are born, and women expect to remain in work until retirement age, so the stress of the caring role for women in their middle years is significant. Healy and Yarrow (1997), commenting on society's view that women have a duty to care, offer examples of the guilt-inducing reluctance of agencies to respond to requests for help from female carers. Similarly, Minkler and Roe (1993) spell out some of the consequences of the challenge for grandmothers and great grandmothers who have taken on the role of raising children of the 'crack cocaine epidemic' in California. Whilst identifying for study a particular group of grandmothers, black women living in Oakland, California who have become caregivers because of drug problems among their children, they show how the stories of this group are both unique to each individual and yet share experiences common to female caregivers across many societies. The response of these women to the needs of their children and their grandchildren is graphically told, highlighting the way in which the roles of parent and grandparent, employee and caregiver are managed, often without support from wider family or the state.

Contextualizing the older person

The experience of grandmothers in California alerts professional practitioners who wish to truly meet the needs of service users to move from an exploration of 'personal troubles' to 'public issues' (Minkler and Roe, 1993) and to contextualize their assessments of users and their carers within an understanding of the history and life experience which all older people bring to the need for care. The pieces of research described above showed that grandparenting is offered in a variety of ways ranging from being the primary caregiver to living thousands of miles away. In the latter case, grandparents may not be unduly affected by the loss of independence implicit in a move into residential care. Grandparenting was already managed meaningfully by some grandmothers across the distance between St Lucia, Pakistan and England. Participants specified the use of letters, telephone calls, home videos and occasional visits as means of maintaining the links. Facilitating the maintenance of this role is important for the well-being of grandparent and grandchild alike and does not need to depend upon the continued ability to live independently in the community. However, for those whose experience of grandparenting has only ever been direct, the breaking of links can cause distress to both parties to the bond. On a recent trip to the island of Montserrat, where relationships of all sorts have been devastated by the volcanic eruption, a grandmother spoke of her helplessness and sense of loss that the absence of her own telephone line meant she was unable even to speak to her grandchildren who had left the island.

Conclusion

In the short time that is usually available to social care practitioners to make relationships with older people as potential service users in the formal assessment of need, the importance cannot be over-emphasized of establishing a meaningful context to this point in their lives. This will most effectively happen within their home setting and is best approached, if possible, through a multidisciplinary assessment which identifies and shares with colleagues a holistic and detailed social and medical history, informed by an understanding of the meaning that history has for the older person. Meanings cannot be assumed. As 'Kate' pleads on behalf of all vulnerable older people, 'open your eyes, open and see not a crabbit old woman. Look closer – see me!'

References

Barrett D, Burroughs L, Schild E and Wells M (1996) Listening to Grandparents. What can we learn from them? Unpublished Paper. Luton: University of Luton

Butler A (1990) Research ethics and older people. In: SM Peace (ed.) Researching Social Gerontology. London: Sage.

CCETSW (1996) Assuring Quality in the Diploma in Social Work (Second Edition, revised 1996). London: Central Council for Education and Training in Social Work.

Challis D, Dunleavy J, Philp I and Roberts H (1994) Social functions of the elderly. In: I Philp (ed.) Assessing Elderly People in Hospital and Community Care, Chapter 8. London: Farrand Press.

Department of Health (1989) Caring for People: Community Care in the Next Decade and Beyond. Cm. 849. London: HMSO.

Erikson E (1977) Childhood and Society. St Albans: Paladin.

Fennell G (1990) Whom to study? Defining the problem. In: SM Peace (ed.) Researching Social Gerontology. London: Sage.

Gearing B and Dant T (1990) Doing biographical research. In: SM Peace (ed.) Researching Social Gerontology. London: Sage.

Griffiths R (1988) Community Care: Agenda for Action. London: HMSO.

Healy J and Yarrow S (1997) Family Matters: Parents Living With Children in Old Age. Bristol: The Policy Press.

Jefferys M (1997) Inter-generational relationships: an autobiographical perspective. In: A Jamieson, S Harper, C Victor (eds) Critical Approaches to Ageing and Later Life. Buckingham: Open University Press. pp. 77–89.

Levy J (1993) In Praise of Grandmothers. An Ageless Treasury of Quotations. Philadelphia: Running Press.

Minkler M and Roe KM (1993) Grandmothers as Caregivers: Raising Children of The Crack Cocaine Epidemic. London: Sage.

National Health Service and Community Care Act (1990) London: HMSO.

Philp I (ed.) (1994) Assessing Elderly People in Hospital and Community Care. London: Farrand Press.

Schild E and Ali N (1997) Listening to grandparents from a range of ethnic communities: the methodological implications. Generations Review, 7(1), 6–8.

Walker R (ed.) (1985) Applied Qualitative Research. Aldershot: Gower Publishing.

A Crabbit Old Woman

Poem by 'Kate' (found in her belongings after her death)

What do you see, nurses, what do you see?
Are you thinking when you are looking at me
A crabbit old woman, not very wise,
Uncertain of habit, with faraway eyes,
Who dribbles her food and makes no reply,
When you say in a loud voice, 'I do wish you'd try!'
Who seems not to notice the things that you do,
And forever is losing a stocking or shoe.
Who unresisting or not lets you do what you will
With bathing and feeding the long day to fill.
Is that what you're thinking, is that what you see?
Then open your eyes, nurse, you're not looking at me.

I'll tell you who I am as I sit here so still,
As I use at your bidding, as I eat at your will.
I'm a small child of ten with a father and mother,
Brothers and sisters who love one another;
A young girl of sixteen with wings on her feet,
Dreaming that soon now a lover she'll meet;
A bride soon at twenty, my heart gives a leap,
Remembering the vows that I promised to keep.

At twenty five now I have young of my own
Who need me to build a secure, happy home;
A woman of thirty, my young now grow fast,

Bound to each other with ties that should last.
At forty my young sons now grown will all be gone,
But my man stays beside me to see I don't mourn.
At fifty once more babies play round my knee;
Again we know children, my loved one and me.
Dark days are upon me, my husband is dead,
I look to the future, I shudder with dread,
For my young are all busy rearing young of their own,
And I think of the years and the young I have known.

I'm an old woman now and nature is cruel,
'Tis her jest to make old age look like a fool.
The body it crumbles, grace and vigour depart,
There now is a stone where once I had a heart.
But inside this old carcass a young girl still dwells,
And now and again my battered heart swells;
I remember the joys, I remember the pain,
And I'm living and loving life over again;
I think of the years, all too few, gone too fast,
And accept the stark fact that nothing can last.

So open your eyes, nurses, open and see
Not a crabbit old woman. Look closer – see ME!

Chapter 7
Psychotherapy with Older People

ALISON CULVERWELL and CAROL MARTIN

Much writing about working psychotherapeutically with older people still starts with Freud's (1905) quotation offering the opinion that people reaching the age of fifty will have become rigid in their thinking, and that, as flexibility and the capacity to learn are required for psychoanalytic treatment to succeed, age is a contraindication. This is then disputed and the reader reassured that older people can indeed be treated by just the same methods (Hammer, 1972; Hildebrand, 1995; Porter, 1991). Indeed, in the independent sector, it seems that many people choose to enter therapy later in life, at a time when they have the resources and interest for so doing. Increasingly, there are also health service staff offering counselling and psychotherapy to older people. Kernberg (1980) suggests that for some patients, those who are described as narcissistic, psychoanalytic treatment may be the treatment of choice in middle age. It is of interest then that there continues to be reference back to that initial pronouncement of Freud's as if it still needs to be challenged, and as if it still cannot be accepted that Freud may have been subject to his own blind spots, one of which was an ageism he was unable to analyse (Woodward, 1991). Perhaps each clinician has taken in some of those sentiments similar to Freud's, making it a continuing conflict almost a century later.

Introduction

There is a burgeoning literature covering the use and effectiveness of a range of therapeutic approaches with older people (Knight, 1996; Orbach, 1996; Woods, 1996; Yalom, 1989; Yost et al, 1986). This chapter will address some of the issues relevant to therapy with this group with the aim that this will prove useful not only for those readers who are involved in the provision of psychological services but also for those who are interested in the challenges and concerns faced by older people.

In this chapter, many of the issues are relevant to patients aged 65 and above. However, it may be more useful to think in broader terms than biological years alone when categorizing someone as old. In addition, one may consider the varied dimensions that together make up a picture of age. These include health status, attitudinal characteristics, social and work roles and appearance; of course, people may begin to experience these different aspects of growing older at different points in life. For example, a man in his late forties facing redundancy may experience similar feelings of being undervalued, left behind, deprived of opportunity and material resources to those of a person who retires at 65 or to those of a person who unwillingly gives up paid work for the first time at the age of 80.

At the same time, there have been developments in the academic world, where the discipline of gerontology has arisen, producing research, frameworks and journals. There have also been political and societal changes. For example, retirement has become a movable and more variable event; the term 'middle age' is now applied not to those in their late thirties but to those in their sixties; and pension power is a significant force affecting marketing, advertising and thereby our culture. Neugarten and Neugarten (in Kimmel, 1990) suggested that society is moving towards a more age-irrelevant state; the post-war baby boomers have reached their early fifties, shifting the cultural norms upwards as they grow older. As the welfare state, with pensions, health and social security resources, has been in existence for most of their lives, albeit in different forms, it might seem as if the prospects for getting older have never been so good. However, there remain more sobering facts: the problematic aspects of ageing are more commonly experienced by women, whose pensions are smaller and for whom material resources in general tend to be scarcer, whose education and public presence is limited and who more often live alone. While there are those who at least for a time experience retirement as an opportunity to enjoy leisure and other activities in a way they found previously impossible, there are also those who are short of money, limited by poor health or by emotional and social strictures. In general, it is this group who find themselves in contact with statutory services, in institutional settings and (occasionally) with therapists.

One key concept from research is that of the cohort: implicit in this idea is the recognition that each generation has a unique set of experiences, even of the same events. Currently in Britain, there seems to be a group of men coming to therapy after the fiftieth anniversary of the end of the Second World War. They are in distress as their previous strategies for coping with the aftermath of traumatic experiences have begun to break down for a number of reasons, as failing health, mortality and loss and the need to make sense of their lives threatens their equilibrium. People reaching 60 now were born at the start of the Second World War, so that staff working in services for older adults are beginning to see people whose war experiences were not those of soldiering and adult war work, but those of evacuation and disrupted childhoods. This has relevance for therapy: therapists may find themselves changing the frameworks on which they habitually draw to make sense of patients' experiences. For example, models of trauma and post-traumatic stress disorder have been useful when working with older adults whose difficulties include intrusive and distressing war memories. By contrast, attachment theory (Bowlby, 1988) may be of increasing importance when considering the experiences of those who were children during the Second World War.

There is no single comprehensive theoretical model to explain the experience of ageing, and given the number of approaches used to conceptualize the issue, it is probable that there never will be. Nevertheless there has been a noticeable increase in the amount of psychological research and psychotherapeutic endeavour in this area in the last decade or so. Woods (1996) provides an overview of current thera-peutic outcome research. Most practitioners now recognize the value of talking therapies for older people, even though the theoretical and empir-ical foundations for this remain patchy. However, there are several models from psychology and psychotherapy that have direct implications for those who work with older people.

Among these models are developmental frameworks. In spite of the criticisms levelled at it, Erikson's (1968) model of psychosocial develop-ment is still probably the best-known and most influential. Erikson assumes that development is driven by the requirement to resolve the conflicts inherent in life. A number of factors, including biological, psycho-logical and social events, act to bring about situations in which an individual faces conflict and must make choices. His model consists of eight dimensions, each of which may predominate at one time. The first, which he links to infancy, concerns the development of trust in others and the environment as a whole. For example, when life starts well, the child will form an optimistic stance, which allows him to approach later experi-ences hopefully. Clearly, however, blind optimism is as undesirable as a strongly suspicious outlook; a constructive position is likely to be somewhere between the extremes. Although it is tempting to think of Erikson's framework as a series of stages, following one after another, it is more fruitful to consider all dimensions as potential influences at any time. For older people, loss and dependency may bring the capacity for trust once more to the fore.

Such models of psychosocial functioning emphasize the influence of the environment on the process of maturation. In this context, the environment includes social, cultural and interpersonal factors in addition to the physical and material setting. In recent years the importance of the environment on development has been acknowledged to be continually significant, not merely in childhood but throughout the life course (Erikson, 1966; Nemiroff and Colarusso, 1985). Favourable external circumstances enable and promote growth; such conditions are essentially benign, rich in stimulation and respectful of autonomy. If malignant, the environment may inhibit development and lead to constrictive resolutions to the varied conflicts inherent in living. Of course, at any point in life there may be points at which circumstances allow for the development of new attitudes and strategies, even though some of the consequences of earlier life experiences may not be reversible. Nemiroff and Colarusso suggest that developmental models such as Erikson's emphasize the importance of time, and that a task for every adult is to come to terms with the recognition that life is finite and irreversible. For example, someone may develop, for the first time, the capacity for maintaining an intimate relationship in mid-life as a result of therapy or life experience (renegotiating the conflict between intimacy and isolation); sadly, although this achievement may give pleasure, it may also lead to regret for lost opportunities or past failures. Unfortunately, developing the capacity to achieve something does not guarantee success; in these circumstances it is still possible that the person may not meet a potential and available partner. However, people may satisfy a need in other ways and find substitutes. Someone in these circumstances who is childless may not be able to have their own child, but may satisfy their developing wish to nurture future generations in some other way, such as through teaching.

Psychoanalytic models

Psychoanalytic clinicians are concerned with the relationship between the subjective experience of the individual and their interactions with the outside world. Such models offer ways of understanding how people protect themselves from anxiety, from painful thoughts or from distress by using self-protective strategies which nonetheless distort their experience or beliefs. The tasks of a therapist include identifying and understanding the role of these strategies and at times challenging them. By facing reality, however painful, it is then possible to develop new, more constructive strategies.

A number of psychoanalysts have written on ageing. For example, Jung (1931/1966) suggested that individuals develop an interest in their inner experience with maturity. The challenge of ageing is the task of integrating aspects of oneself in order to feel more whole. This is one way of expressing a more general belief that appears in Melanie Klein's (1963) writing as reaching the depressive position (integration) and in Erikson's model as the wisdom that develops through the victory of integrity over despair. Other writers include, in particular, those who have written on the importance of self-esteem and shame. Otto Kernberg (1980), for example, has described the role of self-esteem (narcissism) after mid-life, both for those who manage life well and for those whose lives are blighted by a fragile sense of self-worth. As people approach the end of their lives, the need to evaluate the experience as a whole increases; many individuals find it difficult to develop a satisfactory narrative that makes it possible for them to maintain a balanced, positive perspective. This task is made harder for those who have dealt with life's difficulties by avoidance or similar strategies; often such people have learned fewer skills, have low levels of confidence, resist change and feel overwhelmed by the feelings they know they may have to face when reviewing their life. Often they feel deprived, have avoided mourning in the past, have not tested themselves, blame external circumstances for their situation and fear regret. Sometimes this may be related to traumatic experiences, in which the person felt overwhelmed and often ashamed of their responses in fearful situations. Such experiences can lead to a reluctance to act in any way that exposes the person to situations that might become equally overwhelming. The fear that particular relationships or situations may become a repeat of a past traumatic experience and lead to breakdown has been described by Winnicott (1973), who describes fear of death as one example of this phenomenon. Fear of traumatic dependency may be another example of this (Hess, 1987; Martindale, 1989; Martin, 1992). This can result in restrictive lifestyles and refusal of help. The exploration of destructive patterns of subjective experience, as discussed by these writers, can make sense of the difficulties faced by those fending off or living through states of extreme disturbance, whether or not the individual is in a psychotherapeutic relationship.

Other frameworks

Psychoanalytic models allow us to make some sense of the ways in which people face or evade the realities of their existence. Relatively few psychotherapeutic frameworks deal well with the spiritual dimensions of life. However, the philosophical underpinnings to the work of existential therapists contribute something more to our recognition of the infinite ways in which life can be lived. Emmy van Deurzen-Smith (1997) offers a useful framework comprising four existential dimensions: physical, social, personal and spiritual. These provide a way of construing issues related to living and dying. Such philosophically based models are useful for considering the experience of older people, whose lives are increasingly permeated by an awareness of mortality, necessity and limitation.

Alongside these theoretical developments, there has been a growth in interest in psychological therapies and counselling in the population at large. This has resulted in a substantial increase in the pool of practitioners available both within the statutory services and privately, a proportion of whom are drawn or are directed to work with older people. Many of these practitioners use humanistic, person-centred or cognitive–behavioural procedures. These approaches in themselves offer therapeutic optimism; they couch their work in terms of growth or change. This optimism, together with the numerical increase of interested staff, has contributed considerably to services for older people as a whole, and is beginning to provide something of a balance to the dominant medical model within health service facilities.

The humanistic tradition holds as central a respect for the person's experience and their capacity to develop and find a way through life's problems. This approach has expectations that patients will be active in the therapeutic process, develop their potential and draw on their creativity, thus underlining the older person's capacity for continuing to shape his or her life. However, this model does not explicitly take into account the extent of the limitations met in later life, nor does it explicitly recognize the amount of suffering involved in understanding and change. However, Yalom (1989), who seems to use both existential and humanistic elements in his work, has described a number of therapies with older people in which they achieved satisfying lives.

The cognitive–behavioural school offers a logical and consistent framework for understanding human behaviour. It has the advantage of being readily understandable and has face validity for both staff and patients. The model invites patients and therapists to be very clear about defining the problems and their goals and to operationalize how change will be measured. It is based on a model of learning that highlights the importance of positive experiences of achievement and of gradual, incremental challenges, as elements in the process of change. This model also has the advantage of requiring the patient to be actively involved in defining the changes they hope to achieve. However, the structure of the sessions, the focus on external change and on trying out new ways of thinking or behaving, can cause anxiety and may seem irrelevant to some of the existential concerns met by people in later life.

Each of these approaches has a significant contribution to make. While separately they are limited, together they provide a complex framework within which a therapist can begin to understand the particular reactions and strategies of an individual, and may then use an approach aimed to facilitate change at whatever level seems best suited to the therapeutic pair and the circumstances within which they are working. Clearly, this requires both knowledge of a range of skills and a level of experience which are hard won and relatively unusual.

Aims of therapeutic work with older people

There are several interrelating difficulties for therapists themselves if they anticipate a post specializing with older people. These include: the lack of an attractive and easily understood framework that enables clinicians to make their work meaningful; limitations in the available models used for identifying and agreeing aims, goals and outcome; and shortcomings in the ways of conceptualizing the impact of age on the therapeutic relationship. These are particularly important when considering how to evaluate therapeutic outcome. Measuring outcome according to the criteria used for younger people may lead to the often observed therapeutic despair.

Success with younger patients is often seen in terms of satisfying intimate relationships, work and children. Such patients often start therapy aware of difficulties which hinder them from achieving life goals. Therapy enables them to understand and manage themselves in a way that makes these goals more realistic or more possible. Working with such patients as they change can be intensely rewarding. Changes in their external reality are more likely to occur in parallel with internal change and they may come to appreciate both the benefit gained from the experience and the joint work.

Conversely, working with older people requires a refocusing of the concept of therapeutic change. With older patients, change may be more to do with understanding and acceptance of limits or surrendering previously held goals. It may consist of internal shifts, rather than more readily identifiable signs of behavioural change or symptom reduction. Therapy may aim to prevent or reduce deterioration. Given this difference in focus, change may be harder to see and harder to evaluate as meaningful or successful.

Therapist and patient may work on minimizing the impact of distressing life changes and consider ways of limiting the disruption brought about by life events. One example might be the loss of a spouse, which may require, in addition to the necessity to mourn, a response to the material consequences, such as the loss of resources or the need to take on the responsibilities previously held by the partner. However, in addition, they may struggle with the patient's strategies for coping with such events. For example, some people come into therapy wanting, in effect, to reverse time and go back to their earlier circumstances, perhaps before bereavement or illness. Such wishes make it impossible to accept current conditions or to take up available opportunities. It is relatively common, when it becomes necessary for a disabled older person to move into residential care, for the change to be seen as a punishment or as abandonment. This does on occasion lead to a refusal to accept both the new environment and those within it. If this refusal is expressed through aggressive behaviour, the potential for developing satisfying relationships with staff or fellow residents may be destroyed.

In all therapies the therapist may have the task of helping patients change aims. For example, it is relatively common that a person comes to therapy wanting a relationship of some type within their life. Within the therapy, if it goes well, the person will recognize that they need to develop some capacity within themselves to enable this to happen, such as an increased tolerance of the imperfections of others. It is also common that the person begins to wish for a more personal relationship with the therapist, and wants him or her to satisfy that need. When working with an older person, a therapist may feel pressured to take on one of many roles, from lost spouse to ideal child. This sort of wish is only one of those that may surface in therapy. Often, when working with older adults, it becomes apparent that the patient is wanting to reverse time and its effects. This happens especially when people are forced to face an unwelcome change, such as death of a spouse, impaired health or a move. When it becomes impossible to hold on to the hope that there will be a reversal of circumstances, there may be periods of protest or despair and a refusal to accept or appreciate what remains. At the worst extremes, this can end in suicide or disturbance, as in psychotic states.

Age and interpersonal issues

Freud's legacy is offered as one reason for the very limited psychotherapeutic services available to older people. There is, however, rather more to this. For example, Hammer (1972) relates therapists' pessimism about the development of psychotherapeutic services for older adults to personal countertransference feelings affecting recruitment, retention and job satisfaction. He also notes that there is a lack of the client group's 'voice', with therefore little 'consumer pressure' to fund posts. (It may be more than a lack of pressure; given the stigma attached to mental health issues, older people may avoid identifying with the issue and being active in campaigning for related services.) Further, psychological and psychotherapeutic services often provide intangible benefits, which prove hard to quantify. In times when services are under-resourced, developing these may seem like a luxury compared to the provision of practical help. All this requires therapists to acknowledge not only limits on therapeutic efficacy but also other restrictions, including their own prejudices and wishes.

This may lead therapists to despair when they realize that they are unable to live up to their previously held standards, whether these are expressed as a conviction that therapy is about helping people to function better, or that therapists are 'scientist practitioners' or 'agents of change'. Alternatively, it may enable them to reconsider older, more stoic ways of construing the task of therapy, to working in terms of facing reality and accepting that sometimes suffering is unavoidable (Craib, 1994). This, however, requires the therapist to be willing to tolerate disappointment, grief, pain and powerlessness in the face of biology, culture and time. It requires the therapist, too, to be able to tolerate experiences that disconfirm the hopes and illusions we all hold about the future, about success, security and our effectiveness. Yet most staff working with older adults are much younger than their patients; few have much experience of ageing except that which comes from their patients. Without much personal experience to draw on, and blind to the effect of the filters we use as a result of taking in stereotypes of ageing, many may feel vulnerable to a sense of helplessness, despair or disgust in the face of what seem to be overwhelming difficulties and unavoidable failure.

Our culture's current emphasis on continued change, the requirement for progress, zero tolerance of failure and the demand for ever more accommodation to change, exemplified in concepts such as flexibility of the workforce or the Learning Society, have a number of implications for older people and those who work with them. These attitudes overvalue change, denying that there are costs to making changes. Such costs include increased uncertainty or anxiety, giving up what is familiar (to which we may be deeply attached), the need to protect our self-esteem in the face of ignorance and the requirement to mourn what is lost, all of which older patients may know only too well.

One common experience that often has profound effects on therapists is close and sustained contact with the futility and detachment suffered by those older patients who find themselves without the resources or opportunities to live as they would wish. In many therapies there is a need to recognize, and maybe face with the patient, the pain arising from the evaluation of time wasted, the effects of having avoided challenges or anxiety-provoking changes, or the effects of past decisions or tragedies. Yet for those who are able to reconsider, there is a gain to be made in their use and enjoyment of current circumstances. The therapist, however, may have to tolerate distress and helplessness while the patient struggles to accept and work through their difficulties. The achievement of sadness or sorrow can, however, be extremely poignant and requires the therapist to share the recognition that therapy will never allow the patient to make up for what has been done or omitted in a life that seems mis-spent.

Therapists may find some therapeutic encounters difficult because they have to deal with patients who envy them their youth, freedom, health and opportunities. These feelings may remain hidden because they are so difficult to accept within oneself, and they may be based on the patient's assumptions of the therapist's life. One way of avoiding the pain of pleasures no longer available is to try to live vicariously through others, including the therapist. This may lead to requests for information about the therapist's life so that he or she can feel to have experienced it at one remove. Alternatively, other people or circumstances may be idealized, which leaves the patient with a devalued idea of their own lives and maybe of the help available to them. A patient may want the environment to change, to provide the answer, while the therapist ends up feeling impotent and may be inclined to try to put things right. For example, the therapist might feel tempted to accede to requests to provide transport for patients or to help with practical tasks, hoping to reduce their guilt for leaving the patient in an unsatisfied state. The realization that there is no happy ending for anybody, but only a variable number of happy moments, partial successes and continual compromises in life is then avoided. Perhaps it is the necessity of facing this stark realization that makes the work so unpopular.

There are, however, some older people who find such a review too difficult and will avoid such evaluation; Kernberg (1980) discusses this issue in some depth and offers some guidelines to help to distinguish those two groups. Those who are able to feel regret and concern to some degree are more likely to benefit from therapy than those who react with rage and by blaming others. One task therefore for any therapist is to assess how much both they and their patient can manage. The patient may be self-limiting, through anxiety or despair; the therapist will also have limits, often including an anxiety of doing harm. Risk is inherent in all therapy. Given that there may seem to be less potential gain for older people to balance the pain they may experience in therapy, it is important that the patient knows enough of the process to give as informed a consent as possible. It is also important to recognize that to some extent these benign experiences are not restricted to therapeutic relationships, but may develop between family members and other carers.

Families, institutions and services

Family members and others concerned with an older person often face situations in which they have to cope with difficult responsibilities and distressing feelings. Sometimes these can be too much for those involved to manage, leading to crises and to situations which worsen through the understandable, but unhelpful, reactions of those involved. Furthermore, institutions and services often strive in various ways to compensate for the losses an older person is experiencing or anticipating. In some instances, this may be both appropriate and beneficial; for example, people who are experiencing a loss in their capacity to think and remember are indeed helped by measures that reduce the cognitive load, and address the associated anxiety. Such compensatory environments enable the person to make better sense of their surroundings and their place within them. They may help people to feel more contained and hence less anxious, to go on being as much in control as possible and able to function as fully as they are able.

Sometimes, however, families and professionals may look to ways of enriching or enhancing the environment, only to find that their efforts are rejected or denigrated, or that they fail to fill the gap adequately. Renewed efforts by carers may be met by resistance and even overt rejection, which may take the form of disturbed or disturbing behaviour. Attempts to achieve a happier situation can lead to a pattern of imposing constraints on the older person with the intention of changing their behaviour to something more acceptable. Sometimes the strategies that carers use to protect themselves from their own distress combine with those characteristics projected onto them by the patient to exacerbate the situation (Menzies Lyth, 1960), resulting in both patient and carer becoming increasingly distant, desperate and angry. The carer's capacities for empathy and being alongside the older person are compromised, and consequently the quality of care diminishes. When a carer is driven to make attempts to take control in order to protect himself or herself against feelings of despair and helplessness, this may all too easily lead to a cycle of tyranny, abuse, retaliation and revenge.

Menzies Lyth's pioneering work in the 1950s highlighted the intensity and the sources of anxiety experienced by nursing staff who were caring for frail elderly people, and offers us a way of understanding one organization's unconscious attempts to manage this anxiety. She observed how many of the nursing practices had the function of distancing the nurse from those she was caring for, impersonalizing the relationships and minimizing through routines and delegation the nurses' need to think or take responsibility for their decisions. Whilst this strategy for managing anxiety protected the nurses from the arousal of intense feelings, it also seriously impoverished both the patients' and the nurses' existence. Within such an environment the potential for insensitive or abusive interactions is easily imagined.

The experience of reaching the point at which one is hurting either the person in one's care or oneself is familiar to many carers, both professional and relatives. Similarly there are periodic reminders from the media of instances of institutional abuse or neglect of older people. Initiatives such as 'Zero tolerance to domestic violence' and more specifically, discussion about elder abuse, whilst highlighting the problem and its unacceptability, have not moved on to consider the input or resources necessary to prevent the recreation of cycles of abuse within relationships and institutions. Kernberg (1980) comments that it is to be expected that the environment will include aggression, sadism, corruption and envy, offering a reminder that the potential for harm is omnipresent, not isolated within a few individuals or institutions. There is a challenge for those offering care. Often the environment objectively falls short of the ideal. However, at least as important are the conscious and unconscious views of the environment developed by the older person. Sometimes, however good the environment, it will be seen as unsatisfactory. If the person wishes for a particular situation, perhaps to live with a spouse as in earlier years or an adult child, and is unprepared to suffer the disappointment and frustrations of the current circumstances, conflict may develop. However, repeated referrals for problem behaviours can be a sign that there is a problem within the institution. It may be failing to provide an atmosphere in which respect for the individual, choice and procedures for resolution of differences are possible.

The current system of Primary Nursing, in which one or two individuals are charged with the responsibility of getting to know well and being responsible for the care of specific patients, could be seen as a reaction within health care against the previous impersonal system. In many ways this new system mimics aspects of the relationship that family have with their dependent relative; it provides the opportunity for attachments to be made, but also requires staff to find ways of processing the intense feelings that can be aroused within such relationships in order to protect themselves and their patients. The need for carers to have access to the support, resources and perspective offered by a concerned third person has been identified by several writers. Winnicott (1973), in considering how the needs of the baby are met, describes the need of the mother for another, often the father, to keep at bay external demands, to nurture her and to help her contain and make sense of the baby's feelings. Research has repeatedly identified high levels of stress within staff and relatives caring for elderly people; similarly the incidence of depression and supposed behavioural problems among those being cared for in residential and nursing homes is higher than would be expected for the general population. Terry (1997) described his work in long-stay hospital settings in a similar fashion, highlighting his emergent role as a moral advocate, aiming to defend the needs of staff and patients against external circumstances in which they seem to be at risk of deprivation and neglect.

Attachment theory (Bowlby, 1988) provides us with a model for considering factors that might constitute elements of a 'good enough' environment. Attachment theory postulates that we are driven by a need to be in relationship with others. Secure attachments, it is argued, are needed for early survival, and also enable the individual to develop, providing a safe base from which to explore the world. They also contribute to the individual's development by providing a container for distressing feelings, and helping the individual to tolerate and make sense of their anxiety and arousal. These qualities are necessary for the successful provision of care, whether by an individual mother, or by those working in an institutional setting. However, institutions often fall short in providing a psychologically secure base; they are often experienced as unpredictable, frightening and disempowering. This may increase the residents' anxiety and confusion, precipitating requests for reassurance and other care-seeking behaviours. For those with deprived or abusive memories of childhood, it is possible that such institutional settings engender feelings of fear and helplessness similar to these early experiences. As Adshead (1998) outlines, the attachment histories of the caregivers will affect their relationships with their patients. Ingebretsen and Solem (1997) explore the same issue in relation to family carers of those with dementing illnesses, describing the implications for interventions with carers.

Good intentions are not sufficient. The compulsive caregiving pattern, often present to varying degrees in professional carers, attracts comment from both writers. Adshead (1998) argues that the over-involved caregiver both denies the patient the opportunity for improvement and retaining independence, and also risks violating boundaries. This may be especially true of those who have experienced abuse in childhood. Similarly, those carers who are dismissive of emotions and vulnerability may respond to patients' care-seeking behaviour by neglecting their approaches and needs, and showing intolerance of their anxiety and depression.

Conclusion

From this chapter it is possible to conclude, firstly, that psychotherapists are increasingly prepared to work therapeutically with older adults, and have begun to use a more sophisticated cluster of frameworks for understanding and intervening. This has developed into a valued, albeit scarce, resource for older people. Secondly, such work with older adults means that the therapist faces the requirement to develop a perspective that encompasses the experience of older people. This perspective will enable him or her to empathize with the experience of older people in distress. It will also make it easier to live with the knowledge that life is limited both in terms of time and opportunities without feeling overwhelmed by futility or despair. Thirdly, it is clear that this perspective can potentially benefit staff working with older people in other capacities; for example, Ardern et al (1998) discuss the use of psychotherapeutic concepts within the work of a mental health team for older adults.

It is just as much an illusion that older people develop wisdom through the passing of the years alone as is the view that people necessarily decline. There is enormous variation, and like wines perhaps, some mature better than others. With maturity comes an independence of thought that may bring one up against others and this needs to be distinguished from that opposition that comes from discontent and rage. It may be, however, that the most durable source of contentment comes from the development of precisely this. Many examples come to mind of both extremes, real and fictional, from Miss Haversham to Miss Marple. The tasks of ageing are many and include a capacity for acceptance of the transience of feelings; that disappointment, pain and loss are unavoidable, but that their existence need not spoil whatever good is available; that one is no worse a person because one is suffering; and that through enjoying the pleasures and achievements of others, in spite of sadness at the passing of time, one may gain, both through reliving aspects of one's own past and through the recognition and attachment of others.

Working with the elderly requires, perhaps even more than does work with younger people, that therapists define the tasks of therapy with care, so as not to deny the potential for internal growth and change, but equally not to collude with the desire for an unrealistic outcome. This may include the sad recognition that some older people, even with the best care available, may not be able to reach a state of contentment or acceptance. Sometimes, the problem may, however, be exacerbated by the environment and the relationships of others to the person. Although a psychotherapeutic solution may not be found to every psychological problem, a formulation in psychological terms can optimize the provision of care, ameliorating conflict and reducing unnecessary distress for the older person and carers.

References

Adshead G (1998) Psychiatric staff as attachment figures. British Journal of Psychiatry, 172, 64–9.

Ardern M, Garner J and Porter R (1998) Curious bedfellows: psychoanalytic understanding and old age psychiatry. Psychoanalytic Psychotherapy, 12, 47–56.

Bowlby J (1988) A Secure Base: Clinical Applications of Attachment Theory. London: Routledge.

Craib I (1994) The Importance of Disappointment. London: Routledge.

Deurzen-Smith E van (1997) Everyday Mysteries. London: Routledge.

Erikson E (1966) Eight ages of man. International Journal of Psycho-Analysis, 47, 281–300.

Erikson E (1968) Identity; Youth and Crisis. New York: Norton.

Freud S (1905) On Psychotherapy. Standard Edition, vol. 7. London: Hogarth.

Hammer M (1972) Psychotherapy with the aged. In: M Hammer (ed.) The Theory and Practice of Psychotherapy with Specific Disorders. New York: Charles C Thomas.

Hess N (1987) King Lear and some anxieties of old age. British Journal of Medical Psychology, 60, 209–15.

Hildebrand P (1995) Beyond Mid-life Crisis. London: Sheldon Press.

Ingebretsen R and Solem PE (1997) Attachment, loss and coping in caring for a dementing spouse. In: B Miesen and G Jones (eds) Care-giving in Dementia: Research and Applications, vol. 2. London: Routledge.

Jung CJ (1931/1966). The aims of psychotherapy. In: The Practice of Psychotherapy, Collected works of C.J. Jung, vol. 16, pp. 36–52. Princeton, NJ: Princeton University Press.

Kernberg O (1980) Internal World and External Reality: Object Relations Theory Applied. London: Jason Aronson.

Kimmel D (1990) Adulthood and Aging, 3rd edn. New York: Wiley.

Klein M (1963/1975) On the sense of loneliness. In: The Writings of Melanie Klein, vol. 3. London: Hogarth.

Knight R (1996) Psychodynamic therapy with older adults: lessons from scientific gerontology. In: RT Woods (ed.) Handbook of the Clinical Psychology of Ageing. Chichester: Wiley.

Martin C (1992) The elder and the other. Free Associations, 27, 341–54.

Martindale B (1989) Becoming dependent again: the fears of some elderly patients and their younger therapists. Psychoanalytic Psychotherapy, 4, 67–75.

Menzies Lyth I (1960) Social Systems as a Defence Against Anxiety. London: Tavistock.

Nemiroff RA and Colarusso CA (1985) The Race against Time: Psychoanalysis and Psychotherapy in the Second Half of Life. New York: Basic Books.

Orbach A (1996) Not Too Late. London: Jessica Kingsley.

Porter R (1991) Psychotherapy with the Elderly. In: J Holmes (ed.) Textbook of Psychotherapy in Psychiatric Practice. London: Churchill Livingstone.

Terry P (1997) Counselling the Elderly and their Carers. Macmillan Press.

Winnicott DW (1973) Fear of breakdown. In: G Kohon (ed.) The Independent Tradition (1986). London: Free Association Books.

Woods RT (1996) Effectiveness of psychological interventions with older people. In: A Roth and P Fonagy (eds) What Works for Whom? A Critical Review of Psychotherapy Research. New York: Guilford Press.

Woodward K (1991) Aging and its Discontents. Indiana: Indiana University Press.

Yalom I (1989) Love's Executioner and Other Tales of Psychotherapy. London: Bloomsbury.

Yost E, Beutler L, Corbishley M and Allender J (1986) Group Cognitive Therapy. Oxford: Pergamon Press.

Chapter 8
Reminiscence

MARY TILKI

The aim of this chapter is to examine the use of the principles and practice of reminiscence with older people and to consider how these can benefit the older person, formal and informal carers, the organization and society as a whole. It is inspired by the author's reminiscence work with older Irish people living in Britain and by clinical links with services for older people in an area of London with a high proportion of Black, Asian and White minority ethnic clients. It is motivated by a concern that the increasing numbers of older people in the population are confronted by ageist attitudes in wider society and in health care practice. Reminiscence affords a rich seam of information which has the potential to enhance the quality of life for older people by enabling professionals to listen to the real needs of clients. It can raise awareness of the invidious nature of social and professional ageism as well as the other forms of oppression that exist in society and are amplified in old age. It can have a particular value in enhancing understanding of those about whom little is known, such as people from diverse cultures and traditions and those suffering from dementia. If recorded and debated, it can contribute a rich and illuminating body of knowledge to the disciplines of health psychology and sociology. It can inform health and social policy and underpin anti-discriminatory and anti-oppressive approaches to professional practice. It has educational potential and cultural value as social history, documenting the experience of ordinary men and women, and can particularly record the history of emigration and the experience of exile in a place that may not feel like home.

The author's reminiscence work was with older Irish people living in London and attending a day centre jointly provided by the Irish voluntary sector and a local authority. The reminiscence groupwork revealed the hardship experienced by the participants in Ireland before they migrated. It highlighted the discrimination and hostility they experienced on migration and still suffer now, in relation to housing, employment and most aspects of life in Britain (Tilki and McEvoy, 1996), an experience shared with other minority ethnic groups. It afforded a different perspective on the health beliefs of older Irish people and went a long way to explaining their health behaviour and their attitudes to life. It illuminated the reasons for low self-esteem, insecure identity and explained some of the factors which contribute to the high incidence of illness and disability in this community. It showed how people coped or did not cope, materially, psychologically and socially. It demonstrated the similarities between all communities including the host community, and confirmed that where differences occur they are within the individual minority ethnic group. It has been a humbling experience which enriched the author's understanding of her own Irish culture, and as a professional, gave a framework for practice with Irish people and other minority groups. The lessons learnt through reminiscence have proved far more valuable and alive than any lecture or textbook.

Reminiscence

Reminiscence is a natural and universal process that all people engage in and can have a positive outcome (Butler, 1963). It can involve a number of senses and may be triggered by the feel or the image of an object, a sound, a smell, or a taste. It can lead the individual to experience a variety of emotions such as sadness, happiness, anger and elation. Reminiscence is more than recall of facts. It is a process that allows people to relive personal experiences in a meaningful and vivid way (Coleman, 1994). It involves reliving events in a way which is shaped by personal experience, by memory and by psychological coping mechanisms which select what to remember and how to remember it.

As a recreational or therapeutic activity, reminiscence can be encouraged on an individual basis or in groups. It can take a number of forms like conversation, displays, outings, sing-songs, dances, recreational and educational activities. It can be used in hospital, residential, community, day care, educational and recreational settings, as well as in the older person's own home. Reminiscence has a place as an activity in its own right and can provide enjoyment, support and therapy. By drawing on its underpinning principles it has the capacity to enhance the quality of care and thus the quality of life for older people (Gearing, 1994; Dant et al, 1990).

The history of reminiscence

Attitudes towards reminiscence have undergone a fundamental reappraisal in the past 30 years (Gearing, 1994). Although from an early age all humans engage in reminiscence, it is usually associated with old age (Coleman, 1988). There was until recently a tendency to view reminiscence in older people as dysfunctional, outside of the person's control, non-selective, and purposeless (Bornat, 1997), as well as a reflection of older people's inability or unwillingness to adjust to modern society. Serious consideration of the process of reminiscence began, following the publication of a paper by an eminent American psychologist, Robert Butler (Butler, 1963). Quoting his own clinical experience as well as a range of literary authorities, Butler made the case for viewing reminiscence as a normal activity in old age, and life review as a process that people undergo in order to come to terms with life as it has been lived (Coleman, 1993). Prior to this seminal work, reminiscence or 'living in the past' was viewed as pathological, morbid and to be discouraged. It was recognized that although it could be volitional and pleasurable, it was best avoided because it provided escapism (Butler, 1963).

There were fears that remembrance of things past could cause or deepen depression and attempts were to be made to divert or distract people through a range of activities (Dobrof, 1984). Despite these instructions, many staff felt intuitively that individual biography was crucial to quality of care because they could work with greater sensitivity when they knew something of the past lives of their clients. They were aware that clients enjoyed talking about the past and they themselves enjoyed listening to stories of times irretrievably lost. They continued to use a range of strategies to evoke memories and to trigger conversation (Bornat, 1997). Butler's writings legitimated workers' instinctive feelings of what was appropriate for older people.

Although Butler's work is commonly seen as the inspiration for reminiscence, Peter Coleman suggested that the much maligned theory of disengagement of the same period (Cumming and Henry, 1961) had a major part to play. This theory, which has since been lost in negative criticism, served the purpose of challenging the deteriorative 'theory of ageing' of the time (Coleman, 1994) and provoked new ways of thinking about old age. Despite its flaws, it was the first theory which did not focus on intellectual decline. It demonstrated that as people grew older, they focused inwards and became more preoccupied with their own thoughts and reminiscences rather than engaging in external activities. It also demonstrated that they were happy with this shift in orientation. Whilst the study neglected the social forces that caused people to disengage, it looked at developmental change which included the tendency to reminisce. However, the backlash against disengagement theory meant that reminiscence was also seen with negative connotations (Coleman, 1993).

Butler's article was followed by a number of other significant contributions which enhanced the understanding of reminiscence. McMahon and Rhudick (1964) reported how a group of war veterans were particularly well adjusted despite engaging in a considerable amount of reminiscence.

Contrary to previous ideas they appeared free from depression. The reminiscence of these men was of a story-telling nature, meant to be entertaining and instructive, similar to anthropological descriptions in primitive societies, preserving and handing down traditions and customs. In the UK, Malcolm Johnson's work (Johnson, 1976) influenced thinking about the value of considering older people's past lives and their relevance to their present needs. As with Butler's work in the USA, Malcolm Johnson's paper emphasizing the importance of biography struck a chord with professionals who had become increasingly dissatisfied with the low priority accorded to older people (Gearing, 1994).

The decades that followed saw a mushrooming of interest in reminiscence therapy and throughout the 1970s and 1980s reminiscence therapy was widely practised in all settings. It was in keeping with the spirit of the times and matched other moves within oral and community history movements, as well as the development of more assertive and militant roles for older people such as those propounded in the USA by Maggie Kuhn (Bornat, 1997).

Reminiscence therapy or activity?

Early research studies into reminiscence were disappointing and failed to demonstrate empirically the benefits that were consistently reported. Invariably studies related the enjoyment that was observed but more substantial benefits had not been demonstrated (Coleman, 1994). Despite anecdotal evidence which generally proclaimed the value of reminiscence, there was little empirical evidence to confirm its therapeutic effect (Merriam, 1980; Bornat, 1989). This lack of evidence influenced decisions about the nature and extent of provision. The term therapy suggested that reminiscence had 'therapeutic' effects over and above those which occur in ordinary activities and implied that it would be undertaken by 'experts' qualified to maximize its therapeutic potential (Buchanan and Middleton, 1994). Yet there was no evidence to support its effectiveness as a therapy. For some providers and professionals this signified that reminiscence had no benefits and should be abandoned. Others took the view that whilst it might not be therapy, it did not follow that it did not have therapeutic effects and they began to use the terms reminiscence 'groupwork' or 'activity' rather than therapy (Bender, 1994; Gibson, 1994). The absence of research-based evidence for the therapeutic effectiveness of reminiscence coincided with changes in provision for older people. While clear therapeutic benefits were not established, there was evidence of enjoyment, greater understanding of the client by staff and of forming relationships with other clients. Professionals began to detach themselves from reminiscence and increasingly it was delivered as a social activity by non-professionals and volunteer workers.

Research into reminiscence

Although questions about the effectiveness of reminiscence had an impact, a more critical look at the literature raised questions about the methodology of many of the studies. Research was often anecdotal rather than quantitative. There were many limitations in the studies, such as a failure to use control groups or a reliance on small numbers. Some studies attempted to evaluate reminiscence over a limited time span or with a specific group, or failed to consider differences in individual and group approaches (Haight, 1988; Coleman, 1994). Studies generally failed to distinguish between the different functions of thinking and talking about the past such as life review, identity maintenance and story telling. The social function of reminiscence received little attention and more emphasis was given to the intrapsychic functions (Coleman, 1994). There was also an absence of attention to the role of reminiscence in teaching and informing because of an emphasis on the teller rather than the listener (Coleman, 1994).

An absence of clarity about the variety of expressive and functional communications of reminiscence was noted by Wong and Watt (1991). They identified six different forms of reminiscence which need to be considered in addition to the context and culture of individual situations. Research studies also lacked attention to the impact on the listener or on society in general. Perhaps the most significant omission was the failure to look at the social interactional effects on the individuals, on group members, on staff and on wider society (Coleman, 1994).

However, more recent studies have been more rigorous and have shown more positive results. Fielden (1990) has demonstrated the effectiveness of reminiscence in improving well being and socialization. Haight (1988) has shown that systematic life review with individual clients over a prolonged period was beneficial. Researchers appear to have learned the importance of the intentions of the therapeutic intervention as well as the phenomenon under scrutiny (Coleman, 1994).

Functions of reminiscence

A number of functions are cited in the literature on reminiscence and it can, if used in different ways, serve a variety of purposes for clients, carers and society. Butler (1963) described the process of life review as an important aspect of coming to terms with life as it had been lived and regarded reminiscence as a means to achieve integrity prior to death. It was believed that through the process of life review older people stood to gain from a greater understanding of negative experiences and to draw lessons from them in order to develop a sense of peace and wisdom. Although Haight (1988) demonstrated encouraging results with structured life review there is little empirical evidence that the value of life review has been realized (Coleman, 1993, 1994).

Life review and self-preservation are both concerned with the client's sense of identity. While life review is about finding an acceptable identity with which to face death, self-preservation relates to maintaining worth in dramatically changed circumstances. McMahon and Rhudick (1964) considered reminiscence as an instructive process, handing on traditions and as such significant in the maintenance of self-respect and identity. It was believed that greater identification with past lives and past achievements helped adjustment and loss and enhanced a sense of identity and self-esteem. They noticed how older people tended to exaggerate the past and suggested that this enabled them to face the losses of role and function in the present.

Coleman (1988) showed that talking about the past and drawing lessons from it led to greater life satisfaction and protection from depression. Tobin (1991) suggested that the capacity to make the past vivid in the presence of a sympathetic listener could help maintain psychological health, not necessarily resolving conflict or gaining insight but beneficial in allowing the older person to be seen as they were, rather than as they are now. Self-respect is maintained by investing in the image of what one has been and stressing its importance (McMahon and Rhudick, 1964)

The role of reminiscence in preventing depression has been considered by a number of writers (Haight, 1988; Fielden, 1990). Risk factors associated with depression in old age are low self-esteem, physical illness, a history of life crisis and the absence of a confiding relationship (Murphy, 1982). To claim that reminiscence could prevent depression is somewhat ambitious but it may help some older people maintain a sense of coherence which in turn contributes to health. Reminiscence activity may offer opportunities for social interaction in those impaired by physical frailty. Whilst it cannot change the reality of decline it may change perceptions of the ability to cope and reduce feelings of isolation. Reminiscence may allow those affected by loss and bereavement to grieve and obtain comfort (Coleman, 1988). It can afford the chance for those who have experienced adverse life events to recognize that force of circumstances rather than individual failings were to blame. Fallot (1980) noted that older people self-reported that mood was elevated after reminiscing conversation but not after non-reminiscing conversation.

However, it was not the social contact itself which had the capacity to improve psychological health. Murphy (1982) highlighted the importance of a confidante in preventing depression. Reminiscence offered a foundation for the development of friendship (Fielden, 1990). Opportunities for social relationships through reminiscence had positive psychological effects by reducing isolation and enhancing social support. Fielden (1990) demonstrated an increase in self-reported relationships and perceptions of intimacy as a result of reminiscence in sheltered housing. It was also shown that reminiscence had a positive overspill outside the reminiscence group into aspects of everyday life, maintaining contacts and relationships sometimes in the wider community (Fielden, 1990). Reminiscence could also be a lifeline for those caring for frail or dementing relatives, giving them opportunities to share experiences, express pent-up emotions and establish confiding relationships.

A number of studies of older people in hospital and residential settings expressed concern about the low level of activity and social interaction (Goodwin, 1988; Crump, 1991; Lowry and Ryan, 1993; Armstrong-Esther, Browne and McAfee, 1994). Boredom and ritual activity were a way of life in some hospitals, residential and nursing homes (Lowry and Ryan, 1993). Furthermore, nurses did not see leisure activity as an important part of their role (Crump, 1991). The damage caused by not enabling older people to occupy their time in a meaningful, enjoyable and challenging way was dramatically underestimated (Goodwin, 1988). Recreation according to Goodwin was not a luxury, but a starting point for excitement, meaningful diversion, adaptation and creative activity. Crump (1991) went so far as to suggest that the absence of meaningful activity could be interpreted as abuse.

Activities can contribute to maintaining health, and self-esteem, and can ensure that the basic right to purposeful activity is met (Crump, 1991). However, certain principles must be observed to ensure that clients have access to a range of opportunities. Choice is essential and it is crucial that the older client sets the agenda. Reminiscence is only one of a range of activities but has the added benefit of enabling staff to understand the client and offer activities which are more personalized and appropriate.

Using reminiscence to enhance care

Although reminiscence therapy, groupwork or activity all have therapeutic benefits, there may be practical reasons which prevent them being used. However, there is considerable scope to utilize the principles of reminiscence/biography to enhance the quality of care of older people. Using reminiscence principles to inform practice can enlighten the professional and move beyond ageist assumptions which emphasize debility and dependence rather than interdependence. Biographical information can form the basis of individualized care planning by providing insights into the personality and identity of clients. Familiarity with life history, and knowledge of losses and grief, can lead to personalized empathic and appropriate responses to need. Dant et al (1990) showed that by using a biographical approach, practitioners obtained substantively different information than could be obtained by traditional assessment tools. Reminiscence/biography is not a 'tool' for assessment but an approach that elicits richer and more sensitive information. Although it could be a lengthy rigid chronological process it can also be dealt with flexibly. Urgent presenting needs can be assessed initially, working backwards later as opportunities arise. Using this approach can contribute to greater understanding of attitudes, feelings and experiences. It can be used to clarify family relationships or sensitive social factors. It can enhance understanding and the ability to relate to 'difficult' clients and those with mental health problems (Dant et al, 1990).

Using a reminiscence approach can encourage the client to value the past, learn from experience and utilize coping strategies from an earlier time. It can enable the health worker to help the client adjust to changing circumstances in a way that is familiar and fitting to his or her own lifestyle. It can be successful in identifying elderly people at risk and in providing appropriate packages of care to allow them to remain at home for as long as possible (Dant et al, 1990). Therapeutic techniques that draw upon skills developed in childhood may be useful for clients with physical disability, attention deficit or cognitive impairment.

When reminiscence is an integral part of care, it has the potential to enhance understanding by staff who may have had no contact with older people or who have been trained on the basis of a biomedical model. It can promote therapeutic relationships which are crucial to any health intervention and afford opportunities for client participation in care and for increased job satisfaction for workers. Having positive expectations of clients through an appreciation of their biography can have a self-fulfilling prophecy effect and can lead to more effective rehabilitation, fewer episodes of difficult behaviour and in turn greater reward and job satisfaction.

Reminiscence with people who have a dementing illness

For many years people suffering from dementing illness were excluded from reminiscence work. Recent reappraisal of reality orientation (Woods et al, 1992), attention to validation therapy (Feil, 1982, 1992) and interest in social stimulation and activity (Jones and Miesen, 1992) have led to a consideration of its use with dementia sufferers. Gibson suggested that it was not therapy but 'work' which implied mutuality, shared experience and stressed the positive rather than the negative aspects of behaviour (Gibson, 1994). It emphasized the capacities and abilities that were still intact and healthy and it aimed to exercise these abilities and capacities. This required that carers recognized the personhood of the client and in this sense reminiscence might be truly therapeutic (Kitwood, 1992).

Gibson (1994) demonstrated that people with dementia showed significant pleasure and enjoyment in general reminiscence work. They were delighted with their ability to recall even though their recollections were soon forgotten. Aberrant behaviour was reduced in the groups and agitation, restlessness and loss of appetite were reported to be less during the course of the project. However, although the response may have been slight and transitory, Gibson argued against trivializing brief moments of lucidity and suggested that a fleeting moment of pleasure for a person with dementia did not negate its value (Gibson, 1994). A carer or staff member might well have been encouraged to persist by such transitory but positive responses.

Individualized concentrated personal reminiscence informed by life histories was shown to increase sociability and to reduce aggressive or attention-seeking behaviour (Gibson, 1994). This relied on a detailed knowledge of life history from the carer and where possible the client, which was exploited in different ways, opening up possibilities for conversation, planning outings and other activities. Providing a life story and where possible participating in activities reduced the helplessness of carers and allowed them to feel they could make a contribution (Gibson, 1994).

A number of additional gains were identified (Gibson, 1994). Staff perceptions were challenged and led to a reduction in the tendency to attach labels, thus engaging the client in self-fulfilling prophecy. Changes were made to routines to accommodate long-held habits and attempts were made to recreate familiarity of the client's surroundings. Carers and spouses who felt redundant came to feel valued by being able to contribute in providing life history and reminiscence resources. They were also able to review, rework and revalue the whole life shared with the person who was now becoming a stranger.

Reminiscence and carers

Although there is increasing evidence that reminiscence may be therapeutic, it may prove difficult for family carers (Bruce, 1997). Constant repetition, stories from the past which the carer does not share, or those with which they are uncomfortable, are difficult to cope with. Contrary to popular belief, long-term memory may be inaccurate, scrambled and even contrived and this may be a source of irritation to an already stressed carer. Bereaved of the person that was, and of their emotional support, a family carer may be reluctant to engage in reminiscence which the client enjoys and may find therapeutic. Left alone to be listeners, family carers do not, or cannot, always respond with enthusiasm. But experiencing reminiscence with another person can have a huge impact (Bruce, 1997). Another person can respond more positively, take an interest in the client and show that they value that life. It can provide opportunities for the carer to add to the story and reaffirm pride in the person they care for.

However, the carer must also be encouraged to keep in touch with his or her own feelings and vulnerabilities and to transform them into positive resources. Carers need help to be involved, to value reminiscence and to use knowledge of the past to help the present. Reminiscence can help a family carer to maintain a sense of coherence which will enable them to face caring as a challenge rather than as a burden and to cope with that challenge. Baro et al (1997) use Antonovsky's work (1994) on sense of coherence to suggest that the ability to cope depends on the comprehensibility, manageability and meaningfulness of the caring experience (Baro et al, 1997). Sense of coherence can be enhanced by professionals through assessment and support programmes to address the needs of carers, reducing the caregiving burden. Work is currently in progress by the European Alzheimer's Clearing House to develop, implement and evaluate such a programme.

Comprehensibility relates to understanding disease and helping the client to understand and cope with the difficulties. Manageability relates to feelings of control and to personal and other resources. However, meaningfulness is the most crucial dimension, which prevents breakdown in the face of stress (Antonovsky, 1994). It relates to the motivational component and the degree of commitment. The person who can construct a stable and strong idea of personal identity from past memories will see the world as a coherent whole.

Older people from minority ethnic groups

Reminiscence has the potential to benefit older people in general but has a particular merit for older people from minority ethnic groups. There are increasing numbers of older people from different minority ethnic groups who are growing old throughout Europe, far from their original homelands (Walker and Maltby, 1997). Although many in Britain are still relatively youthful, numbers are increasing rapidly and little is known about their life history, their health beliefs or the impact of the ageing process (Blakemore and Boneham, 1994). There is a need to highlight a neglected group of people who are coming to terms with growing old in societies where old age is devalued and where there is increasing xenophobia and widespread institutionalized racism.

There is evidence of poor physical and mental health in older people from most minority ethnic groups (Warnes, 1997). The limited existing research into old age in minority ethnic groups has tended to focus on access to services with little or no attention to the experience of migration, life in another country and especially to feelings about growing old. Little is known about health beliefs or behaviours, even by professionals from the same ethnic backgrounds who have largely been acculturated by Western models of health care (Tilki, 1998). Reminiscence affords many opportunities to explore these issues in order to underpin culturally safe approaches to health care provision. This can best be facilitated by workers from the same cultural background.

All the functions of reminiscence are appropriate to older people from minority groups but because of their experiences of disadvantage and marginalization some are more relevant than others. Contrary to myths about the extended family, many older people from minority groups are isolated and alienated and this is especially true of older Irish people in

Britain. Culturally informed reminiscence can provide enjoyment and social contact in a safe cultural environment and may enhance opportunities to develop friendships and meaningful relationships (Fielden, 1990). Opportunities for life review are particularly appropriate for older people from minority groups. The majority of older people have always viewed themselves as migrants rather than emigrants. They left home to take up opportunities for training, education or to earn better money, and after a temporary exile anticipated returning home in glory. For many, the dream never transpired. The reality of hardship was hidden from the family and repeated lack of progress was absorbed as self-blame, echoing the negative stereotypes in society. Reminiscence can help share these unfulfilled hopes, explore the reasons why, highlight the real achievements and acknowledge the courage and determination needed to surmount the obstacles. They can be helped to recognize the structural forces which led to low income, poor housing and other forms of disadvantage. They can be encouraged to reinterpret what might have been thought of as failure, to value the challenges they have overcome and to prize their achievements. These processes can afford opportunities to rebuild self-esteem and to secure identity. The ability to make the past vivid in the presence of a sensitive listener is a key resource in psychological health as people can be seen as they once were and not as they are now (Tobin, 1991).

Older people from minority ethnic groups are frequently in an ambiguous situation, having psychological links with two societies but not belonging in either. For many the wish to return is strong. But as they age, the realization that family or economic reasons may prevent them from ever seeing home again becomes a painful reality. Life review can enable older people to begin to grieve for what might have been and to marshal the support of their peers. It can also enable them to maintain a psychological link with their cultural roots and retain cultural ways of coping. Reminiscence can be used to keep in touch with the picture postcard image of home. Some will grieve for their homeland and families long left behind but can be encouraged to reflect on their current life in a more positive way. Although this may be easier for staff who share either the cultural background of the client or the experience of migration, such sensitivity may be developed through participation in reminiscence. Reminiscence can ensure that that culture continues to be passed on, although modified and shaped by wider social influences.

Although some minority ethnic group members prefer culture-specific services, many are happy to join with people from other communities (Boneham et al, 1997). Sharing learning about similarity and difference can begin a process of challenging ethnocentric ideas and valuing diversity and can be enriching personally, professionally and socially. If appropriate, specific cultural knowledge can be analysed and recorded so it can be subsequently incorporated into training for culturally competent care. Knowledge gained can inform policy and practice and can improve provision for those who have contributed to the development of the host society and ensure their citizen rights are upheld.

Benefits of reminiscence for staff

Using reminiscence principles in practice can have benefits for staff as well as clients. Whilst primarily designed to evoke memories in older people there was also a notable impact on staff who not only identified with the content but became more aware of their own strengths and competencies (Bornat, 1997). Some shone as facilitators or collectors of ephemera, while others were keen to monitor the impact of reminiscence within the wider organization.

Reminiscence can have a transforming effect on the client/care worker relationship (Gibson, 1989; Norris, 1989). One of the attractions of reminiscence is its empowering potential (Bornat, 1989) but it is this which may present a dilemma for care staff. Listening to and hearing people may become more important than maintaining policies and following routines more concerned with physical care (Gibson, 1989). This may pose conflicts for the worker whose enhanced knowledge of the client suggests different and more individualized approaches to treatment and care.

Challenging ageism in clinical practice

Although there is as yet no evidence that exposure to reminiscence can address ageism in professional practice it has been suggested that just as Butler's writings in the 1960s led to a shift in practice, so also today a widespread use of reminiscence with an explicit anti-discriminatory focus might counter aspects of ageism (Harris and Hopkins, 1994). However, it is dangerous to assume that reminiscence in itself is anti-discriminatory. In order to challenge ageism it must be subject to review and evaluation. In order to be effective, reminiscence needs to avoid presuming shared experiences that deny issues of class, race, gender and sexuality. If reminiscence is to be truly anti-discriminatory it must begin from the ambiguities, tensions and contradictions in people's earlier lives and allow them to reflect on their past and present and interpret these in new and different ways (Harris and Hopkins, 1994).

Whilst there is a danger that reminiscence work can reinforce ageist beliefs by confirming preoccupation with nostalgia and personal thoughts (Harris and Hopkins, 1994), it also has the potential to challenge discrimination. Reminiscence can be a medium by which ageism is articulated in a safe and supportive environment. Negative images of older people persist and influence professional practice in a number of different ways. Economic constraints can disadvantage the older person whose needs are seen as less important than those of children or younger adults. There may be an increasing tendency to refuse care and treatment purely on the basis of age. Such ageist ideas are perpetuated by staff who practise from a biomedical model which fails to recognize the older client as a person who has the same rights as any other citizen. A knowledge of the life history of the older person or older people in general, can serve to remind practitioners of the contribution of the previous generation and their rights to quality services now.

Challenging discrimination relies on a recognition of the multiplicity of oppressions and diversity of experience of older people. It is invariably assumed that the 'elderly' are a homogeneous group rather than one diversified by age, gender, class, ethnicity and life experience. Challenging must begin from the ambiguities and tensions that surround people's lives and allow experiences to be interpreted and reconstructed in new and meaningful ways. It particularly requires the client to shape the content and process of reminiscence work rather than being the passive recipient of organized activities.

Although reminiscence is not the best mechanism by which older clients are holistically assessed, it has the capacity to raise awareness of the personhood and biography of the individual. Biomedical models still focus on the problems of old age without considering the abilities or the wider meaning of health and illness. Reminiscence cannot claim to redress the evils of ageism, but it can serve to remind staff of the personhood and individuality of their clients.

The need for culture and history

Coleman argued that Western societies had lost a sense of culture and that it must be regained, with older people playing a lead role in regaining it (Coleman, 1994). Reminiscence should not, according to Guttman (1987), be a means of self-defence but should provide a way of cultural support and enrichment passed from one generation to the next. Guttmann recognized that older people were deroled by modern Western societies and saw that reminiscence could provide an inspiration, a source of encouragement and not a retreat from everyday concerns. It was an opportunity for them to recover their involvement in the life of the community. The value lay not in the personal nature of reminiscing but in its translation into literature, history and autobiography (Moody, 1984).

However, reminiscence was not just about self-preservation. It had a wider dimension in preserving culture and cultural ways of coping (Coleman, 1994). The history of people from minority groups was lost twice, firstly to the home culture and secondly by antipathy to the host culture. Reminiscence had the capacity to record the history of ordinary people and in particular, marginalized members of society. This was an important part of social history, and if used effectively, had the makings of a living vibrant, intergenerational educational tool.

Sadly, the value attached to oral history is limited, but there is little doubt that modern professionals have a lot to learn from folklore and anthropology. In Ireland and other labour exporting countries there is a tendency to neglect the experience of migration and to deny its impact on life and health and its impact on the home community. Reminiscence with older people allows examination of this experience. It should enable policy-makers to formulate frameworks that help avoid the mistakes of the past and facilitate planning in an informed way for the needs of future generations.

Reminiscence can and should be translated to oral and written history, to record the lived experience of ordinary people. This history is enriching for both the home and the host community. In particular, the process of diaspora and the biographies of those who migrated and those who remained at home must be recorded to reflect social history accurately. This human history must inform developing bodies of knowledge such as cross-cultural and health psychology.

There is a genuine interest in the concept of quality of life for older people in health and welfare circles in Britain today. Quality of life should be concerned with the subjective experience of old age and not just functional ability. Greater attention must be paid to what quality means for the individual and in particular to the type of environment which contributes to happiness and encourages older people to flourish (Draper, 1997). It is not sufficient to focus on the here and now, as individuals are a product of their life history and the experience of old age is shaped by the past. Later life should not be seen as an event or a stage but as a continuing intricate pattern throughout life where older people adapt to change by using strategies linked to their past experiences of themselves and their social worlds (Atchley, 1989). These arguments are perhaps more relevant than ever today when market principles and financial cutbacks disadvantage older clients. Exclusion from the paid labour market, ageist images and public discussions about the burden of old age do little to preserve the self-esteem of the older person. Using reminiscence techniques and the principles of reminiscence can help maintain self-esteem and enable practitioners to work with clients to find the most appropriate ways of adjusting to ill health or infirmity. Perhaps more importantly, reminiscence can provide an important educational resource to tackle the neglect of age and ageing which exists in most programmes of professional preparation.

References

Antonovsky A (1994) The sense of coherence: an historical and future perspective. In: HI McCubbin, EA Thompson and A Thompson (eds) Sense of Coherence and Resiliency. Madison, WI: University of Wisconsin Press and (1998), London: Sage.

Armstrong-Esther C, Browne K and McAfee J (1994) Elderly patients: still clean and sitting quietly. Journal of Advanced Nursing, 19, 264–71.

Atchley R (1989) A continuity theory of normal ageing. Gerontologist, 29(2), 183–90.

Baro F, Keirse E, Meulenbergs L, Ruelens L and Van Liempt A (1997) Remembrance and dementia caregiving: supporting the sense of coherence. Widening Horizons in Dementia Care. Blackheath Conference of the European Reminiscence Network, 15–18 May 1997.

Bender M (1994) An interesting confusion: what can we do with reminiscence groupwork? In: J Bornat (ed.) Reminiscence Reviewed: Perspectives, Evaluations and Achievements pp. 32–45. Buckingham: Open University Press.

Blakemore K and Boneham M (1994) Age, Race and Ethnicity: A Comparative Approach. Buckingham: Open University Press.

Boneham M, Williams K, Copeland J, McKibbin P, Wilson K, Scott A and Saunders P (1997) Elderly people from ethnic minorities in Liverpool: mental illness, unmet need and barriers to service use. Health and Social Care in the Community, 5(3), 173–80.

Bornat J (1989) Oral history as a social movement: reminiscence and older people. Oral History, 17(2), 16–24.

Bornat J (1997) Reminiscence reviewed. Widening Horizons in Dementia Care, pp. 34–40. Conference of the European Reminiscence Network Age Exchange, London.

Bruce E (1997) Reminiscence and family carers. Widening Horizons in Dementia Care, pp. 40–6. Conference of the European Reminiscence Network Age Exchange, London.

Buchanan K and Middleton D (1994) Reminiscence reviewed: a discourse analytic perspective. In: J Bornat (ed.) Reminiscence Reviewed: Perspectives, Evaluations and Achievements pp. 61–74. Buckingham: Open University Press.

Butler R (1963) The life review: an interpretation of reminiscence in the aged. Psychiatry, 26, 65–76.

Coleman P (1988) Issues in the therapeutic use of reminiscence with elderly people. In: B Gearing, M Johnson and T Heller (eds) Mental Health Problems in Old Age, pp. 177–85. Chichester: Wiley, in conjunction with Open University.

Coleman P (1993) Adjustment in later life. In: J Bond, P Coleman and S Peace. Ageing in Society: An Introduction to Social Gerontology pp. 97–132. London: Sage/Open University.

Coleman P (1994) Reminiscence within the study of ageing: the social significance of story. In: J Bornat (ed.) Reminiscence Reviewed: Perspectives, Evaluations and Achievements pp. 8–20. Buckingham: Open University Press.

Crump A (1991) Promoting self-esteem. Nursing the Elderly, March/April, 19–21.

Cumming E and Henry D (1961) Growing old: the process of disengagement. New York: Basic Books.

Dant T, Carley M, Gearing B and Johnson M (1990) Final report of care for elderly people at home; a research and development project in collaboration with Gloucester Health Authority. Milton Keynes: Open University Press.

Dobrof R (1984) Introduction: A time for reclaiming the past. In: M Kaminsky (ed.) The Uses of Reminiscence: New Ways of Working with Older Adults. New York: Haworth Press.

Draper P (1997) Nursing Perspectives on Quality of Life. London: Routledge.

Fallot RD (1980) The impact of mood on verbal reminiscing in late adulthood. International Journal of Aging and Human Development, 10, 385–400.

Feil N (1982) Validation: the Feil Method. How to Help Disoriented Old-Old. Cleveland: Edward Feil Publications.

Feil N (1992) Validation therapy with late onset dementia populations. In: G Jones and B Miesen (eds) Care Giving in Dementia: Research and Applications Vol 1 pp. 199–218. London: Routledge.

Fielden M (1990) Reminiscence as a therapeutic intervention with sheltered housing residents: a comparative study. British Journal of Social Work, 20(1), 21–4.

Gearing B (1994) Series editor's preface. In: J Bornat (ed.) Reminiscence Reviewed: Perspectives, Evaluations and Achievements pp. ix–xi. Buckingham: Open University Press.

Gibson F (1989) Using Reminiscence: A Training Pack. London: Help the Aged.

Gibson F (1994) What can reminiscence contribute to people with dementia. In: J Bornat (ed.) Reminiscence Reviewed: Perspectives, Evaluations and Achievements pp. 46–60. Buckingham: Open University Press.

Goodwin S (1988) Working and Playing. In: S Wright, Nursing the Older Patient pp. 209–21. London: Harper & Row.

Guttmann D (1987) Reclaimed Powers: Towards a New Psychology of Men and Women in Later Life. New York: Basic Books.

Haight BK (1988) The therapeutic role of structured life review process in homebound elderly subjects. Journal of Gerontology, 43, 40–4.

Haight BK (1991) The state of the art as a basis for practice. International Journal of Ageing and Human Development, 33(1), 1–32.

Harris J and Hopkins T (1994) Beyond anti-ageism: reminiscence groups and the development of anti-discriminatory social work education and practice. In: J Bornat (ed.) Reminiscence Reviewed: Perspectives, Evaluations and Achievements pp. 75–83. Buckingham: Open University Press.

Johnson M (1976) That was your life: a biographical approach to old age. In: J Munnichs and W van den Heuval (eds) Dependency and Interdependency in Old Age. The Hague: Martinus Nijhoff.

Jones G and Miesen B (eds) (1992) Care Giving in Dementia: Research and Applications. London: Routledge.

Kitwood T (1992) Towards a theory of dementia care: personhood and wellbeing. Ageing and Society, 12(3), 269–87.

Lowry L and Ryan A (1993) Recreation is not a luxury. Elderly Care, 5(6), 24–6.

McMahon A and Rhudick P (1964) Reminiscing: adaptational significance in the aged. Archives of General Psychiatry, 10, 292–8.

Merriam S (1980) The concept and function of reminiscence: a review of research. Gerontologist, 20, 604–9.

Moody H (1984) Reminiscence and the recovery of the public world. In: M Kaminsky (ed.) The Uses of Reminiscence: New Ways of Working with Older Adults. New York: Haworth Press.

Murphy E (1982) Social origins of depression in old age. British Journal of Psychiatry, 141, 135–42.

Norris A (1989) Reminiscence with Elderly People. London: Winslow Press.

Tilki M and McEvoy D (1996) Culturally sensitive reminiscence. Federation of Irish Societies Bulletin, No 10 July 1996. London: Federation of Irish Societies.

Tilki M (1998) Old Age in Afro-Caribbean and Asian communities in Britain. In: I Papadopoulos, M Tilki and G Taylor (eds) Transcultural Care: A Guide for Health Professionals. Salisbury: Quay Books.

Tobin S (1991) Personhood in Advanced Old Age. New York: Springer.

Walker A and Maltby T (1997) Ageing Europe. Buckingham: Open University Press.

Warnes A (1997) The Health and Care of Older People in London. London: King's Fund.

Wong P and Watt L (1991) What types of reminiscence are associated with successful ageing? Psychology and Aging, 6, 272–9.

Woods B, Portnoy S, Head D and Jones G (1992) Reminiscence and life review with older persons with dementia: which way forward? In: M Jones and B Miesen (eds) Care Giving in Dementia: Research and Applications Vol 1 pp. 137–61. London: Routledge.

Chapter 9
Psychobiography:
Fingerprints of a Lifetime

PAUL HARRIS

Introduction

Each one of the elderly individuals one meets has gained a unique collection of experiences of life in the twentieth century. These are locked up in the memories of themselves, their families and acquaintances, and partly recorded in personal documents such as photographs, letters, diaries, and myriad 'souvenirs' of the past. Discerning the life stories of elderly people is especially relevant and rewarding since their story is more complete than those of younger individuals. They are especially inclined to review their lives in the form of reminiscence and to find 'integrity' or 'despair', or both, from this review (Kimmel, 1974).

Botton (1996) has supplied a poignant reminder of the effort needed on our part to prevent the memories of old people dying with them. He has described how his grandfather spent the final days of his life on a busy hospital ward. The old man was thwarted in his attempt to engage the interest of a nurse in his wartime memories. Botton reflected how his grandfather lacked a biographer since the empathy of other people was limited by their busy lives. The result was that his grandfather died having 'leaked' his biography in fragments 'haphazardly scattered' in anecdotes told to relatives and friends and in his personal souvenirs.

Few people write their memoirs. Of those who do, few find a publisher. Yet any bookshop or library contains a section of autobiographical and biographical books. Almost all such works concern the lives of individuals which society considers prominent in some way, famous or infamous. These tend to include writers, artists, politicians, sportsmen or sportswomen, criminals or others who have been in the public eye or have an unusual tale to tell. Nevertheless, biographers often spotlight ways in which their illustrious subjects are like the reader. The effect is a reminder of the threads of common humanity, an enhancement of the daily endeavour to understand other people.

The notion that only eminent people have a lifetime of experiences worth relating is increasingly being questioned. Every life is as unique as a fingerprint. Deceptively 'ordinary' lives include remarkably out-of-the ordinary moments and episodes. Dr Johnson's thinking was ahead of his time when he observed that 'there has rarely passed a life of which a judicious and faithful narrative would not be useful' (quoted by Botton, 1996).

Clinicians as biographers

As part of their everyday work, health care professionals have a distinct opportunity to become biographers of elderly people. For example, in the course of completing an assessment, psychologists tend to collect and collate biographical information about individuals. Similarly, many forms of psychological intervention, counselling and psychotherapy involve exploring in depth 'scripts', personal themes and unresolved issues. In routine clinical work there is a tendency to abbreviate this process and to take a problem-orientated approach focused upon relevance to present problems. This partly reflects constraints on the time available for clinical casework. Since the act of providing autobiographical details can be therapeutic, if sensitively managed, the therapist's response is worthy of more thought and time than is commonly recognized. In some circumstances the clinician may wish to consider the explicit option of preparing an assisted biography.

The assisted biography is a bridge between autobiographies and biographies, whereby a biographer writes down the autobiographical account of the person concerned. Modern aids to this interview process can include not only a notebook but also a tape-recorder or even a video-camera. Recent innovations relevant to biographical investigation may also include computer software, for example software for tracing family histories, photographs and all!

The methods selected for assisted biography partly depend upon the level, the breadth and depth at which a life history is to be studied and the professional training of the biographer in the range of methods available. Conventionally, case studies and clinical case histories can vary from the informal to the formal, the unstructured to the structured, or a combination of forms (Bromley, 1977). This may involve interviews ranging from casual conversations to structured interview formats (Johnson et al, 1992), and also the use of personal documents (Wrightsman, 1981), and specialized techniques such as questionnaires, role play and repertory grids (Viney, 1993).

Given the unfamiliarity of many clinicians with biographical methods or their superficial use of such techniques, some initial practice and familiarization is worthwhile. A good place to start is for clinicians to try out some of the methods available on themselves or a willing colleague. For example, the charting of life events is a useful exercise with which to begin.

There is a considerable theoretical and research literature on the measurement of life events. An early and well-known approach is exemplified by the Social Readjustment Rating Scale produced by Holmes and Rahe (1967). More recent refinements include the PERI scale, based upon the Psychiatric Epidemiology Research Interview utilized by Dohrenwend et al (1990). The focus of such scales is usually upon recent life events, for instance, within the past six or twelve months. A similar list can, however, inform a lifelong chronological timescale with the sequence of events for a particular individual elicited during interview. An anonymized example constructed from the author's own clinical work is shown in Table 9.1. The list shown can be constructed or adapted from a structured interview such as that documented by Johnson et al (1992).

A typical sequence of life events includes schooldays, jobs and careers, relationships, marriage and divorce, childbirth and child-rearing, moving home, unemployment and retirement, serving in the forces or war industries, illness and disability, and bereavements. In terms of constructing an assisted biography it is to be realized that life histories are more than a collection of the events in a person's life course. Such events need to be considered within a framework of self and identity theory as being 'structured self-images' (Johnson, 1978; Kohli, 1983). Kohli conceptualized life histories as lifescripts played out through childhood, adolescence and adulthood. Anderson (1981) has cautioned how individuals have 'practised ways of presenting themselves' which the biographer must penetrate to locate the 'secret self, the inner myth' that shapes the person's self-image. Anderson also draws attention to the fact that life events usually result from multiple causes, within which not only childhood precursors but also later influences may be salient.

Memories as reconstructions

An appreciation of personal accounts of life events should recognize that everyone's memories are reconstructions (Funder et al, 1993) rather than strictly accurate and objective records of original events (Baddeley et al, 1995). A particular memory is not retrieved from sixty years ago or whenever but from a more recent occasion when it was rehearsed or recounted. For example, memories of childhood are selective accounts which can be embellished and altered through the process of retelling. Although there is evidence of deterioration in some aspects of memory functioning with the passage of age, this is less marked for some facets of the means by which individuals process information. There is evidence that in older people the ability to recognize memorized information holds up better than tasks demanding free recall. This point suggests that when working with the elderly on assisted biography, it is important to use

Table 9.1. An example of life events chronology (figures refer to age in years)

Born 20 February 1925

Age		
	1	Family lived in north London.
	3	Sister born.
	5	Started school. Brother born.
	8	Family moved house in same street. Maternal grandmother died.
	9	Maternal grandfather died.
	11	Started secondary school.
	14	Second World War started.
	15	Left school. Evacuated out of London. Began factory work.
	16	First boyfriend.
	17	Father killed in war. Met husband.
	19	Married. Moved into own home.
	20	Finished employment. Elder daughter born. Second World War ended.
	22	Younger daughter born.
	23	Miscarriage.
	24	Moved home.
	25	Son born.
	30	Husband unemployed for six months. Returned to part-time employment as shop assistant. Termination of pregnancy.
	31/32	Marital problems.
	33	Best friend killed in car accident.
	37	Gynaecological operation.
	38	Elder daughter left home.
	39	Younger daughter married and left home.
	41	Grandson born. Road traffic accident: whiplash injury.
	44	Son married and left home. Granddaughter born.
	45	First holiday abroad.
	47	Mother's health deteriorated.
	49	Younger daughter separated (and later divorced). Daughter moved in, with grandson, for two years.
	50	Mother died.
	51	Grandson seriously ill.
	55	Grandson in trouble with police.
	58	Younger daughter remarried. Husband's health deteriorates.
	61	Husband took early retirement.
	63	Moved home.
	65	Husband in poor health.
	66	Husband died. Depressed for three years.
	68	Moved to a flat.
	72	Brother died suddenly of heart attack.
	74	Hospitalized for two weeks after fall.
	75	Biographical interview.

materials such as family photograph albums to help 'cue' recognition rather than depend only upon free recall. Memory for pictorial materials tends to hold up quite well with age, unlike, for instance, memory for spatial information (Baddeley et al, 1995). Cemack (in Baddeley et al,

1995) has suggested that autobiographical memories become 'crystallized' through being repeatedly retrieved and in effect become part of the individual's generalized knowledge of the world. In technical terms an implication of Cemack's observation is that key autobiographical memories are stored in the 'semantic' rather than 'episodic' memory bank. Since the efficiency of the semantic memory system is believed to decline less with age than the episodic store, this rich vein of information is often relatively intact well into old age.

Personal construct theory and therapy

Viney (1993) has presented a guideline for applying the personal construct approach, pioneered by George Kelly, to illuminate the psychology of how the elderly construe complex meanings in their long lives. The process whereby individuals continuously interpret and reinterpret their life events is utilized as a cornerstone for psychotherapy with the elderly. Case examples are explored tracing the meaning of personal accounts of retirement, illness and bereavement. Viney has explained how individuals live their lives in terms of 'stories', whereby a sequence of meanings or 'constructs' together form a theme. Such stories maintain a sense of identity and centre upon both the conceptualization of self and other people in relation to the self. Within a personal construct perspective the elderly are viewed as 'growing' psychologically in the same manner as individuals in other age groups. Viney indicates that such growth is achieved because elderly people continue a lifelong attempt to understand, anticipate and construct coherent stories about events. Viney notes evidence of how the thinking and memory processes of the elderly focus upon the distant and recent past as much as upon the here and now. Consequently their stories often refer to personally significant events stored in their episodic and semantic memory rather than being driven by recent memory.

Several personal construct techniques which have been applied by therapists when addressing psychological problems presented by the elderly are outlined by Viney. These include 'self-characterization', a method by which an individual evolves a character sketch of himself or herself.

A more elaborate methodology is role construct repertory technique. The reader is referred to Viney's (1993) text for a detailed account of this approach. In brief, the technique reveals information about the content of constructs and how constructs are related to one another. One formal means for eliciting constructs is called the triadic comparison method. A simple example is to ask a person to think of three individuals significant in their lives and to state how two of them are similar and different from the third. For instance, 'in what way are your husband and daughter-in-law alike and different from your son?' Psychologists sometimes record the replies given on a sheet designed for the purpose in order to produce a grid of ratings of people (or other 'entities') on selected constructs. This sometimes difficult procedure can be modified for use with the elderly and woven into a more informal interview approach.

Viney (1993) has specified additional personal construct methods drawn upon by psychologists who work with the elderly. One of these is termed 'narrative analysis'. This involves arriving at a 'core narrative' from the various themes which emerge from the detailed stories supplied by elderly clients in the course of psychotherapy. The therapist's analysis and interpretation of the story is then checked with the client to yield a mutually agreed version. The implications of the 'core story' are subsequently explored with the elderly client. When appropriate, this can encompass a technical objective of 'loosening' or 'tightening' construal when some change in the person's view of people or events is considered therapeutic. Viney has given a detailed guide to 'story retelling as therapy' specific to psychotherapy with the elderly and presents numerous case examples.

Writing a life story

In comparison with personal construct theory and methodology, a less technical approach more accessible to non-psychologists is to be discovered in Nancy Smith's (1993) stepwise guide to writing an autobiography. Smith's work is a rich sourcebook for methods and tips to unlock and retell autobiographical experiences.

Smith's book includes exercises such as 'memory joggers', 're-creating characters', 'writing in scenes' and 'writing a family history'. Such approaches can be adapted for use not only in construction of an autobiography but also in directing the 'assisted biography' of an elderly person. As an example, in writing a family history Smith lists a number of useful questions to cover when interviewing 'an ageing relative'. Notably, the list of topics which she presents to inspire memory joggers is not dissimilar to the sequence of personal landmarks employed in life events research. Her list contains some worthwhile additions such as 'travel', 'people who have influenced you/characters you'll never forget', 'a special place', 'unfulfilled dreams/ambitions' and 'first love/romance'.

Smith refers to the 'therapeutic value' of committing to paper some of the 'traumas and difficulties' encountered over the course of a lifetime. Since an autobiography is an important statement of personal identity ('who you are'), it can validate or integrate self and 'banish the fear of annihilation of self' which we may 'fear more than death'.

A place in history

The assisted biography of an elderly person cannot be completed without extensive reference to the world and society which the person inhabited

(Le Goff, 1989). Any man or woman aged three score years and ten and more as the millennium approaches has lived through the historical milestones of a century of immense social and technological change.

The catalogue of events that happened around them often spans two world wars and other less global conflicts (the Korean, Vietnam, Gulf and Cold Wars to name but a few). The history witnessed encompasses a nuclear holocaust and the Cuban Missile Crisis, economic prosperity and depression, the rise and fall of governments and ideologies, and a changing cast of international foes and friends. An elderly person in Britain, for example, has observed the death of a king, the abdication of a king, the coronation of a queen, and the death of a princess.

The elderly as a war generation

It cannot be automatically assumed that historical episodes such as the Second World War have special significance for all members of the older generation. For some its impact may have been minimal or overshadowed by other personally significant life events. Nevertheless, for a significant number of today's elderly citizens the wartime era, its precursors and aftermath, have crucially shaped their perception of the world. A review by Hunt (1997) of the 'trauma of war' refers to research which demonstrates how Second World War veterans suffer war-related psychological distress even half a century after the end of the war (see also Robbins, 1994). At a late stage in their lives these veterans have to find new ways of coping with their memories. A psychological process of 'decompensating' in later life can be witnessed in individuals despite previously appearing 'symptom-free'. Suppressing the past may be a successful strategy when in employment and absorbed in raising a family but can become less effective when the war veteran retires and traumatic memories resurface.

Similarly, research relating to both men and women in the Netherlands has indicated higher rates of mortality and morbidity in resistance veterans and pervasive psychosomatic disorders in elderly veterans (Waugh, 1997).

Such consequences of wartime experiences are not confined to men. Waugh (1997) has reported a study of 112 women who experienced the Second World War, either in the armed forces or as civilians. The fear associated with experiences such as doodlebugs and V2 rockets can persist for a lifetime. This author, a clinical psychologist, recalls receiving a referral to treat a case of thunder phobia presented by a woman in her sixties. A clinical interview including a chart of life events revealed that the initial onset of this long-standing phobia coincided with the experience of seeking safety in an air-raid shelter. There was a strong suggestion that the phobia represented a displaced fear of the 'noise of bombs dropping', thereafter triggered by the sound of thunder.

Waugh (1997) found that occurrences such as reports of current wars and the anniversaries of wartime events often rekindled traumatic recollections. While some women viewed wartime experience in a positive light, Waugh cautions against applications of reminiscence therapy that neglect to take into account the personal meaning of the objects of memory. This is especially the case when these associations may be counter to the common or benign experiences of the population at large (see also Hunt et al, 1997).

Davies (1997) has proposed guidelines relevant to therapists working with elderly clients. These include a basic knowledge of the events of the Second World War, a sensitive and cautious approach which is guided by the wishes of the elderly individual, and a need to avoid sanitizing unpleasant events. A general goal is to assist the person concerned to review such experiences in the context of their subsequent life. This involves facilitating an integration of these experiences with the person's view of himself or herself and the world in general. Psychological models have been developed that are suitable for an evidence-based practice approach. This includes Robbins' four-stage model of war trauma treatment for war veterans and Knight's framework for 'maturity specific challenge' (Davies, 1997). Like Waugh, Davies reminds not only therapists but all caregivers working with older people that group reminiscence of wartime experiences should be conducted with caution. In particular, he warns that such an approach with cognitively impaired older individuals is often unwise.

The task confronting not only clinicians but society in general is to explore with the current elderly 'war generation' how 'to look behind the propaganda and jingoism at the war they actually experienced' (Bender, 1994).

Biographical accounts of developing dementia

Several authors have commented upon how there has been considerably more written in terms of the experiences of families and carers than of the direct observations of individuals who are themselves experiencing dementia (e.g. Balfour, 1995).

In recent years several books have been published recounting the first-hand experience of individuals of the process of dementia and related neurological disorders. As Goldsmith (1996) has pointed out, however, such autobiographical stories remain 'discrete accounts' reflecting individualized and not necessarily common or generalizable experiences which do not as yet summate into a 'unifying pattern'. One of the first such publications was Robert Davis's book, *My Journey into Alzheimer's Disease*, published in 1989. Davis offered particularly valuable insights into the confusion and anxieties felt in situations such as public places.

A more recent and significant work is Diana McGowin's (1994) courageous and moving description of the progression of symptoms diagnosed as 'probably Alzheimer's disease'. In heartfelt but unsentimental terms she records her experiences of psychological and medical assessments, which included procedures such as an EEG and MRI brain scan. She retells the moments she learned the results of these tests and her attempt to understand her diagnosis. She charts episodes of despair and a positive struggle to come to terms with the enormity of the changes to her life which ensued. Her portrait of the spectrum of reactions by other people to her predicament, that is, by family, friends and work colleagues, represents a thumbprint of how individuals respond in a variety of ways to the adversity of such situations. The theme of McGowin's narrative can be compared to the literary parable of *Metamorphosis* created by one of the great writers of the twentieth century, Franz Kafka (1961). Kafka's story centres upon the struggle to stay human in the face of physical and personal decline involved in the process of serious illness. McGowin presents a clear statement of the importance of biography as a counter to the threatened despair of confronting Alzheimer's disorder. In her words, 'as my grip on the present slips, more and more comfort is found within my memories of the past' (McGowin, 1994). Her positive spirit was translated into practical measures such as founding an early onset support group for Alzheimer sufferers in her own community, the town of Orlando, Florida.

McGowin's book, *Living in the Labyrinth*, is an invaluable insight into the world of the sufferer from Alzheimer's disease. As an autobiography of the period of 'early onset', it at least requires supplementing with the stories of sufferers of more advanced age. Also, Cayton (1997) has queried the accuracy of diagnosis but not the sincerity of McGowin's perspective. This is a not unreasonable point given that it has been estimated that 15% of individuals initially diagnosed as suffering from dementia are subsequently thought to have been misdiagnosed (Goldsmith, 1996).

First-hand accounts such as that of McGowin remain a rarity. Part of the difficulty in any attempt at representing generalizable experience stems from the pervasiveness of individual differences in experience, relating to variations in personal and social background, personality, type of neurological disorder and stage of illness, and physical health. There are, however, increasing attempts to report and interpret the experience of elderly people experiencing severe impairment of their thinking, memory and behaviour (Goldsmith, 1996; Hunt et al, 1997). It can be suggested that a psychobiographical perspective is consistent with endeavours to engage people with dementia as active rather than passive participants in their care and treatment. Thus for most individuals travelling the lonely journey of dementia, assisted biographies may be a more achievable goal, with widespread value in improving services and the appreciation of the potential role and contribution of professional and family caregivers.

Conclusions

A review of the topic of psychobiography presented in this chapter has highlighted key points to be considered by health professionals and others who work with and care for old people. It is noted that the life histories related by elderly people are embedded within each individual's self-image and identity. Autobiographical memory is comprehended as a process of 'reconstruction' rather than objective recall of events. It is also proposed that life histories need to be appreciated within a historical context. This issue is illustrated in portrayal of the elderly as a 'war generation'. Reference has also been made to biographical accounts of people suffering from dementia and similar changes to the brain affecting their thinking, abilities, memory and actions.

The art and science of psychobiography remains in its infancy but shows encouraging signs of growing maturity (Anderson, 1981; Denzin, 1989). In this chapter it is suggested that psychobiography is an endeavour already sufficiently developed to assist the clinician in recognizing the elderly as unique individuals whose lives are worth recording, in part or whole. Some guidelines have been outlined for how psychologists and fellow professionals can conceptualize and approach this task, at various levels and from complementary directions. The application of psychobiography to working with older people deserves consideration not as a diversionary therapy but as central to understanding and valuing their lives and experiences.

References

Anderson J (1981) The methodology of psychological biography. Journal of Interdisciplinary History, 11, 455–75.

Baddeley A, Wilson B and Watts F (1995) Handbook of Memory Disorders. Chichester: Wiley.

Balfour A (1995) Account of a study aiming to explore the experience of dementia. Psychologists' Special Interest Group In The Elderly Newsletter, 53, 15–19.

Bender M (1994) Symposium on the long-term effects of World War Two. Psychologists' Special Interest Group In The Elderly Newsletter, 48, 25.

Botton A (1996) Kiss And Tell. London: Picador.

Bromley D (1977) Personality Description in Ordinary Language, pp. 162–204. Chichester: Wiley.

Cayton H (1997) Hunting in the dark: what can people with dementia tell us? Unpublished conference paper, XIII Alzheimer's International Conference, Helsinki, Finland.

Davies S (1997) The long-term psychological effects of World War Two. Psychologist, 10(8), 364–7.

Davis R (1989) My Journey into Alzheimer's Disease. Wheaton, IL: Tyndale House.

Denzin N (1989) Interpretative Biographies. London: Sage.

Dohrenwend B, Link B, Kern R, Shrout P and Markowitz J (1990) Measuring life events: the problems of variability within event categories. Stress Medicine, 6, 179–87.

Funder D, Parke R, Tomlinson-Keasey C and Widaman K (1993) Studying Lives through Time: Personality and Development. Washington, DC: American Psychological Association.

Goldsmith M (1996) Hearing the Voices of People with Dementia. London: Jessica Kingsley.

Holmes T and Rahe R (1967) The Social Readjustment Rating Scale. Journal of Psychosomatic Research, 11, 213–18.

Hunt L, Marshall M and Rowlings C (1997) Past Trauma in Late Life. London: Jessica Kingsley.

Hunt N (1997) Trauma of war. Psychologist, 10(8), 357–60.

Johnson M (1978) That was your life: a biographical approach to later life. In: V Carter and P Liddiard (eds) An Ageing Population, pp. 99–113. London: Hodder and Stoughton/Open University Press.

Johnson M, Gearing B, Carley M and Dant T (1992) A biographically based health and social diagnostic technique: a research report. Psychologists' Special Interest Group In The Elderly Newsletter, 43, 3–12.

Kafka F (1961) Metamorphosis and Other Stories. Harmondsworth: Penguin.

Kimmel D (1974) Adulthood and Aging. New York: Wiley.

Kohli M (1983) Biography: account, text, method. In: D Bertaux (ed.) Biography And Society. London: Sage.

Le Goff J (1989) After Annales: the life as history. Times Literary Supplement, April 14–20, 405.

McGowin D (1994) Living in the Labyrinth: a personal journey through the maze of Alzheimer's. Cambridge: Mainsail Press.

Robbins I (1994) The long term consequences of war trauma: a review and case example. Psychologists' Special Interest Group In The Elderly Newsletter, 48, 26–8.

Smith N (1993) Writing Your Life Story. London: Piatkus.

Waugh M (1997) Keeping the home fires burning. Psychologist, 10(8), 361–3.

Wrightsman L (1981) Personal documents as data in conceptualizing adult personality development. Personality And Social Psychology Bulletin, 1, 367–85.

Viney L (1993) Life Stories: Personal Construct Therapy with the Elderly. Chichester: Wiley.

Chapter 10
Occupational Therapy with Older People

RITCHARD LEDGERD and GWILYM ROBERTS

Introduction

The purpose of this chapter is to explore the role of occupational therapy with older people. Changes in health care since the early 1990s have seen a shift from hospital to community-based services and support. Occupational therapy has a fundamental role in ensuring that clients and carers have the ability to cope at home, living as independent lives as possible. This chapter seeks to identify the underlying philosophy of occupational therapy theory and provide an applied knowledge of practical intervention when working with older people. Emphasis is also placed on the necessity for multidisciplinary working, to provide a comprehensive service to meet the needs of older people.

History

Ancient Greek and Chinese civilizations first recognized the therapeutic value of occupation and activity when boredom and inactivity were blamed for a variety of diseases. As a result, programmes of activities were introduced in which good health and the related immortality of the soul were encouraged. As early as 2600 BC the Chinese taught that disease resulted from organic inactivity and used physical training for the promotion of health (Creek, 1997). In 1000 BC, the Persians used problem-solving and physical activities to train recruits for the army. Hippocrates introduced recreational activities as a way of treating illness (MacDonald et al, 1976). Occupational and diversional activities have been accepted throughout the ages as being a positive influence on both the physical and mental well-being of humans.

The World Federation of Occupational Therapists (1993) defines occupational therapy thus:

'Occupational therapy is assessment and treatment through the specific use of selected activity. This is designed by the occupational therapist and undertaken by those who are temporarily or permanently disabled by physical or mental illness, by social or developmental problems. The purpose is to prevent disability and to fulfil the person's needs by achieving optimum function and independence in work, social and domestic environments.'

Occupational therapy (OT) was founded on the firm belief that people can influence their own health by being proficient in occupations which allow them to explore and interact with the environment in an adaptive way.

Occupational therapists (OTs) are health care professionals who assess, treat and educate clients of all ages in order to optimize human performance and function. In addition, the scope for practice also encompasses research, education and administration. In modern day medicine, OTs as well as other health care professionals are concerned with enabling individuals to overcome dysfunction in social and life skills. OTs achieve this by a process of problem-solving through occupational and activity-based programmes. Occupation can sometimes be seen as work orientated, craft or leisure activity; it may focus on creativity, or on functional skills. Everyday practical activities are valued as highly as aesthetic or intellectual pursuits and interests. Assisting others to overcome daily problems has become one of the most fundamental skills of a State Registered Occupational Therapist.

OT is seen as art and science which utilizes the analysis and application of activities specifically related to occupational performance in the areas of self-care, productivity and leisure. Through assessment, interpretation and intervention, the OT addresses problems impeding functional or adaptive behaviour in persons whose occupational performance is impaired by illness, injury, emotional disorder, developmental disorder, social disadvantage, or the ageing process (Engel, 1991).

Treatment is likely to take place in hospitals, day hospitals, resource centres and especially in the community, in areas such as Primary Care Teams. OTs will endeavour to support and provide a service to both the clients and the carers.

Core skills

All therapists should be aware of their primary and generic core skills when undertaking any therapeutic intervention. Research suggests that OTs share many skills with other professionals and these can be termed generic core skills. These include communication, teaching, counselling and interviewing skills. Primary occupational therapy core skills can be identified by analysing those skills that the therapist uses which form the core of their practice.

The College of Occupational Therapists (1994) defines the unique core skills of occupational therapy as:

- Use of purposeful activity and meaningful occupation as therapeutic tools in the promotion of health and well-being.
- Ability to enable people to explore, achieve and maintain balance in the daily living tasks and the roles of personal and domestic care, leisure and productivity.
- Ability to assess the effect of, and then to manipulate, physical and psychological environments to maximize function and social integration.
- Ability to analyse, select and apply occupations as therapeutic media to treat people who are experiencing dysfunction in daily living tasks, interactions and occupational roles.

Models of practice/frames of reference

When questioned, many OTs term their use of models and frames of reference as eclectic. This is true. However, the therapist should be aware of these models and frames of reference when understanding the theory underpinning their practice. Working with older people requires the therapist to draw on many approaches to assessment and treatment. The therapist should be able to trace their practice to the frames of reference and models identified below. These are derived from five predominant theoretical principles that have been adapted from Hagadorn (1992):

The physiological frame of reference: Two predominant and diverse approaches are derived from this frame of reference, namely the neurodevelopmental approach and the biomechanical approach. Most aspects of physical intervention are related to this frame of reference.

The cognitive frame of reference: Cognitive theories and approaches have a strong place within OT intervention and relate to the clients' memory, insight and conceptualization process. Intervention can focus on working with retained abilities and can improve the client's awareness and understanding of their function and themselves.

The behavioural frame of reference: Behavioural theories and approaches may be used in interventions which include behaviour modification and programmed learning.

The humanist frame of reference: The underlying components of this frame of reference relate to the philosophy of humanism. This is important, as many related client-centred approaches to treatment are derived from this school of thought and therapists should be aware of related issues.

The rehabilitation model: This encapsulates the many frames of reference and moulds them into a therapy-related concept. This should be explored to give a direction to theoretical knowledge relating primarily to OT.

These models and frames of reference are suggestions by the authors and it is strongly recommended that the OT should undertake further reading to clarify the theories associated with these schools of thought.

Interview

When undertaking any interview or discussion with a client it is essential that the therapist respects the individual's rights as a human being and also as an older person. Respect for the individual's life experience and subsequent knowledge is necessary to maintain the therapist/client working partnership. It bridges the age difference and gives an opportunity for a mutual learning experience.

Undertaking an interview with a client is important. However, it is necessary to appreciate that the client may be apprehensive at the thought that he or she is being 'assessed'. Recognizing that older people have a wealth of life experience is important, as is acknowledging that the client has encountered many types of situation and personalities before. Interviewers should be aware that older people are accustomed to the different techniques used by others to ascertain their personal information. They will be reluctant to tolerate any disguised attempts to make them divulge personal information. Older people rarely suffer fools gladly and do not respond kindly to patronizing attitudes that can sometimes be conveyed in the interviewer's style. Older people are usually extremely honest in their thoughts and opinions and will readily tell the interviewer their perceptions of a situation, question or request.

Some clients who are experiencing memory deficits are defensive about their problems and become agitated during formal and informal testing. They may have an awareness that they are being interviewed and are sometimes still conscious of their memory problems. The key skill to undertaking the interview is honesty. A clear, jargon free, basic explanation is required of the OT's purpose, what it is hoped to achieve and how this will benefit the client.

Assessment

Activities of daily living (ADL)

Initial intervention should involve spending time with a client and discussing how he or she spends the day. Older people can have varied and fulfilling lives and it is wrong to assume, because they are older, that they do not have interests beyond the home. It is assumed that if a client is referred to an occupational therapist, he or she is experiencing problems in managing skills of daily living. This can be through physical or mental health problems, or commonly both.

As people grow older their needs focus predominately on the mainte-nance and preservation of independence in the basic skills of activities of daily living.

Activities of daily living are an essential component in using an individual's daily occupations as therapy. Activities of daily living can be described as the 'performance of self-care, work and leisure activities' (Punwar, 1994).

Establishing the client's activities is fundamental in formulating a personalized assessment and treatment plan. It is essential to ascertain the true picture of an individual's lifestyle and not to assume, or generalize the routine and specific actions that a person undertakes every day. The OT's assessment and treatment are based on the client's lifestyle and are usually undertaken in the home.

Home environment

A client's home is his or her domain. Homes reflect the individual's choice and preferences and this is an important consideration for anyone entering into a client's environment. It should be acknowledged that some older people have lived in their present accommodation for many years and fiercely defend their right to remain in their home. They are aware of their environment's structure and know how to compensate for obstacles and objects that have become part of their daily routine. Many properties may not have been updated and their resources may be dated.

Consideration of the environment may initially include access, how the client can manage to gain entrance to his or her property, ability to manage keys in the door or cross the threshold step. Increasing numbers of clients are remaining housebound and therefore this may not be a consideration. Provision of grab rails and ramps can assist door mobility and the OT uses professional skills in ergonometry to advise on the safest and most purposeful positioning of the equipment.

It is important to remember that a client's living style may be different from one's own. Judging a client's home environment by personal standards is not an objective assessment. Obviously, if the home has serious environmental risks to hygiene and safety, then the necessary agencies should be alerted; however, this is a rare event associated probably with severe cognitive impairment and long-term isolation from social intervention. Each home is as different as the client. Structures and designs of homes vary and an OT's problem-solving ability develops to adapt to each unique home.

Mobility

Mobility is fundamental in the assessment of a client's ability to undertake activities of daily living. The client may mobilize independently, aided or unaided, or may be completely immobile. Liaison with the physiotherapist is essential, to clarify the assessment findings and subsequent prescription of walking equipment or mobility exercises. The OT may establish a client's ability to use the prescribed equipment in the home environment. Many household dangers include the numerous loose unsecured mats and carpets which are situated around the home. These can be removed or taped down with double-sided or border tape.

Experience suggests that some clients will not use the recommended equipment or walking pattern and will continue to use their own unsafe yet preferred methods of mobility. The therapist faces an ethical decision. Is the client to be allowed to continue to use the unsafe method of mobilizing, documenting that the client is at risk and no further intervention is possible? Although this is an essential part of good practice, the OT has an obligation to ensure that the client's environment is made suitably safe from obvious dangers, which could result from the client's non-compliance with the recommendations. It may be more appropriate to recommend provision of further grab rails which may not have been necessary if the client used the recommended walking pattern. In many cases a discussion with the client about his or her reluctance to use the recommended equipment can solve many problems. OTs should also be aware of the budgetary constraints linked to prescription of non-basic equipment. A priority is to have regular liaison with the physiotherapist regarding his or her intervention and to provide regular feedback regarding OT recommendations.

Wheelchairs

A client may require assessment and prescription of a wheelchair. It is recommended that the OT should have undertaken training and updates in the prescription of wheelchairs. Considerations for the correct prescription may include the client's physical and mental ability to self-propel a wheelchair. Attention to the home environment is necessary to establish suitability for the size of chair prescribed and also whether the doorways require widening or ramps require fitting, or in some cases whether an application for rehousing should be sought. Prescription of electric wheelchairs also requires careful consideration. Vision, cognition, safety are key components of the assessment. The majority of wheelchairs issued are attendant propelled. Carer ability and dexterity should be a primary consideration.

Pressure care is important when contemplating the prescription of a wheelchair. Suitable assessment scales are in operation in most wheelchair providing units. Common scales include the Waterlow and Braden scores. Any scale is designed to measure the risk involved to a client's skin due to prolonged posture in a wheelchair. It is necessary to review the scores and the client's needs regularly, and carers should be educated to recognize any visible signs of skin deterioration. Where possible the client should be encouraged to voice any discomfort in seating from an early stage.

Stairs

Stairs are an important feature of an individual's environment. Both internal and external stairs can vary in size, length, height and width. Provision of additional banister rails, grab rails and stairlifts can assist stair mobility. Liaison with the physiotherapist can clarify the client's ability and any prescribed exercises. A problem-solving technique frequently used is the relocation of the bed downstairs to avoid use of the stairs. Indeed, this can be used as an interim measure prior to provision of major adaptations. It is important to note that clients with severe cognitive impairment can sometimes become distressed and confused when using a stairlift and clients with any memory problems can also have difficulty operating the stairlift safely.

Transfers

Regular transfers in the home environment are bed, chair, toilet and bath/shower transfers. As above, close liaison with physiotherapists is essential to coordinate therapeutic intervention and feedback regarding the client's ability to undertake transfers within the home.

Bed transfers

How the client is able to get on/off the bed is a primary consideration in promoting independence in the home. This involves not only the client's ability to sit to stand from a bed but also to place the legs into the bed, manoeuvre up and down as necessary and also cover themselves with the bed clothes. Some beds can be raised or lowered to improve sit to stand transfer. Another way can simply be to reposition the bed so the client transfers from the other side. This can make a tremendous difference for some clients and does not require the provision of any equipment. Other safety measures include provision of an overbed table, pillow raising cradles, cot sides and/or bed lever. Access to light switches and communication devices is also an essential component in client ability to transfer on and off the bed.

Chair transfers

Clients invariably have a preferred chair for daily use. Over the years they have found compensatory methods to improve their transfers in and out of a chair. This can include numerous cushions being added to a chair and in the case of one memorable client, the use of a wooden box on the seat to improve the height. Safety remains an essential component in chair transfers. Prescription of chair raising equipment is the most commonly used method to improve height. The products on the market cater for most styles of chair. Other equipment can include reclining chairs, both electric and manual, and also 'ejector' chair seat pads. These can enable a client to sit to stand with minimal effort. However, caution is advised in prescribing such pads for clients with neurological problems, especially those with Parkinsonian features, as compensatory and corrective reactions are not always present with this client group. Static height-adjustable chairs are commonly prescribed; again some clients are reluctant to sacrifice a previous chair.

Toilet transfers

Location of and ability to access the toilet is considered when assessing the home environment. Toilets can vary in height size. Prescription of grab rails, raised toilet seats, and free standing and floor fixed toilet frames can assist transfers. Product styles available are widespread and can play an essential part in client safety in the home.

Bath transfers

Transferring in and out of the bath requires complex coordination, agility and good physical dexterity. Many healthy, fit adults have experienced difficulty transferring in and out of a bath at some point in their lives. It is important to consider that a client may have stopped using the bath many years prior to occupational therapy intervention. In most of these cases the client has become accustomed to a stripwash or assisted wash. It is therefore not practical, safe or objective for the therapist to insist that the client trials and restarts using the bath with adaptive equipment.

Many clients referred to OTs experience difficulty with bathing and wish to continue using their bath. Prescription of bath boards, electronic and static bath seats, or grab rails can assist transfers. Another useful household item is a non-slip bath mat. Provision of a walk-in shower can be of tremendous assistance to an older person. However, many social service providers will have strict criteria to fund provision. Showers can alleviate many transfer problems faced by elderly carers.

Prescribing bathing equipment should be undertaken with caution when dealing with a client with cognitive impairment. Learning skills are not always intact and therefore the client will have little or no recollection of what the equipment was initially prescribed for or how to use it safely. Clients have reinvented bathboards as over sink dish drainers and turned bath seats into flower pot stands! Safety and client awareness are paramount in recommending any non-static equipment.

Personal and domestic activities of daily living

Personal and domestic ADL are important elements of how the client functions in the home environment. These assessments can give valuable insight into the client's mental and physical health. Liaison with the client and carers will clarify home support services that are currently deployed/needed.

Many people perceive the OT assessment of these skills as a simple process. However, an OT can identify numerous capabilities and problems when assessing these complex and intricate tasks. Liaison with members of the multidisciplinary team can enable the client to benefit from specialist intervention from colleagues. Speech therapy, physiotherapy, social work, dietetics, podiatry and nursing can provide a multidisciplinary approach to facilitate independence in a client's activities of daily living.

Personal ADL include maintenance of personal hygiene, feeding, toileting, washing and dressing. Domestic ADL include meal and drink preparation, shopping, budgeting, laundry and cleaning. All these skills are necessary to maintain a client's independence at home.

Attempts should be made to assess these skills in accordance with the client's daily pattern and timing. All too often therapists attempt to undertake these assessments at the convenience of their own schedule, but the question should be raised about the purpose and validity of such an approach. Is it reasonable to expect to assess a client's ability to wash and dress at 9 a.m., simply because that is the time the therapist starts the working day? Similarly, is it reasonable to expect a client to prepare the evening meal at 3.30 p.m. so the therapist can finish work on time? The answer to these problems is to encourage therapists to remain flexible with their working hours, so the needs of the client can be appropriately met.

Observation of a client's ability to undertake personal and domestic ADL can identify how safely the client undertakes the tasks they perform daily to maintain independence.

Personal activities of daily living (PADL)

Assessment findings may include:

- Physical ability with transfers, fastenings and range of movement.
- Safe use of hot and cold water.
- Correct use of prescribed equipment.
- Recognition and correct use of clothing.
- Hygiene.
- Body image and neglect/body scheme.
- Cognition, memory, sequencing, vision.

Domestic activities of daily living (DADL)

Assessment findings may include:

- Mobility around the kitchen environment, with and without kitchen utensils.
- Ability to use gas and electrical appliances safely.

- Coordination and physical dexterity.
- Food storage, recognition of sell-by dates, food product preference and nutritional intake.
- Hygiene.
- Cognition, memory, sequencing, vision.

As the assessments are completed, the OT can identify the level of independence the client attains in undertaking these tasks. These can be broadly categorized and can form an observational based conclusion to the assessments. The terms below can be used to summarize specific or global abilities of ADL.

- A client who receives no verbal or physical assistance can be termed independent.
- Clients requiring minimal or maximum verbal prompts can be termed as requiring supervision.
- Clients who require minimal or maximum physical assistance can be termed as requiring assistance.

The OT should clarify clients' abilities and problems in detail prior to using the above terms.

Mental state

It is assumed that good rapport is established between therapist and client during the assessment process, thus promoting clients' trust in the relationship. Throughout OT intervention, the therapist becomes aware of a client's mental level of functioning. This can be assessed both formally and informally.

Formal standardized assessments for use with the elderly can highlight areas of competence and deficit. These include MMSE (Mini Mental State Examination), CAPE (Clifton Assessment Procedures for the Elderly) and SOTOF (Structured Observational Test of Function). The therapist must research the requirements and protocols of the desired test.

Informal testing can occur when the client is undertaking activities of daily living and the OT can help to clarify a client's thoughts, perceptions and difficulties. The value of occupational therapy is that assessment focuses primarily on function and therefore clients who have poor scores on a standardized assessment may still be able to undertake certain ADL independently. Clients may also feel more comfortable performing their usual activities in their home surroundings and may therefore not be as guarded or apprehensive as when they are aware that they are undergoing a formal assessment.

From the OT assessment of ADL the therapist may also establish that the client displays:

- confabulation;
- aggression;
- repetitive behaviour;
- anxiety, depression;
- insight;
- psychosomatic symptoms;
- paranoia, delusions, hallucinations;
- social skills;
- difficulty with sequencing skills;
- communication skills;
- recognition;
- sensory motor deficits;
- disorientation;
- variable memory performance.

Rehabilitation

The OT is always aware that treatment should be a graded and purposeful activity. There are numerous approaches to undertaking rehabilitation with older people. Commonly, therapists engage clients by rehabilitating them using their activities of daily living. From the assessment findings the OT is able to formulate a plan of intervention focused on the client's needs. This is done in conjunction with the client and in some cases the carers.

Individual and one-to-one activities

Techniques involved in the rehabilitation of clients may include regular practice of transfers and personal and domestic activities of daily living. It may also be necessary to continue practising with a client the ability to use prescribed equipment safely.

Provision of equipment designed to assist independence in dressing can also be beneficial. Items can include stocking and sock gutters, long-handled shoe horns, Velcro fastening garments, and button hooks. Useful techniques can also be taught to clients who have paralysis including educating the client how to dress using one upper limb.

Provision of equipment designed to increase independence with domestic activities of daily living may also be appropriate. Items can include kettle and jug tippers, adapted cutlery and crockery, kitchen trolleys, tap turners, tin openers and also repositioning of household utensils or adaptation to work surfaces.

Other areas of rehabilitation may focus on budgeting, healthy eating and lifestyle, ability to undertake shopping, cleaning and laundry. This would understandably require the client's outdoor mobility to be established and also education in energy conservation techniques.

Groupwork

OT treatment groups are unique in that they are therapeutic groups which make use of activity as treatment. They are different from other groups because they have therapeutic aims – they seek to maintain or change personal functioning. Groupwork can also build group skills where the emphasis is not specifically on making members more effective group participants but on remediating and effecting change across all aspects of the self. Because activity is the main focus of the group, the use of activity makes OT groups substantially different from other groups. Since the OT is concerned with areas of dysfunction in the client's physical and mental health, functional and purposeful activities are used to treat specific problems encountered by the older person. Any hospital or community facility that provides occupational therapy for the older person should be utilized in order to help to maintain sensory, motor and cognitive functions.

Groupwork benefits

Groups are often seen as a supportive resource as members should feel a sense of belonging. Individuals are encouraged to work towards fulfilling the group goals. Benefits of group work can include:

- Comparing attitudes, feelings, thoughts, skills and learning.
- Experiencing directly the effects of actions, attitudes and emotional expression on others.
- Increasing knowledge of self, attitudes and beliefs.
- Exploring learning and interpersonal skills in the group: using the group to test new behaviours, roles, and skills in a safe environment.
- Developing social interaction.

An effective OT group may also provide a safe setting to explore feelings, such as sadness and disappointment. The older person may be encouraged by the OT to ventilate the feelings that are addressed in the group and learn that they need not be overwhelmed by them. A group can provide an opportunity for members to learn to acknowledge and accept their feelings and learn more adequate ways of expressing them.

Planning and understanding

Therapists should remember that when planning or undertaking any therapeutic intervention, clients should not be modelled into existing group structures, simply because it meets the needs of the organization's timetable. OTs must ensure that clients' needs are a priority and that, given the flexibility allowed within the service, structures should be adjusted or developed to meet these needs.

The OT's skill lies in reinforcing learning in many dimensions and helping the older person to see why doing the activity benefits him or her.

If these skills are not used, the benefits of doing the activity are greatly reduced. OTs, carers and the client should understand the types of learning that may be reinforced:

* Learning about personal physical dysfunction.
* Learning about themselves and others.
* Gaining conceptual knowledge.

Groupwork application

The OT may reinforce some or all of the above areas, depending on the clients' needs. For example, a group of clients may participate in a creative group, whereby magazine pictures are collated and mounted on a collage. The aim of this group is to enhance communication in a social setting. In that single activity the individuals within the group could discover:

* Aspects of the physical self regarding dexterity, coordination, organizational skills.
* Aspects of the cognitive self and the individual's ability to concentrate, conceptualize and choose pictures required.
* Aspects of the self-concept and how individuals see themselves in certain roles.
* Aspects of the interpersonal self and whether individuals work best alone, or in cooperation with others.
* Communication skills with other group members.
* Aspects of health and safety.

The OT does not just deal with a body and its dysfunction in a physical setting nor with psychological or emotional problems in a mental health setting. An elderly cardiac client may have more need at one point to develop a new self-concept than to concentrate solely on physical rehabilitation.

Use of up-to-date media can prove valuable in the treatment of older people in groupwork. Groupwork suggestions may include:

Comedy group: Using current and historical television comedy programmes, sharing embarrassing moments and joke telling can sometimes prove beneficial in exploring the use of humour and laughter as a form of therapeutic intervention.

Chart music group: A juke box jury style group based on clients discussing and scoring music played on compact disc, audio or video tape. Video media can increase client awareness of technology and advances in production techniques. This group not only gives clients the ability to have an informed choice of music, it encourages communication with younger family members and an informed knowledge of media personalities' abilities. It also benefits the client to share personal opinions with the group. As music is so personal, no other person can tell them they are wrong for having their own views.

Mobile reminiscence group: Using a car or other transport to enable clients to travel to various local landmarks without having to leave the vehicle. Discussion can be carried out in the vehicle and this can benefit clients who have impaired mobility to experience a group outside of the assessment/rehabilitation environment.

Diagnosis groups: These can be an essential form of communicating to the client specific areas of diagnosis and presenting problems. This can be useful in a variety of clinical settings including stroke rehabilitation, cardiac, neurology/neuroscience, pain management and in various mental health settings.

Carer support: These groups can be an invaluable source of support to the carer in dealing with issues relating to caring for an individual. The opportunity to share and exchange information can provide tremendous support to carers, in particular, the support and advice from other carers who may have experienced similar problems.

Areas for future development in occupational therapy with older people

Occupational therapy is an adaptable and forward thinking profession. OTs have a valuable opportunity to adjust their skills to accommodate changes to meet individuals' and society's ever changing needs. Suggestions for future developments for occupational therapy with older people are outlined below.

- Community-based assessment and rehabilitation programmes incorporating health, social services, voluntary and private sectors.
- Integration with domiciliary services including carer organizations and coordination of support worker roles from multidisciplinary backgrounds.
- Continued occupational therapy involvement in practical and technological advances in the development of equipment and adaptations designed to suit the needs of the older person.
- Developing occupational therapy services to meet the needs of older people living in residential and nursing home accommodation.
- Occupational therapists should remain actively involved in *continuing professional development*, updating their knowledge and skills in this specialized area. They should continue to publish their research findings to ensure growth and progression within their profession.

References

College of Occupational Therapists (1994) Core Skills and a Conceptual Framework for Practice – A Position Statement. London.

Creek J (1997) Occupational Therapy and Mental Health. Edinburgh: Churchill Livingstone.

Engel CE (1991) Not just a method but a way of learning. In: D Boud and G Felleti (eds) The Challenge of Problem Based Learning pp. 23–33. London: Kogan Page.

Hagadorn R (1992) Occupational Therapy: Foundations for Practice. Models, Frames of Reference and Core Skills. Edinburgh: Churchill Livingstone.

MacDonald M, MacCaul G, Mirrey L and Morrison E (1976) Occupational Therapy. London: Baillière Tindall.

Punwar AJ (1994) Occupational Therapy Principles and Practice, 2nd edn. Baltimore: Williams and Wilkins.

World Federation of Occupational Therapists (1993) Professional Practice Committee. World Federation of Occupational Therapists.

Further reading

Core skills

Hollis V (1993) Core skills and competencies: Part 1, What is experience? British Journal of Occupational Therapy, 56(2), 48–50.

Hollis V (1993) Core skills and competencies: Part 2, The competency conundrum. British Journal of Occupational Therapy, 56(3), 102–6.

Hollis V (1993) Core skills and competencies: Part 3, Excellence made explicit. British Journal of Occupational Therapy, 56(4), 135–9.

Hollis V (1993) Core skills and competencies: Part 4, Application and expectation. British Journal of Occupational Therapy, 56(5), 181–4.

Joice A (1989) Discussion on the skills of an occupational therapist working within a multi-disciplinary team. British Journal of Occupational Therapy, 52(12), 466–8.

Phillips N and Renton L (1995) Is assessment of function the core of occupational therapy? British Journal of Occupational Therapy, 58(2), 72–4.

Renton LB (1992) Occupational therapy core skills in mental handicap: a review of the literature. British Journal of Occupational Therapy, 55(11), 424–8.

Models of practice

Creek J and Feaver S (1993) Models for practice in occupational therapy: Part 1, Defining terms. British Journal of Occupational Therapy, 56(1), 4–6.

Creek J and Feaver S (1993) Models for practice in occupational therapy: Part 2, What use are they? British Journal of Occupational Therapy, 56(2), 59–62.

Jenkins M and Brotherton C (1995) In search of a theoretical framework for practice, part 1. British Journal of Occupational Therapy, 58(7), 280–5.

Jenkins M and Brotherton C (1995) In search of a theoretical framework for practice, part 2. British Journal of Occupational Therapy, 58(8), 332–6.

Groupwork

Benson JF (1991) Working More Creatively with Groups. London: Routledge.

Chapter 11
Independence and Rehabilitation

LIZ RANDALL and LIZ GLASGOW

Physiotherapy plays a key role in physical rehabilitation and the promotion of independence. The physiotherapist's aim in rehabilitation is to assist people back to a situation where they are able to function at their maximum capability, which is achieved by working on joint mobility, muscle strength, balance and pain. Through training, the physiotherapist has an intimate knowledge of how the body should move within the bounds of normality and is able to recognize aberrations. Using this knowledge and trained skill, the physiotherapist attempts to normalize movement, sometimes discouraging the fast quick fix with its trick movements that appear good initially in favour of a slower approach that will in time give the client a more correct and efficient result. Physiotherapy is a 'hands-on' profession, using exercise, hydrotherapy, therapeutic electrical modalities, joint mobilization, relaxation and massage as methods of treatment. Continence physiotherapists provide specialized treatment to help alleviate the all too common problem of incontinence.

Independence

Physiotherapists are involved in helping clients to remain independent through the promotion of exercise throughout life as a means to retain health and fitness.

The benefits of exercise and its positive impact on clients' health is an underlying belief of all physiotherapists. Regular exercise causes reduction of blood pressure, decreases the incidence of heart attack, allows easier weight control and leads to better concentration and relaxation. Physiotherapists incorporate education about the benefits of exercise wherever possible, for example, the benefits of weight-bearing exercises in the prevention of osteoporosis and the advisability of warming up and cooling down periods plus stretching when exercising in order to prevent exercise-induced injuries.

Prevention of falls programmes, graded exercise classes, and recreation or sport are areas where physiotherapists can be involved either as organizers or advisers. Walking, golf, swimming, aquaerobics, bowls, croquet, table tennis, badminton, dancing and T'ai Chi are some of the pursuits that active older people enjoy.

Care has to be taken to ensure that exercise regimes match the capabilities of the participants for both physical and psychological reasons. While most activities can be modified to allow a greater participation for those with physical difficulties or limited stamina, it is always essential for all participants to gain a medical clearance before commencing any exercise programme.

The aim of all rehabilitation physiotherapists, wherever they work, is independence for their clients. This should be taken to mean not only that the clients are able to look after themselves and/or return to a situation that is as close to their previous way of life as possible, but also that they are equipped with a self-management plan which allows them to deal with any recurrences of their problems.

As well as aiming for independence in mobility, it is important to support people in their wish to stay in their own homes until they reach the stage where this becomes impossible. Bearing in mind the enormous age and physical range that is present in an Aged Care setting, 'independence' may be a relative rather than total state. Sixty year old clients may be aiming to get back to bush walking or bowls once they have recovered from their fractured necks of femur, whereas the same fracture in 80 year old clients may threaten their ability to continue living in their own home and could result in them, at best, being independent in mobility indoors but needing help outdoors or for longer distances. There are many community-based services which can be accessed to help ensure this type of independence for the client, thereby easing some of the burden on family, friends and neighbours. The physiotherapist needs to be aware of all these options in order to be able to make appropriate recommendations, referrals and treatment.

Continence

Incontinence is the inappropriate loss of urine or faeces in the wrong place at the wrong time. It is common and may be one of the factors in causing a person to no longer be able to live at home. It may first become apparent in early childhood and is particularly common in women of child-bearing age and men and women over the age of 65. Without proper assessment and treatment, incontinence can be distressing, embarrassing and uncomfortable. It has a restricting and often devastating effect on quality of life and lifestyle, as well as on self-image. Many people never seek help for this problem. In fact, it is estimated that less than 30% of people with incontinence have consulted their doctor about it.

Incontinence in males is less common in the younger age groups than in females. However, as age increases so does the incidence of urinary incontinence so that, by the age of 65, men and women have a similar incidence. Males generally suffer from urgency, frequency and overflow incontinence, but may suffer from stress incontinence if they have had chronic constipation or straining, e.g. heavy lifting in manual occupations or in obstructive conditions as in an enlarged prostate.

In achieving and maintaining continence, certain elements are required:

- Knowing where to go.
- Being able to get there: mobility – is the person able to get out of bed at night?
- Being able to hold on. This requires an awareness of the distance to the toilet and a certain level of mobility.
- The ability to void on the toilet. This consideration of physical disabilities may involve the height of the seat as well as cognitive awareness.

Many older people have impaired mobility, impaired memory and/or multiple pathologies. In the physiotherapy management of older clients with incontinence, it is important to optimize mobility so that the person can get to the toilet. This might be achieved by adjusting the environment – for example, putting a commode next to the bed at night.

The aim of a Continence Service, which may be hospital or community based, is to help restore people's continence or reduce the severity of their symptoms. If this is not possible, the aim is to assist the person to achieve 'social continence'. This is where appropriate aids or appliances such as pads for women, condom drainage for men or intermittent self-catheterization are used to help minimize the severity of the incontinence, thereby permitting a more normal lifestyle. If night continence becomes intractable, washable plastic-backed protective bedding is readily available. Ideally, continence problems should be discussed with and treated in a multidisciplinary facility comprising a specialist medical practitioner, continence nurse and continence physiotherapist. Taking into consideration that incontinence is a symptom not a disease, a comprehensive assessment with an accurate medical diagnosis of each individual is essential.

In the past twenty years there has been an increase in research into bladder dysfunction, pelvic floor anatomy and physiology. New investigative techniques for diagnosis have been developed and new physiological concepts have emerged based on recent findings. This has led to investigative procedures such as urodynamics and to the establishment of special multidisciplinary continence clinics. Incontinence is not an inevitable part of ageing, though physical disabilities, physiological changes and multiple pathologies related to ageing, e.g. stroke, can add to the difficulties of maintaining continence. The physiotherapist has therefore an important role. In addition to the normal assessment of these clients, the physiotherapist must be aware of the type of incontinence. It is important to determine whether it is associated with immobility or lack of dexterity compounded by an inappropriate toileting regime or whether there are other factors to be taken into account. Some of this information can be gained from the client and other team members. Observation and charting will establish whether there is a definable pattern of micturition and whether incontinence is by day, by night, or both. A distinction must be made between clients who are aware of the urge to micturate and those who are unaware.

There are three main types of incontinence: stress, urge and overflow.

Stress

Stress incontinence is the involuntary loss of urine during an increase in abdominal pressure in the absence of a detrusor contraction such as in coughing, sneezing, laughing or lifting. The amount of urine lost depends on the specific cause of the leakage, e.g. neurological or soft tissue damage, and the severity of the problem. Stress incontinence can be caused by weak pelvic floor muscles. It can also be associated with:

- being overweight;
- strain – e.g. constipation;
- surgical trauma;
- direct injury, e.g. motor vehicle accident, fractured pelvis;
- birth trauma.

This type of incontinence can often be treated with pelvic floor muscle rehabilitation, surgery and/or oestrogen therapy.

Urge

Urge incontinence is one of the most common forms of incontinence in older people and is associated with an unstable bladder. This gives rise to a sensation of needing to go to the toilet urgently. If the person cannot get to the toilet, an accident – loss of urine, often the whole contents of the bladder – will occur. Stress and urge incontinence can occur together in men and women. Conditions such as diabetes, stroke, Parkinson's disease and multiple sclerosis can be associated with urge incontinence. Underlying pathology such as urinary tract infections needs to be addressed and treated, as these can be a cause of urge and frequency.

Overflow

Overflow incontinence is the leakage of urine from a bladder that is always full. This is often caused by a blockage of the bladder neck, e.g. enlarged prostate or tumour. The urine seeps out and the bladder never empties completely at void. With time, the bladder stretches because it is never completely empty and the urge to void returns frequently. Thus the unstable bladder and prostate problems are commonly associated with incontinence in older men. This type of incontinence is treated with surgery to remove the blockage and/or medication to promote bladder emptying. Bladder retraining may be necessary.

Faecal incontinence

Faecal incontinence is defined as the unintentional loss of gas, fluid or faecal matter from the anus. This again is a symptom of an underlying condition and needs to be carefully assessed before treatment is commenced. There are many causes of faecal incontinence: trauma, neuropathic, congenital, disease, mechanical, motility or constipation.

- Trauma may be direct or spinal, or surgical trauma such as anal dilatation, haemorrhoidectomy, lateral sphincterotomy or fistula. Childbirth trauma is becoming increasingly recognized as a cause of damage to the external anal sphincter (90%) or the internal anal sphincter, especially after a forceps delivery or a third or fourth degree tear.
- Neuropathic causes include those that occur during straining or heavy lifting, spinal cord lesions, neurological diseases or during childbirth trauma.
- Congenital causes are fistula, atresia and spinal lesions.
- Disease causes include tumour, infection and inflammation.
- Rectal prolapses, haemorrhoids and rectal ulcers are mechanical causes.
- Motility problems such as hypersensitivity (low compliance, proctitis and ulcerative colitis), giant rectal waves, irritable bowel syndrome and colorectal surgery can also cause incontinence.
- However, the most common cause of faecal incontinence in the elderly (and in children) is constipation. Severe constipation becomes impaction in older people, the symptoms of which are diarrhoea and loss of control of the anal sphincter, which can result in soiling several times a day. Impaction can be detected by an abdominal X-ray or by rectal or vaginal examination and treatment has to be supervised by a health professional.

The pelvic floor muscles play a large role in the ability to defaecate effectively. Positioning for evacuation is important. Squatting allows the anal canal to be opened more fully from front to back, making an efficient tunnel so that faeces pass through easily. Using a stool approximately 15 cm high to rest the feet on ensures that the pelvic floor is braced, providing support for the anus as it opens. It is important to use the abdominal and pelvic floor muscles together in order to empty the bowel effectively. If this is not done, then the result could be obstructed defaecation.

Many different types of management approaches are available although a large basic component can be pelvic floor rehabilitation. Physiotherapists have an important role to perform in the teaching of correct abdominal and pelvic floor muscle dynamics in both emptying techniques and the treatment of obstructive defaecation disorders. With their knowledge of muscle function and coordination they are the ideal health professionals to treat these conditions.

Rehabilitation

Rehabilitation in older people is never as straightforward as it is in those striving for fitness after a car accident or sports injury. Independence is so multifaceted that no one clinician can expect to deal with all aspects. In many cases, in addition to the presenting problem, there may also be:

- co-morbidities often resulting in a cocktail of medications being ingested daily which may result in iatrogenic problems;
- disempowerment as a result of financial worries associated with no longer being able to earn money, loss of status, or the perception of having nothing more to offer society;
- in some, a varying degree of senile or presenile signs;
- family concerns;
- isolation (relative or absolute), often as a result of the above or for those in their late eighties and nineties because they have outlived their friends and in some cases, their family as well.

Any of the following additional problems – impairment of hearing or sight, dizziness, incontinence, eccentric behaviour or unsafe living environment – create extra barriers to recovery. However, all these problems can be addressed by the appropriate specialist professions and consequently Aged Care Teams (both assessment and treatment) are a particularly efficient way of working. Within the team the physiotherapist primarily addresses the problems of pain, mobility, muscle weakness, joint stiffness and balance.

Clients access rehabilitation teams through referral from their local doctor, their specialist, self-referral, or as part of the discharge plan of an acute hospital. After receiving a community-based referral, one or more members of the Aged Care Assessment Service may visit the client's home to assess exactly what services and therapies are needed. If the client is at a stage where supported accommodation may have to be considered, the Assessment Service members will determine which level of care is appropriate. Staffed by a geriatrician, community nurse, physiotherapist, occupational therapist and social worker, they are an excellent resource for general practitioners and provide an efficient method of tapping into community services and supports. There are also Aged Psychiatric Assessment Teams which provide a parallel service.

Rehabilitation can take place in a special rehabilitation hospital or ward within an acute hospital, as part of a Rehabilitation in the Home scheme or at a Community Rehabilitation Unit.

A stay in a rehabilitation unit, with its holistic approach, can also bring to light evidence of unsuspected problems such as failure to cope properly at home, the beginnings of dementia or hidden health or continence problems. A period of rehabilitation, therefore, enables the team to do more than merely look after the current health problem and enable a return to the pre-morbid state; the team can also:

- establish the individual's capabilities at that time, providing a base level for future reference;
- provide an exercise programme that will make sure they are as fit and physically capable as possible on departure from the unit;
- alter or withdraw medication under the close supervision of medical staff and rationalize the dose so that it can be easily managed by means of a dosette box;
- organize community supports as needed;
- educate family and friends so as to ensure a successful discharge home;
- provide information on the options for socialization through family, friends or a social group of like-minded people, e.g. University of the Third Age, and encourage its use. For many people isolation and its inherent loneliness creep up slowly as their group of friends either gradually drift away or die. The team needs to be alert to this possibility and encourage the use of community socialization options;
- give advice on the level of care that the treating team feel is appropriate and provide clients with information and completed forms to enable them to follow that advice, if so desired;
- provide access to continence clinics;
- screen clients for depression or dementia;
- refer clients on to other specialist medical services as required.

The rehabilitation team

Typically the team comprises the following professional disciplines: doctor, physiotherapist, occupational therapist, social worker, speech pathologist, dietitian, podiatrist, nurse, continence specialists (nurse and physiotherapist).

Each client is treated by the appropriate therapists, with the overall management of each individual reviewed at the team meeting, which occurs on a formal basis at least once a week. There should always be close liaison between all therapists and medical staff, to ensure appropriate onward referral and seamless treatment with the minimum of duplication.

Using the team as a hub, there are other specialized therapists that can be called on as the need arises. Examples of this are the neuropsychologist, the remedial driving instructor and tester, the audiologist, the low vision educator, the orthotist or prosthetist and the neurological mobility service. This service, headed by an occupational therapist, teaches clients with hemianopia to optimize their scanning ability.

The success of the team depends not only on the professional skills of each member and their ability to use their time efficiently, but also on the personalities within the team for, as with sport, working in a team is a skill that not all possess. Team members have to be able to take a holistic viewpoint, recognize conditions and needs that fall well outside their basic professional training and be willing to refer on to others in the team. In effect all team members have to gain a basic knowledge of every other discipline within the team in order to be able to help the client fully.

Clients of a rehabilitation unit

The average age of the clientele seen in an Aged Care/Rehabilitation facility providing treatment for both inpatient and community clientele is in the 80s. However, the spread of ages can be from 19 to 108, as it is considered that the condition that the person presents with has to be taken into consideration as well as age.

Clients attending most rehabilitation units have problems that can be categorized under the following broad headings:

• Neurological
• Orthopaedic
• Other, e.g. post polio syndrome
• Failure to cope at home/debility/poor balance/after major surgery.

Clients may be in more than one of these groupings.

Neurological

Generally these will be victims of stroke or Parkinson's disease but some will be exhibiting signs of neurological damage which require a period of further investigation to determine its origin.

Stroke

Stroke sufferers are admitted to rehabilitation units only if the admitting doctor considers their rehabilitation prospects are favourable. It is generally accepted that this can be gauged at one week post event by independent sitting balance and continence. Age and initial motor ability are also taken into account, as are cognitive function and perceptual problems.

Physiotherapists have a large role in stroke rehabilitation, working on upper and lower limb movement, motor control, balance and gait re-education. There are many approaches to stroke rehabilitation, but most clinicians choose to use a mixed approach rather than following one method alone.

Most clients who have had a stroke are admitted relatively soon after the episode once they are medically stable. However, occasionally some arrive much later and will almost certainly have a few extra problems associated with a period of immobility. Twice daily physiotherapy treatments give the greatest benefit providing the client is able to deal with the amount of work and concentration. Fatigue is often one of the limiting factors in the early stages of stroke recovery. Close attention needs to be paid to the client's ability to learn and to retain information, as poor performance in this area limits the success of rehabilitation.

Of all the presentations following stroke, those exhibiting the so-called 'pusher syndrome' still appear to cause the most difficulty for therapists unused to stroke rehabilitation. Clients presenting with the symptom of leaning heavily onto their affected side but who have the feeling that they are in fact vertical often do very well once the correct sense of verticality has been re-established through visual and tactile facilitation.

After a period of rehabilitation, decisions have to be made as to whether or not safe ambulation is possible and whether gait aids or ankle/foot orthoses are needed. Close liaison with an orthotist is important with any rehabilitation team, either as a visiting specialist, or in bigger hospitals, as a regular member of the team.

Family members are encouraged to watch and take part in physiotherapy sessions to help them with the adjustments that will have to be made in their lives and to educate them in the home exercise programme the client will have on discharge.

Parkinson's disease

Whilst quite a few older clients will exhibit Parkinson-like symptoms not all will have Parkinson's disease, suffering instead the side effects of medications or other diseases such as Steele Richardson's syndrome, multisystem atrophy, cerebral atrophy or essential tremor.

The Kingston Centre in Melbourne, headed by Professor R. Iansek and Associate Professor Dr M. Morris, have done considerable work in helping people with Parkinson's disease and associated movement disorders. The book, Parkinson's Disease: A Team Approach (Morris and Iansek, 1997), is an excellent introduction to their methods in which the team approach to treatment is paramount, with the client and carer the hub of the team. This method, in contrast to the usual medical management with referrals to other isolated disciplines, can better be described as an interdisciplinary approach, where all members of a rehabilitation team work in interchangeable roles. A similar model has now been adopted by the Peter James Centre in Melbourne. The interdisciplinary team should comprise a neurologist, neuropsychologist, nurse, physiotherapist, occupational therapist, speech pathologist, dietitian and social worker. When establishing and appointing staff it is essential that the personnel employed are strong team players.

All clients treated using this model receive an individualized programme of management. They are prescribed medications designed to meet their needs and given at times to provide maximum efficiency throughout their day. Individual waking times, meal times and work/leisure activities are all taken into account when a medication schedule is being planned. This method allows empowerment for individuals to maintain a lifestyle of their choosing. The medication schedule is not confined to the doctor, client and nurse but involves all members of the rehabilitation team sharing their knowledge of the client's peak function time. In a client who has been on long-term levodopa management and is no longer receiving benefit, the disease is easier to manage with only one drug. In this case the treatment of choice is liquid levodopa, which can be given hourly and can be titrated as finely as 1 mg increments each hour to best meet the client's needs.

The physical management of Parkinson's disease using the interdisciplinary model is also individualized to the person's own daily needs and has a functional basis concentrating on what the individual wishes to do each day. These activities may include housework, continuing in the paid workforce, writing letters, typing, using public transport, shopping, playing sport and so on. Personal care and social activities are also addressed.

While the specialist team works in a central location, there is value in home visits to ensure safety of the environment and also to educate family members, friends, caregivers and others as necessary in the strategies being used to assist the person with Parkinson's disease.

Orthopaedic

The most common orthopaedic problems in an Aged Care setting are falls resulting in fractures mostly of the wrist and hip, rehabilitation following joint replacement surgery, osteoarthritis, rheumatoid arthritis and degenerative spinal problems.

Physiotherapy treatment is aimed at improving joint range of movement and muscle strength, decreasing pain and improving gait. This is achieved by exercise, hydrotherapy, joint mobilization, gait re-education and therapeutic electrical modalities.

In the case of clients who have fallen, in addition to treating the presenting problem, physiotherapists analyse the cause of the fall(s) and either add another aspect to the treatment or, where appropriate, refer the client onto other disciplines, e.g. podiatrist for advice on footwear, occupational therapist for advice on safety in the home.

Hydrotherapy is especially beneficial for clients with orthopaedic problems, either as a treatment by itself or as part of a therapy package. The buoyancy of water enables weak muscles to work more easily and the pressure of the water against the body provides support, allowing easier walking for those who struggle on dry land. Since buoyancy also prevents full body weight going through the legs, clients who are not allowed to walk without support after fracture or joint surgery are able to do so in the water. The temperature of a the water in a hydrotherapy pool is in the region of 33°C, thereby providing a warm environment that assists stiff joints and promotes relaxation.

Provision of hydrotherapy sessions for self-help arthritis groups allows those clients with long-term orthopaedic problems access to a general exercise class in a warm supportive environment.

Post polio syndrome

The generation that suffered with the worldwide poliomyelitis outbreaks in the years after the Second World War is now approaching the older age group. Their struggles to overcome the disabilities of childhood or early adulthood may return in their later life. The treatment during their initial illness was to exercise their way back to independence and they tend to want to do the same thing when the disabilities return. However, the treatment of choice now is to teach them energy-saving strategies and to avoid over-exercising affected muscles. Providing clients can deal with the temperature of the water and the ambient temperature of the pool room, hydrotherapy is beneficial. Some education from the orthotist may also be needed regarding splinting, as the clients' memory is of the heavy, awkward splints of their youth which many opted to do without.

Failure to cope at home/debility/poor balance/post major surgery

Some of the clients being admitted to a rehabilitation unit are there because they are having difficulty in coping at home with no specific medical problem having been discovered. Reasons for this could be poor nutrition, a urinary tract infection or merely accumulated fatigue from having to exert themselves beyond their capabilities just in order to keep going. A spell of restorative care, plus a detailed medical check-up, rationalization of medication and provision of more help at home may be all that is needed. However, since all clients are checked over by the physiotherapist, it is often discovered that they also have poor muscle strength, poor balance, tight calf muscles and wear inappropriate footwear. A general strengthening exercise programme is useful, with added work on balance and calf stretches combined with advice on footwear by the podiatrist and possible provision of a gait aid. Clients exhibiting poor balance are given a thorough assessment by medical and therapy staff to establish the cause of the problem before an appropriate programme of treatment is followed. Others who need a general exercise programme are those recovering from major abdominal or chest surgery. Clients who are in a generally deconditioned state may initially find a full programme too much and may well be better treated by the bedside until their stamina has increased.

Provision of gait aids

Part of the rehabilitation process in many cases is the temporary or permanent use of a gait aid. Physiotherapists and occupational therapists work together to ensure that the client is given the correct gait aid, as this may be the difference between returning home or going into assisted accommodation. The physiotherapist chooses which sort of gait aid is appropriate for the client (frame, crutches, sticks) and teaches their correct use. The occupational therapist ensures the gait aid will allow the client to be safe within the home environment and, if necessary, recommends changes to gait aid or home.

Whilst many, if not most, people do not mind using sticks to help them walk, there is often considerable resistance to the use of a frame. This reluctance has in part been solved by the recent arrival of a series of four-wheeled frames in racing green, electric blue and wine red colours.

Goal setting

Within the team each treating therapist sets their own goals for their clients. The team goal is generally considered to be the discharge destination of each client. Goal setting must be client driven, flexible and appropriate. It should be done following discussion with the client and perhaps the carers, and should be functionally based. Physiotherapists have to accept that sometimes the goal they know the client can be helped to achieve is more than the client actually wants to aim for. The use of daily goals is often particularly successful for the despondent older person or for a client who has had a long spell of illness.

Education

Education is not only limited to the client. Family members, friends and carers are invited to visit the physiotherapy department to see how the client is progressing and to observe what is involved. When it is apparent that a lot of help will be needed to ensure a safe and successful discharge, carers are encouraged to learn how to mobilize the client safely. Walking with whatever gait aids and splints are needed, going up and down stairs, transferring from chair to chair and from bed to chair need to be practised, with stress being placed not only on the safety of the client but also on that of the carer and his or her back. The carer's health is often a vital factor in the ability of the client to remain at home.

As most clients are discharged with a home exercise programme, carers also need to be advised of the correct way to do the exercises. Many clients find continuing exercise programmes at home quite difficult and need the added impetus of someone monitoring them. Teaching family and carers the individualized home exercise programme combined with the provision of well produced illustrated exercise sheets goes a long way to ensuring the exercises continue to be performed properly.

Conclusion

Satisfactory mobility, dexterity and continence add considerably to an older person's quality of life and independence. Physiotherapists give 'hands-on' treatment, providing not only physical benefit, but also an element often missing in the life of an isolated older person – the sense of touch. Physiotherapy is practical in its application and is evolving constantly in response to the search for improved solutions to common problems. Interdisciplinary work is emerging as one way of providing a seamless service for particular groups of older people. Postgraduate courses are available for physiotherapists wishing to specialize in aged care, rehabilitation and continence and the demand for more training and research will no doubt increase in step with the increasing numbers of people who are living to a great age and who require assistance in sustaining independence.

Reference

Morris M and Iansek R (1997) Parkinson's Disease: A Team Approach. Blackburn: Buscombe Vicprint.

Further reading

Sapsford R, Bullock-Saxton J and Markwell S (1997) Women's Health: A Text Book For Physiotherapists. London: WB Saunders.
Schussler B, Laycock J, Norton P and Stanton S (1994) Pelvic Floor Re-Education. London: Springer-Verlag.

Acknowledgement

The authors acknowledge with thanks the assistance of colleagues at the Peter James Centre in the preparation of this chapter.

Chapter 12
Family Care – 'How Do I Cope?'

MARY LIGHTFOOT

The nature of the care of the family for its elderly members reflects the society in which the family lives. 'By the way in which a society behaves towards its old people it uncovers the naked, and often carefully hidden, truth about its real principles and aims' (de Beauvoir, 1972). Simone de Beauvoir shows in her chapter on ethnological data that concerned care for the elderly members of a community depends on economic and cultural factors. The old person becomes unproductive. Care requires a reasonable level of resources and a culture of valuing the elderly. Children who are not cherished will in turn neglect and abuse the older family members, when they become frail. Religious and mystical beliefs and customs can give significance and status to old age, as the elderly person may be seen as nearer to the after-life and having special powers. Whilst still in possession of mental powers, an elderly person may be valued for his wisdom, but loss of mental powers tends to result in loss of respect from younger members of the community.

Community care legislation following the Griffiths Report (1988) and the White Paper, Caring for People (DoH, 1989), and including, for example, the Community Care (Residential Accommodation) Act 1998, contains information about society's 'principles and aims' in this last decade of the twentieth century. It is the interpretation of legislation (see Tinker, 1997), the extent to which modern society allows older people dignity and respect, and whether adequate resources to back the law are made available, which indicate more clearly current social values. Certainly the present emphasis is on the education of the young, who may be seen as society's future source of wealth. The White Paper described its main objective as enabling people to 'live as normal a life as possible in their own homes or in a homely environment in the local community'. Services should 'respond flexibly and sensitively to the needs of individuals and their carers' and 'intervene no more than is necessary to foster independence'. The National Health Service and Community Care Act

162

1990 included a provision to make local authorities responsible for working collaboratively to assess needs for community care services.

Example

An elderly woman, living alone, was often seen by neighbours walking down the middle of the road, poorly clad. The mattress from her bed was in the garden, soiled with faeces. She was thin. She collapsed in a shop and was taken to hospital. On discharge, she was returned home with meals delivered to her and a neighbour was asked to keep an eye on her by a visiting social worker. The elderly woman cancelled the arrangement for meals, the neighbour worried and wondered what to do, and soon after the elderly woman collapsed again, was again taken to hospital and died. Social Services arranged for the house to be cleaned. This woman had previously worked as a college lecturer. The neighbours remembered her as a pleasant person who was always willing to be helpful to others. She had two children.

This example, which took place in 1997, together with those which follow, are provided by individuals with recent experience of caring for an elderly person.

This woman was known to a number of services. She had a variety of needs which were not addressed by the provision that was made for her and the planning did not appear to allow for action when the original provision did not work. Neighbours have no legal responsibility or power to intervene and in this case the children assumed no responsibility. When children are not able to provide day-to-day practical care, other important contributions such as giving advice based on knowledge of the parent's previous personality, and acting as advocates and in a protective capacity, should be valued.

Tinker (1997) comments on the 'outpouring of advice from the Department of Health' since the 1990 Act which could indicate some difficulties in its implementation and lack of clarity. Section 47 of the National Assistance Act 1948 still enables a local authority to seek a court order for compulsory removal to hospital or other suitable place, if an elderly person cannot care for himself or herself and is not being cared for. However, Tinker notes that this power is rarely used.

Taking responsibility for an elderly parent is difficult if children are living far away. This society encourages workers to be mobile, not only within the country but between countries. The European Union is designed to enable labour to be flexibly mobile across national boundaries.

Women are more frequently out of the home at work and therefore less available to act as carers. This is not yet offset by working at home using such technological devices as computers and e-mail. When women are at home working as carers, they are at a financial disadvantage. Their earning power is reduced, they miss opportunities for promotion, and in due course they will receive a smaller pension. Pitkeathley (1989) argues that women will become progressively less willing to adopt a carer role in the future. Such a trend would be in conflict with community care legislation, which aims to keep dependent elderly people in the home environment. Political concern and legislation about an ageing population, as well as social trends in this capitalist society, require an understanding not only of the needs of elderly people but also of the needs of family members who take on an often enormously heavy task of providing care.

Becoming old

Ageing is the lot of every member of society providing life is not cut short by illness or accident. Erik Erikson (1982) describes old age as part of the natural life cycle – 'the last stage'. It follows on from 'adulthood', which is the 'generative stage', the basic strength of which is 'care', which he defines as 'to be care-ful', 'to take care of' and 'to care for'. He speaks of taking 'care of what one truly cares for' (Erikson, Erikson and Kivnick, 1986). He sees each phase as being 'developmentally related to any other'. 'Old people can and need to maintain a grand-generative function', and to have 'a minimum of vital involvement' in order to stay 'really alive'. 'Care' can be expressed not only in adult 'care' for biological children, but also in a sublimated form, for example, caring for non-biological children. Looking after elderly and dependent relatives can be seen as another aspect of this caring function. Erikson sees old age as a time when developmental concerns from previous stages can be faced again in a process not only of 'involvement' but also of 'disinvolvement' (Erikson et al, 1986). The concept of 'elder', with its implications of wisdom and having more or less successfully negotiated life's developmental stages, implies that such older people may have much to offer, but in a society that values speed, change, new inventions, wealth and power, the elder may seem irrelevant and be given little regard. The current term for the nation's care of its less able members is 'The Nanny State'. This is a derogatory expression which manages to insult women, older people and caring simultaneously. It ignores the key role which many grandmothers play in looking after grandchildren, who will be the future wealth-earners, whilst mothers go out to work. Support of children and grandchildren, passing on skills, being a uniting, integrating force in the family are key functions of grandparents and aspects of their 'vital involvement'.

Old age is a time to bring together life's experiences but it is also a time to prepare for ending, a time of letting go and facing loss, and a time for regret for the past and fearfulness about the future. Erikson describes the emotion of 'despair', which he sees as part of this stage of life (Erikson et al, 1986). Pace is slower, everything takes longer. Deterioration in physical health requires waiting in waiting rooms for various medical appointments, collecting prescriptions, taking the hearing aid back for repair, dealing with incontinence pads and extra washing, waiting for the chiropodist, the home carer, the social worker and other professional visitors who cross the home boundary. Being able to buy help is a great advantage, but the income of most disabled pensioners is derived from state benefits (Finch, Hugman and Carter, 1993).

The ageing process can be emotionally stressful not only because of the loss of hearing, sight, mobility, perhaps through stroke or arthritis, and other abilities, but also because of the loss of partner, contemporary friends, home and perhaps autonomy and independence. Individuals react to the ageing process in different ways, some meeting it more than halfway and others denying it or aspects of it. Some continue with activities or develop new ones more suited to their abilities. Others withdraw from activity.

Priorities in old age may change, but the basic needs are for protection, good food, warmth, company, interests, a comfortable bed, good medical care, a clean environment and help in dealing with negotiations with bureaucracy, financial matters and other formal communications.

The family

A model of the family and its development is described by Olson (1988). Using Erikson's life cycle model, he describes seven stages of the family life cycle and concludes with 'Empty-nest families' at Stage 6 (i.e. families where children have left home) and 'Retired couples' (male over 65 years) at Stage 7. He uses three dimensions of family behaviour from a systems perspective. These three dimensions are 'family cohesion', 'family adaptability' and 'family communication'.

'Family cohesion' is defined as that 'emotional bonding that family members have toward one another' (Olson et al, 1983). Four levels of family cohesion are described, 'disengaged', 'separated', 'connected' and 'enmeshed'. These range from high levels of autonomy and limited attachment, to a system where there is over-identification and consensus in the family, preventing individual development.

'Family adaptability' is defined as 'the ability of a marital or family system to change its power structure, role relationships, and relationship rules in response to situational and developmental stress' (Olson, 1986). There are also four levels of family adaptability, 'rigid', 'structured', 'flexible' and 'chaotic'. This dimension describes the family's ability to change when appropriate to meet changing circumstances.

'Family communication' is either positive (empathic, supportive, being good at listening) or negative (containing double messages, double binds, criticism). Positive communication facilitates movement on the other two dimensions. The three dimensions of family behaviour can be related to the way in which families address the changes that occur as family members face the ageing process. This can be stressful and requires changes in role and adaptation to loss. Families functioning in the midrange of cohesion and adaptability, which also have positive patterns of communication, will be able more readily to cope with the issues of ageing in family members.

Family cohesion and attachment behaviour

The concept of family cohesion and 'emotional bonding' in families implies that an attachment process has taken place. Family carers are usually prompted by family attachments and not just caring as a matter of duty, though a sense of obligation may also be a factor. Cicirelli (1983) uses attachment theory as a model to explain the care of an adult child for elderly parents. Drawing on Bowlby's work (Bowlby, 1979, 1980), he suggests that emotional and affectional bonds between a child and parent continue through life. When children leave home, closeness is maintained through phone calls, letters, visits and perhaps by living near. The adult child engages in protective behaviour or caregiving, when there appears to be a threat to the parent's existence through illness or disability. This caregiving is aimed at helping the elderly parent to survive and maintaining the emotional bond. Nevertheless, in the end, survival is not an option, as old age leads inevitably to death. The marriage vow is 'till death do us part', but adult children and other carers may also wish to care until the elderly person's death.

However, it would be a mistake to assume that because there are available family members, they will always be able to take on the task of caring. An obvious example is the situation where a daughter has been abused by her father. It would be unreasonable to expect her to carry out personal physical tasks for him should he become disabled, but she is likely to find it difficult to talk about why she is unwilling. Appropriate family boundaries have not been maintained and the daughter's need for individual development has not been respected. Anger, guilt, and poor self-esteem are emotions which are common to this experience. There are also other circumstances, which may lead to adult children being unable to care.

Example

An adult daughter, and only child, described emotions of fear, resentment, guilt and feeling trapped when faced with an expectation that she would care for her elderly, dependent mother. She realized that it was impossible for her to fulfil the request. She had no recollection of ever having experienced any demonstration of warmth or affection from her mother. Touching, cuddling and kissing had all been absent in their relationship. An additional ingredient had been that there was conflict between her parents with verbal unkindness. She was put in the position of which side to take and protected herself by 'sitting on the fence'. The family atmosphere was destructive and her whole aim was to shake off the difficulties of the family relationships in order to survive. In these circumstances, the demand to care for an unloved parent was terrifying and to attempt it would have been disastrous. Family cohesion in this case would be described as 'disengaged' and negative emotions and communications outweighed positive ones.

Family adaptability and loss and change

Changes occur in families throughout the family life cycle. These bring loss, for example when children go to school or leave home, or loss of work routine at retirement, but they may also bring gains and the opportunity to make new attachments. Children at school develop new skills, make new friends; leaving home can result in more freedom for parents and growing understanding and maturity in children, as well as new lifelong partnerships. Retirement provides opportunities to make social contacts, to engage in leisure activities and for reflection. However, the ageing process also results in a series of losses, resulting at last in death. These losses are experienced not just by the elderly person but also by family members who have attachments to that person. Peter Marris (1974) explains our need for continuity and the process of mourning, akin to bereavement, which occurs even with less major changes. Physical changes such as being unable to walk, becoming blind or deaf, developing incontinence, all require a process of mourning.

Example

A 90 year old man had suffered a number of physical losses as well as the loss of his wife, who had dementia. He had sight in only one eye following an unsuccessful cataract operation, he had problems with mobility, and he needed help with getting food and looking after the home. He became more irritable and less patient and then his hearing deteriorated significantly. It was no longer possible for his son to joke with him. It was 'impossible to make him laugh'. He coped with the other losses, but 'he could not cope with being deaf. He just gave up and died.'

McKenzie-Smith (1992) discusses this experience of loss and separation in old age. She describes the effect of a stroke, which may result in a person being confined to bed or a chair permanently, and also the loss that results when an elderly person goes into a nursing home or other institution.

Example

An 89 year old woman had a stroke which left her unable to walk or care for herself. Her son, who lived some distance away, arranged for her to go into a nursing home. The home was not well staffed and she endured a hard chair in the day and a hard bed at night with over-bright fluorescent lighting. She attempted to adapt to the new situation and began to make a positive bond with the other elderly woman with whom she shared the room, but the other woman soon became ill, was confused and had memory loss, so that they could no longer communicate. The first woman then became completely discouraged, also fell ill and died soon after. The son made arrangements for the house and her possessions, but rarely visited. He believed that his mother was 'well looked after'.

When the quality of life becomes too poor and the extent of loss becomes too great, death may be welcomed. This feeling may also be shared by carers. They may wish that their elderly relative would die and they experience the guilt which this brings. This wish may be because of difficulty in facing the painful reality of ageing, or a wish to avoid the demands that are brought by the relative's dependent state. It may arise through empathy with what the elderly person is going through, or the exhaustion and stress which the task of caring can bring.

Example

An elderly woman adapted well to loss of physical abilities, even the loss of her sight. She had had several children and outlived some of them, including a daughter who cared for her after her husband's death. Following the daughter's death, the daughter's eldest daughter arranged a rota of family care. The granddaughter reported that following the death of another son, her grandmother said 'I don't want to bury any more children.' The granddaughter described feelings of resentment at her grandmother's loss of abilities, and her difficulty in adapting to this was expressed in her insistence that her grandmother continued to make egg custard for her, even when this became very difficult.

The egg custard symbolized the care that her grandmother had given her and the affectionate bond between them. The granddaughter was able to provide very good and competent care herself, but her difficulty in accepting the progressive loss she was experiencing was expressed in her insistence on this representative action. This example also highlights a process by which one person in a family takes the key role in caring, even where others are also involved.

Communication

Researchers have confirmed that the most stressful problems for carers are incontinence, disturbance at night, difficult behaviour, need for constant supervision and communication problems (Gilleard et al, 1984; Levin, Sinclair and Gorbach, 1989). These problems can lead to carers losing their temper and then feeling upset about it. Levin particularly focused on the situation of carers of elderly people with dementia as these carers experience the most stress and these elderly people are heaviest users of services. Dementia does not always result in difficult behaviour, but it can lead to a change in personality, which adds to problems of management and communication. Because of memory loss, the same questions or statements may be repeated over and over again.

Example

An elderly woman developed dementia. She was cared for mainly by her daughter-in-law. She had always been a private person but this became more pronounced and she refused to undress in front of anyone or to have help with bathing. She was restless during the day and at night. She was incontinent, but it was impossible to persuade her to manage this appropriately so that her daughter-in-law had to deal with unpredictable messes and could only change the wet bed when her mother-in-law was in another part of the house. The daughter-in-law became physically and mentally exhausted and reached breaking point.

This example illustrates all the main stress factors. A key element in it is the communication problem. Communication implies that ideas can be exchanged between people, which can affect behaviour, understanding, knowledge and emotions. Interaction through language enables people to play, for example, through puns and jokes. Here communication was negative with the parent being unaware of the wishes of other family members, being unable to discuss issues and saying people were 'strange' if they did not do what she wanted. When she was given food, she said 'I'm not going to eat that rubbish.' The daughter-in-law felt irritable, anxious and frustrated. 'You wonder what you're doing wrong all the time.' Other family members had to adapt to the changes as this elderly woman deteriorated. The demands, particularly on the daughter-in-law, left her no room for herself as an individual.

The link between communication, attachment, and loss and change is illustrated by this statement by a carer who said, 'When my mother began to develop dementia, it was in the early stages that I felt most angry about her not being there for me. Once she got worse, it was easier to accept.'

Another disability that makes communication difficult in old age is severe deafness. This problem can make elderly people isolated, even when they are with other people. Family members have to speak slowly and clearly and even then may not be understood. Conversation becomes hard work for both sides and the normal easy family interchange with asides and jokes is impossible.

In these circumstances communication, which may have been very good in the past, can become markedly poorer and more strained, especially when carers are short of time because of additional caring tasks.

Family care – coping

Is it possible for family care for an elderly person to be a satisfying experience? Cicirelli (1983) refers to a diminishing of positive feeling from adult children to parents when parents become less healthy and more dependent. When a family member is ill, other family members are worried. The loss of normality and individual freedom, the threat to security and continuity can result in feelings of anxiety, anger and resentment. Pitkeathley (1989) shows the adverse effects on carers including increasing isolation, financial disadvantage and health problems. In spite of these factors, caring for an elderly relative can give satisfaction. 'We were very thankful we were there to help him.' 'We got to know her better; she had a sweetness of character, which had not been so obvious before.' Caring for an elderly relative is about managing an ending well. Facing the prospect of caring for her mother as her mother's health deteriorated with age, a carer posed herself the question 'How do I cope with this?'

Family functioning

The first requirement for successful family care is good family functioning that is cohesive, but not enmeshed, able to respond to change and facilitated by good communication. If a family is not functioning well, family care may be impossible or undesirable. Relationships can continue to develop even up to the time of death. Simone de Beauvoir (1964) sensitively illustrates the complexity of family relationships and attachments in her account of her mother's death and shows the importance of being able to carry out caring tasks prior to such a significant loss. The majority of carers are spouses. In the marital relationship there is a contract to care 'in sickness and in health'. Marital relationships can also evolve in old age. What may have seemed a less than satisfactory partnership can become closer and more harmonious. Children do not have a contract to care but carry out caring tasks prompted by feelings of attachment and a sense of duty, and in response to need.

Example

Throughout their married life, a couple experienced tensions. The husband was better educated than the wife and tended to belittle her. She always felt that she was not good enough for him and not sufficiently intellectual. As they grew older the wife developed dementia and became confused, easily upset and inflexible. She wanted her husband always to be with her and he became a devoted carer. It seemed that he responded to her dependency. They became more aware of their love for each other and he was heartbroken when she died.

Communicating with elderly people

The importance of giving time to listen to the communications of elderly people is demonstrated by McKenzie-Smith (1992). In her observations of elderly people who had been moved into an institution, she found that what the elderly people said had a significance that was not appreciated by busy staff. People with dementia may have more understanding than they are able to express.

Example

A niece visited her aunt in a nursing home. She had not seen her aunt since the aunt's sister had died. Although the aunt was suffering from dementia and was unable to remember her niece's name, she immediately began to try to tell her about her sister's death. On subsequent visits, the aunt would speak as if her own parents were still alive. Seeing her niece for the first time after the major loss of her sister, she struggled to get in touch with this recent event and to communicate it to the niece. Time was essential to allow her to express this important feeling.

Family members may be in the best position to understand these communications. They need time to be able to do this and to be able to make the links between distantly related ideas. This can be difficult if a family carer is over-stretched with other family or work responsibilities. Most elderly people, however, do not suffer dementia. They are still able to make good decisions, even though this may be harder, if they are depressed through increased stress and loss, and failing energy. Carers and the elderly person may not always take the same view about what is best, and it is important to give due weight to the wishes of an elderly person.

Example

An elderly woman had been living with her son and daughter-in-law. It was not working out well. She decided that she would prefer to live on her own again even though she had various fairly serious physical disabilities. She was a determined person with a strong personality. After some discussion between family members, it was decided that she would take a warden-supervised flat that had been offered to her. The relative who supported her in this decision was criticized by other members of the family and told that it would 'kill her'. She lived there successfully with support for over seven years.

Communicating with carers

Listening to carers and sharing information with them is now a better understood priority, but there is still much that needs to be done. Carers often make decisions for and with the elderly person. They are likely to be most aware of that person's wishes, and their own lives are often being affected in a major way by the task of looking after the relative. Because of these factors, it is important that the key carer or carers should be recognized and time given for discussion with them. Professional staff in contact with the family need to bear in mind the effect of the responsibility of care on the physical and emotional health of carers. Carers say that those not directly involved with the task of caring underestimate the difficulties with which they are dealing. This is true of professional people as well as relatives and friends.

Example

An only daughter in a Jewish family cared for her parents when they grew old and infirm. She experienced poor communication. Her mother was moved from one hospital to another three times, without there being any consultation with her. She had been visiting her mother in hospital for three months when a junior doctor asked her how she was feeling. No one else had enquired. She was accompanied by a cousin's husband to the Jewish Burial Authority when her mother died. The cousin's husband had come with her out of curiosity and only shared in this one task, but all remarks were addressed to him.

This carer found that it was difficult for her to be treated as the responsible person because she was a woman, even though she had carried out the task of caring for her parents alone.

Information

Information and advice need to be made available to the general public as well as to carers, as anyone may be involved in looking after others at some time in their life. Carers want to know how best to cope with someone who is deteriorating physically and perhaps mentally and how best to manage practical tasks. Managing difficult behaviour may be part of this. 'You don't know what it's all about and you haven't a clue who to ask.' This carer 'really wanted to talk to someone about the situation'. A carer may know in theory how to lift, but for someone who is busy and tired, it can be difficult to know how to apply this to getting someone out of the bath and this may result in a back injury. TV and radio dramas and soap operas have not yet addressed the problem of caring for the elderly, but this could be a fruitful way of giving people information in a palatable way. Printed information could also be made available about local services, such as the adviser for the hearing impaired, through general practitioners as they are the people who are most likely to be asked for advice in the first instance. Advice about what to do when a person dies would also be helpful and should take into account the practices of different religious groups.

Sharing care

Real sharing of care makes the task less stressful. The tendency is for carers to become isolated (Pitkeathley, 1989; Finch et al, 1993). Once a carer has taken on the role in the family, other family members tend to withdraw. Carers also become less able to make social contacts. It may be difficult to leave the elderly dependent person and others may be less willing to visit – 'But there's your mother, isn't there?' Sharing care can be arranged within a family or with the help of community services. Family members may share out tasks between themselves, if there is good communication. This is more likely to happen if the elderly person is not living with a family member.

Example

An elderly lady, who lived for over 100 years, managed to remain in her own flat almost until she died. She was looked after by a rota of relatives and friends. The main responsibility for planning was taken by the women in the family, but the male relatives also carried out significant caring tasks, including cooking meals for her.

Example

An elderly man was cared for by his daughter, who lived nearby, but his son visited each weekend and bathed him, cooked for him, did his washing and also some of his shopping.

Personal tasks, such as bathing, can cause embarrassment for family members. The practical situation often means that embarrassment has to be overcome, but this is a task where assistance from a competent person from outside the family may be indicated.

Example

A daughter looking after her elderly mother shared the caring tasks with a helper, who had worked for the family for years. This helper took responsibility for bathing the mother. This enabled the mother to retain her privacy and dignity in relation to her daughter and relieved the daughter of one of the stresses of caring.

Sharing care spreads the responsibility and also provides carers with opportunity for breaks, whilst someone else takes over.

Breaks

In order to care successfully, it is also necessary to have breaks from caring. Research by Levin, Moriarty and Gorbach (1994) shows that it was the opportunity of planned breaks that enabled many of the carers they studied to continue. Day care and respite care can provide breaks for carers and breaks can also be provided by having someone to come in to be with the elderly person.

If an elderly disabled person is left alone, then some judgement has to be made about the level of risk that people are prepared to take. Being able to have a holiday, go to work, pursue a hobby or meet with friends gives a mental break which can help in maintaining the carer's emotional and mental health. Levin et al (1994) also found that even with help, the care of a demented elderly person can become too much and residential care is then necessary. The researchers found that on average the mental health of the carers then improved. The effect on children of these family stresses has to be borne in mind.

Example

Two children whose grandmother was living with the family and suffered from dementia began to close doors to keep her out of the room where they were. They had become impatient of her asking the same questions repeatedly and they had been disturbed by her coming into their bedrooms and feeling their faces in the night. When she was admitted to residential care the children's behaviour changed completely and the family experienced a tremendous sense of relief and freedom.

Support services

Standards of care from agencies outside the family is an issue raised by family carers. One of the most needed services is that of the home carer. Families are pleased with this service when it is consistent and of a good quality, but comment is often made about changes of carer, irregularity of service and no clear standards of care. Elderly carers in particular need this form of help as they may themselves be disabled and have health problems. If elderly people are not able to carry out tasks themselves, they are likely to need all the normal home caring tasks done for them. Home carers may not be allocated enough time with their clients and if the service is overstretched there can be long gaps between visits and the tasks performed fall short of what is needed to keep things in good order over a period of time.

One of the problems of old age is that of needing more services and having more difficulty in getting to them. Providing services at home goes some way towards helping with this difficulty. Hairdressing and chiropody are examples of services that can be available at home, but additional services at home such as eye tests, dentistry and other medical services would be welcomed, both by carers and by elderly people. 'His sight was failing and he needed new dentures, but he couldn't cope with going.'

Change

Ageing is a process that leads to increasing disability. Families and elderly people and public services need to plan for change. At a point in time when an old person has an increased need for help because of a period of less good health, it is often not possible to see whether the additional help will be a permanent requirement. However, it is likely that this state will be reached again and that the need could then be permanent.

Being able to face change is also about being able to face loss. 'Dad didn't want to use a stick – he didn't want to feel he was old. He couldn't accept that change. He was still interested in things. His mind was very active.' This is the 'vital involvement' of old age described by Erikson et al (1986), but this elderly man was having difficulty in adjusting to the losses he was undergoing. At what point does a person need a stick, or a walking frame, or a rail for the bath, or to wear incontinence pads? 'She accepted losses without resentment. She didn't like it but she coped well.' In some cases the family will have to move house in order to manage the elderly person's needs. Being able to anticipate the changes and act on them is an important part of the family carer's ability to cope successfully. Public services also need to take this view and to reassure carers that because they have refused a service at one point in time, it does not mean it will not be available at a later date. Everyone needs to plan for change and to meet needs as they arise.

Knowing how to respond to change is nevertheless often not easy.

Example

A daughter caring for her father became increasingly concerned about the deterioration in his appearance and self-care, his diminishing ability to manage household matters (he was leaving food to decay) and the fact that he continued to drive his car, even though she believed it was not safe for him to do so. He thought that she was 'worrying too much', and his strong personality presented his daughter with problems about how she could intervene.

The process of change raises issues of timing. When is the time right – to stop driving, for example? It may be necessary to wait until an opportunity arises and the balance of things has shifted, before responding to change. This requires the carer to bear the anxiety of waiting and perhaps the disapproval of others outside the situation, who may think the carer neglectful or not to be taking the right actions.

Finances

The Invalid Care Allowance recognizes that carers encounter additional costs in the task of caring. However, it has serious limitations. It is only available to those on a low income, it is not available to those over 65 years and it is linked to the Attendance/Disability Living Allowance. Pitkeathley (1989) and Levin et al (1994) comment on its inadequacies. Caring can involve the carer in additional costs, for example for incontinence pads, travelling, telephone bills, laundry and many other contributions. Society is saved money by the work that carers do. It would be helpful if there could be more general acknowledgement of the costs of caring, for example by restoring the tax allowance and taking into account loss of earnings and benefits which can result from looking after a disabled relative.

Elderly people of course want to continue to contribute to household or petrol costs, often as part of retaining their self-respect and feeling of independence. 'Father wanted to pay the household bills, but eventually I had to take them on.' 'There were the costs of visiting her frequently, but she paid £5 towards the petrol, though she didn't have very much money and when she died there was only enough left for her funeral.'

After death there can be issues about how possessions and money should be shared even when there is a will. Disagreements and hurt feelings can arise and have long-term effects on relationships. 'His grand-daughter did most of the caring for him but she didn't inherit anything and that's been a problem.' 'My sister was the last one to leave home and she seemed to think she should have everything.' This was resolved by the adult children taking it in turns to say what they wanted most, so that everyone had something that they particularly valued. The meaning of things associated with the person who has died makes their disposal a significant emotional act. 'It was all fairly amicable and there were no real problems between us, but I am sorry we got rid of things so soon.' Acknowledging what family members and others have done in a concrete way and, if possible, giving time to wait until familiar objects have lost some of their emotional impact and family members are ready to part with them, helps with the final process of separation.

Death

Although family carers see the process of failing abilities and health prior to death, the actual time of death remains unknown until it actually happens. However, there can be a shared awareness that it is imminent.

'Dad was aware that he was dying. He said 'You know where the will is.' 'We both knew she was getting much worse and that she could not live much longer. She said "I won't be here in September".' 'Disinvolvement' (Erikson et al, 1986) can be expressed through tasks that are carried out prior to death with family members in mind. Making a will is an obvious example of this. An elderly woman went through all her many books with her daughter before she died, so that she could tell her what she should keep, and decide together what to give away. Her daughter said that she could not have faced this task after her mother had died.

Death can be a relief for carers, but is also accompanied by sadness about the lost relationship. 'I feel I want to discuss things and he isn't there.' 'I was very relieved. I was worried for the last two years. He should have been allowed to go then. I felt I should do more to help but I couldn't.' 'It was a strain visiting, but it was a terrible loss. We were very close.' 'It was hard to leave him after the weekend. I miss him more than I expected I would.' 'It was a tremendous relief to know that she didn't have to struggle on any more, but the most difficult thing is realizing that she isn't there when I come home.' All these comments show a strength of attachment which had prompted the family member to care in spite of the difficulties. Relationships are never perfect and there needs to be acceptance of the things that were difficult. 'I mourned in advance. I accepted the things that had not been resolved and my mother knew me almost up to the time she died.'

References

Bowlby J (1979) The Making and Breaking of Affectional Bonds. New York: Tavistock.

Bowlby J (1980) Attachment and Loss, Vol. 3. Loss, Sadness and Depression. New York: Basic Books.

Cicirelli VG (1981) Helping Elderly Parents: Role of Adult Children. Boston: Auburn House.

Cicirelli VG (1983) Adult children and their elderly parents. In: TH Brubaker (ed.) Family Relationships in Later Life pp. 31–46. Beverly Hills and London: Sage.

De Beauvoir S (1964) A Very Easy Death. Harmondsworth: Penguin Books.

De Beauvoir S (1972) Old Age. London: André Deutsch.

DoH (1989) Caring for People: Community Care in the Next Decade and Beyond. London: HMSO.

DoH (1998) Community Care (Residential Accomodation Act) London: HMSO.

Erikson EH (1982) The Life Cycle Completed. London and New York: Norton.

Erikson EH, Erikson JM and Kivnick HQ (1986) Vital Involvement in Old Age. New York: Norton.

Finch J, Hugman R and Carter J (1993) Family Care of the Older Elderly. Shankill Co. Dublin. European Foundation for the Improvement of Living and Working Conditions.

Gilleard CJ, Belford H, Gilleard E, Whittick JE and Gledhill K (1984) Emotional distress amongst the supporters of the elderly mentally infirm. British Journal of Psychiatry, 145, 172–7.

Griffiths R (1988) Community Care: Agenda for Action. London: HMSO.

Levin E, Sinclair I and Gorbach P (1989) Families, Services and Confusion in Old Age. Aldershot: Gower.

Levin E, Moriarty J and Gorbach P (1994) Better for the Break. London: National Institute for Social Work.

McKenzie-Smith S (1992) A psychoanalytical observational study of the elderly. Free Associations, 3(Part 3, No. 27), 355–90.

Marris P (1974) Loss and Change. London. Routledge and Kegan Paul.

National Health Service and Community Care Act (1990) London: HMSO.

Olson DH (1986) Circumplex Model. VII: Validation studies and FACES III. Family Process, 25, 337–51.

Olson DH (1988) Family types, family stress, and family satisfaction: a family development perspective. In: CJ Falicov (ed.) Family Transitions: Continuity and Change Over the Life Cycle. London. Guilford Press.

Olson DH, McCubbin HI, Barnes HL, Larsen AS, Muxen MJ and Wilson MA (1983) Families: What Makes Them Work. Newbury Park, CA: Sage Publishing.

Pitkeathley J (1989) It's My Duty, Isn't It? London: Souvenir Press.

Tinker A (1997) Older People in Modern Society, 4th edn. Harlow: Longman. Social Policy in Britain Series.

Chapter 13
The Quality of Formal Care Services for People with Dementia

DAWN BROOKER

This chapter focuses on that small group of older people who have a dementia illness such as Alzheimer's disease. Although the percentage of people with dementia is only around 5% of the over sixty-fives, the care of this group represents a major challenge to our society. Dementia is the shadowy nightmare that most older people fear, only overshadowed by the institutional care that is seen to go hand in hand with it.

The author has worked with people with dementia and their families since the late 1970s, first as a nursing assistant, then through various jobs as a professional clinical psychologist and also as a health service manager with responsibility for quality assurance. This chapter reviews why it has proved so difficult to provide excellence in the quality of formal care for people with dementia. There is now a much clearer idea of what excellence should look like and some centres have put some aspects of excellence into practice. The chapter concludes with some reflections on how excellence can be maintained.

The problem

'If Mental Health is the Cinderella service of the NHS then the service for people with dementia is the carbuncle on Cinderella's foot.' (Anon)

This quote sums up the subjective experience of many working in services for people with dementia. The services older people receive are often appalling and yet it is rare that complaints are made. Occasionally, scandals hit the media but they usually focus on issues of physical abuse or malnourishment. These episodes are not commonplace. The commonplace abuse is psychological rather than physical. Incomplete assessments, no-one contacting clients and carers when they promised, feeling deceived, lack of privacy, indignity, insensitivity and disrespect are all very familiar features to those on the receiving end of dementia care. The erosion of human and legal rights, and the overwhelming feeling that nothing personal is sacred, is the day-to-day experience of people with dementia.

The Health Advisory Service Review Teams (HAS, 1997) in their visits to ten health districts reporting on services for older people in England and Wales noted:

> '... inconsistencies in practice, overlaps and gaps in the provision of care, inequity of care, problems with funding, lack of proper assessment and reassessment, ... and inadequate communication between commissioners, providers, the voluntary sector and the independent sector.' (HAS, 1997, p. 1)

A postal survey of the views of carers (Alzheimer's Disease Society, 1997) found that 10% of the 1,421 questionnaires returned cited cases of mistreatment or neglect of their relative within residential or nursing homes. More than 150 specific examples of abuse were described by carers. Thirty per cent rated personal care as average or poor, 29% rated continence management as average or poor and 69% thought that the amount of stimulating activities available was average or poor.

Complaints, however, are rare. The reasons for this are many and complex. Generally, those who are receiving formal care are too damaged and demoralized to complain and their relatives are too browbeaten and scared to complain. Very often, those who are fit and well find the spectre of mental illness in old age too distressing to take it on as a crusade and would rather focus their energy elsewhere. Generally, those responsible for funding services working within a cash-restricted budget dare not look too closely for fear of the cost of putting it right. Set within an inherently ageist society, the collusion of silence continues.

The organization of care

Services for people with dementia are often marginalized because they do not fit neatly with any single organization's care remit. More than any other group, they require an holistic assessment and package of care but the chances of the 'whole' coming together are hampered by the fact that the services they require come from so many different sources. Their mental and physical health is often compromised. They require inputs from both specialist Psychiatric and Physical Health Care Teams as well as the Primary Health Care Team. Because of their level of disturbed behaviour and need for sensitive emotional support, they are most usually referred to psychiatric services. However, dementia often coexists with other physically disabling disorders which require the attention of geriatric medicine or other acute hospital services. Helping people with dementia remain physically fit and clear of acute disorders that can lead to further acute confusional states requires a high degree of skill from general practitioners.

The primary responsibility for providing specialist health services for people with dementia lies with Mental Health Services. Commissioning within mental health, however, often focuses its attention on the needs of younger adults with mental health problems. In the 1997/1998 NHS handbook, for example, no mention whatsoever is made of the care of people with dementia in the section on mental health (Muijen and Shepherd, 1997).

As well as significant health care needs, people with dementia often require help with social care issues. Their needs for social care are often complex. The private and voluntary sectors now play a much bigger part in all levels of service provision than they did ten years ago and care packages may involve input from many different agencies. Care packages will usually entail practical and emotional support for the family in arranging day care and respite care, assistance in sorting out finances and applying for benefits; in addition, home care services may need to be arranged and eventual assessment and placement in permanent care may be a possibility. Community care for the most disabled people with dementia now means institutional placement in residential or nursing home care rather than in a long-stay psychiatric ward. Although the institutional physical environment is much more pleasant than it was for thousands of elderly people in care, they are still at risk of the social and emotional ravages of institutional care.

At the receiving end of these multiple services is a very confused and often traumatized person with dementia and their worried family. It is little wonder that services are perceived as fragmented and that gaps exist in service provision. Breakdowns in service quality often occur at the transition points between one agency and another. The very way in which services are provided for people with dementia means that continuity and consistency in the quality of services they receive are likely to be poor.

The way in which health and social care is organized within the UK has undergone radical changes within the past decade. The establishment of the internal market, the purchaser/provider split, fundholding GPs, the creation of trusts, mergers, contracts, information technology, value for money, quality assurance, clinical audit, inspections, evidence-based practice, Patient's Charter, Community Care Charter and the care programme approach have all emerged over the past decade. This culture of continual change is now accepted as the norm by many managers and care practitioners.

As Britton and Woods (1996) comment, however, the speed of change has left many professionals unsure of their roles and many elderly people confused as to who has the responsibility for providing which services. Gilleard (1996) draws similar conclusions and quotes evidence to show that elderly people and their carers have very little information and limited expectations about what services they could receive.

The 1990 NHS and Community Care Act set the legal framework by which care was to be achieved. The Act separated the role of purchasing and providing health and social care, with the health authorities being given the responsibility for purchasing health care and local authorities the responsibility for purchasing social care. As people with dementia have long-term coexisting needs for both types of care, this has proved very challenging for purchasers and providers to manage. Embodied in the Act is the need for care to be planned and costed and based on assessment of need. Authorities have spent a great deal of energy in trying to get their assessment 'right' by trying to draw a clear line between health and social need (HAS, 1997). The reality is that the line is not there. Even when the line appears to be clear, variables such as social environment and physical health can change it very rapidly when providing services for people with dementia.

Cost and quality

The major tension in the planning and delivery of services for any section of society is between cost and quality. The changes in how care for elderly people is organized for people within the UK has added to the tension of who pays for which aspect of care. This tension is set to become even greater in the next three decades as the number of elderly people sharply increases. By 2020 the number of people over the age of 85 will have increased by 65% from the 1990 figures (DOH, 1992). Those over the age of 85 are much more likely to suffer from chronic disabling conditions which make them the major consumers of health and social care. The availability of informal carers is also set to decrease, with an increasing number of elderly people living alone or with an elderly spouse (see DOH, 1992). The 'Rising Tide' (HAS, 1982), and its effect on health and social services into the next millennium, is a major challenge facing policy-makers. Which services should be funded for which groups in society and how the money should be raised remains a contentious area of political debate.

'Rationing' services on the basis of age is an emotive issue and has received publicity on a number of occasions over the past few years. Models that take into account the number of years a person is expected to live alongside measurements based on the quality of that life – popularly known as QALYs (quality adjusted life years) – have been around since the late 1980s (see Lane, 1987). When it comes down to making decisions about denying people health care, the British public has very little stomach for it, as evidenced by the newspaper reports of people being refused treatment on the basis of age.

Human rights and dementia

Alongside this emphasis on the economic problems of providing for an ageing population, there has been an increasing recognition over the past decade that people with dementia should have equality in human rights. A number of key publications have caused this factor to enter into the care equation at a more strategic level of service planning. The publication, Living Well into Old Age (King's Fund, 1986), was very important in this respect. It provided a clearly stated set of principles, which became known as the King's Fund principles, that people with dementia had the same rights and values as anyone else in society. Although this had been an implicit assumption held by practitioners schooled in the theories of social role valorization (Wolfensberger, 1983), it had never before been stated explicitly by such an authoritative body as the King's Fund in the context of dementia care.

The King's Fund principles found themselves embedded in the mission statements of most elderly services during the following decade. The fact that there is often a 'cooling effect' between mission statements and operational practice has been documented with this client group (Booth, Bilson and Fowell, 1990). There have also been many barriers to the application of social role valorization with people with dementia (see Stirling, 1996).

The psychological needs of older people with dementia

Britton and Woods (1996) identify a threshold of change occurring in the mid-1980s in how psychological needs were construed in this group. Psychological research in dementia in the mid-1980s was limited mainly to traditional areas of behavioural and cognitive assessments. Throughout the past ten years there has been a huge increase in the numbers and sophistication of assessment tools that are available to the elderly specialist. The choice of tests and assessment tools is now very comprehensive (Davies, 1996; Little and Doherty, 1996) with most publishers of assessment materials having a specialist section on ageing.

The mid-1980s saw the increasing use of psychotherapeutic interventions with those with dementia. For example, reality orientation (Holden and Woods, 1988), reminiscence therapy (Coleman, 1986) and validation therapy (Feil, 1982) all had their proponents. A number of excellent texts which outlined good psychological care, in terminology that could be easily understood by the majority of caregivers, were published in the late 1980s and early 1990s (e.g. Bender, Norris and Bauckham, 1987; Twining, 1988; Stokes and Goudie, 1990; Kitwood and Bredin, 1992). Stokes and Goudie (1990) used the term resolution therapy to describe the usefulness of counselling skills with people with dementia.

The work of Kitwood on personhood in dementia over the past decade clearly has its roots in those humanizing therapies (Woods, 1995). His writing on the person centred approach to care (Kitwood, 1997) has helped clinicians to see behind the disability and to engage positively with the person rather than with the disease. A growing number of psychologists are now interested in using psychotherapy with people with dementia (e.g. Hausman, 1992). The use of non-verbal complementary therapies such as aromatherapy, massage and Snoezelen has grown rapidly in recent years (Threadgold, 1995; Brooker et al, 1997; Burleigh and Armstrong, 1997).

The New Culture of Dementia Care

The New Culture of Dementia Care (Kitwood and Benson, 1995) has clarified where thinking has come from and where it is heading, in the move away from purely biomedical models of dementia. Kitwood (1995) drew ten points of contrast between the new and old cultures, which are paraphrased in Table 13.1 and expanded on below.

Table 13.1. A summary of the contrast between the practice of Old and New Culture

Old Culture	New Culture
Backwater	The crest of a wave
Disease	Disability
CT scans	Care plans
Laboratory research	Applied research
Us and them	All of us
Living death	Living
Deficits	Unique abilities
Problem behaviour	Communication
Denial	Openness
Grit	Diamonds

1. From backwater to the crest of a wave

Apart from a few obvious exceptions, dementia care was what professionals did if they were not good enough to do anything else. The work was physically demanding but boring. This attitude is still prevalent among those practitioners who have not got the skills to work in dementia care or who are temperamentally unsuited to it! Within the dementia literature there has been a distinct shift towards seeing this as the area of care that demands the highest levels of interpersonal skills and creativity. Excellence in dementia care demands the synthesis of good practice in psychological, physical and social care. The move away from a custodial model of care towards a more humanizing model for people with dementia has been seen in the training and practice of professionals working with the client group.

2. From disease to disability

There has been a shift in many services in recognizing that the progressive neurological impairment in dementia does not mean that 'nothing can be done'. Seeing dementia as a disability rather than as a disease means that practitioners have a clear role in ensuring that rights are protected, that individuals are empowered and that compensatory strategies are introduced to minimize the effects of the disability. Only when this premise is accepted does the endeavour of improving the quality of care become a main focus of interest.

3. From CT scans to care plans

Related to this shift is the recognition that the most valuable information about the person with dementia can be obtained not from an image of the degree of neurological impairment (the CT scan) but from those skilled practitioners that are involved in day-to-day care. Most of the new ways that have developed in working with people with dementia have their roots in practical care. *The Journal of Dementia Care* is full of examples from practitioners of all types deciding to try a different way of doing something, recognizing its beneficial results and telling other practitioners about it.

4. From laboratory to applied research

The medical cure for dementia has been 'just around the corner' for a long time. Research into the neurobiological basis of dementia is obviously important. However, it has, as yet, made very little impact on the lives of ordinary families despite the vast amounts of money that have been spent. Social and psychological research in dementia is now much more academically acceptable than it was ten years ago and it has impacted already on the lives of people with dementia.

The launches of *The Journal of Dementia Care* in 1992 and of *Aging and Mental Health* in 1997 reflect the growing multidisciplinary interest in evidence-based practice and research in this area. The number of conferences available on the social and psychological aspects of dementia care has also mushroomed over the past few years. Most of the social science publishers have whole sections devoted to the psychological texts on ageing.

5. From us and them to all of us

There has been a fundamental shift in the New Culture away from the power differential operating within institutionalized care which marked out those with neurological impairment as set apart from the rest of humanity. Seeing people with dementia as less than human makes it easy to treat them in degrading and inhumane ways. The emphasis in the New Culture is on seeing all people as human beings regardless of cognitive ability or disability.

6. From living death to living

In the Old Culture the task was safety and basic physical care. This could result in ensuring the person was kept alive physically but with extremely impoverished quality of life. In the New Culture the task is to provide care which maintains and enhances each individual's personhood. This involves care practitioners enabling the person with dementia to remain socially confident within an environment that supports their special needs.

7. From disease deficits to unique abilities

Kitwood (1995, p. 10) says:

> 'There are as many manifestations of dementia as there are people with dementia.'

The Old Culture focused on stage theories that emphasized the general decline that people should expect as the disease progressed. The New Culture concentrates on the uniqueness of individuals and recognizes that if people are going to live life to the full, then those caring for them need to know as much as possible about the person's preferences, values, interests and abilities. This requires more than just a shift in language, it requires a shift to seeing person first and disease second. In Dementia Reconsidered, Kitwood (1997) describes this graphically as a shift away from the 'person with *dementia*' to the '*person* with dementia'. The shift is in seeing the person as the key determining factor in the care they receive rather than the disease.

8. From problem behaviours to communication

The Old Culture labelled many of the actions of those with dementia as problem behaviours that needed management either by pharmacological or by psychological means. In the New Culture these actions would be seen as a means by which the person with dementia struggles to make their needs known and understood. The challenge for care practitioners is to try to understand what they are being told by the person with dementia and to act accordingly in the interest of everyone, including the individual with dementia.

9. From denial to openness

The Old Culture encouraged care practitioners to repress their true feelings so that they could do a job which was distasteful, often desperately sad and under-resourced. Burnout and abuse of power are evident in this sort of culture. In the New Culture, care practitioners are in touch with their feelings and use their emotional energy creatively as a positive resource in their work.

10. From grit to diamonds

This rather unpleasant metaphor refers to how organizations treat staff who care for people with dementia. In the Old Culture they were seen as fairly unimportant and plentiful in supply as they were doing low status work. In the New Culture, if staff are to deliver the top quality care outlined above, then they too have to have their personhood maintained and enhanced. Staff need to feel emotionally supported themselves in order to provide long-term support to those in their care. Involving and empowering staff within quality assurance programmes (Brooker, 1994; Brooker et al, 1998; Brooker and Dinshaw, 1998) can be one of the ways of achieving this shift.

From vision to reality

In recent years, this contrast between Old and New Cultures of Care has been presented by the author to many different audiences. The presentations are usually met with many nods of agreement but when asked, many people do not feel they work wholly in the New Culture. Although Kitwood has provided a vision of the New Culture, and many elements of it can be recognized, it is still a rare creature in its pure form. Three examples from the author's personal experience of the changing culture of dementia care are provided below. These are offered as a means of understanding what it is that leads to change in care cultures.

Example one

In 1979, the author worked as a nursing auxiliary in a psychiatric hospital and remembers doing a Sunday morning shift on the geriatric ward (as it was known). The shift consisted of hurriedly getting up 24 'boys and girls' (as they were known to the staff) or 'mixed ambulant and non-ambulant dements' (as they were known to the medics). She is sure she was not told the names of any of her charges and eye contact was not achieved with any of them.

When all the patients were cleaned and fed, the staff read the Sunday papers for the rest of the morning. One of the male residents urinated in his chair. The author remembers getting up to help him, only to be told in fairly sharp tones that the staff had done their work for the morning. He was eventually changed along with everyone else before lunch (which arrived at 11.30 to fit in with staff breaks). As a young auxiliary, the author avoided working on the ward again mainly because she did not like being told off. She would like to say that she found the treatment the residents received distressing but, to be honest, she just assumed that they had no human feelings whatsoever because every staff member behaved as if they did not. She was a young newcomer trying to fit in with the culture.

This is a clear example of Old Culture. Staff received absolutely no reinforcement for providing care to residents that enhanced psychological well-being. Care staff received positive strokes for ensuring that the ward was kept quiet and tidy with all the patients sitting down. The rewards for achieving these goals were fairly straightforward. Once this had been achieved, staff could take a rest from direct patient contact. Dealing with the residents as quickly as possible was a skill that was clearly rewarded as a nursing auxiliary. The accolade of being 'a quick pair of hands' was very much sought after by new staff. On a Sunday morning, when staff were absolutely sure that no nursing officer would appear, they took their rest quite literally. On weekdays staff would take a break from direct patient care by making the beds to precision neatness, or in sorting out laundry or making coffee for the doctors or in other such 'caring' tasks. If these sorts of tasks were not done, then there would be a negative consequence for staff in the shape of comments from the ward sister and nursing officer. This criticism was to be avoided at all costs. The organizational style and defences fit almost exactly with those described by Kitwood (1997).

Example two

When the author took up post as a quality assurance manager within the same health district in 1992, not much had changed. The terminology had changed but not the attitudes. The ward was now called 'Elderly Care' and the people living out their lives were called 'residents'. The place looked and smelt prettier than it had done ten years previously. The staff were very proud that they had a 'personalized laundry system' which covered everything apart from undergarments.

The ward sister was now called a 'ward manager'. As a manager herself, the author was no longer privy to seeing what really went on when all the managers had gone home. However, staff were still imbued with enough Old Culture to tell her about dreadful practice without realizing that it was dreadful. The ward manager told the new quality assurance manager that what they offered was 'terminal care' because dementia was a terminal illness. When asked about basics such as vision and hearing problems that residents experienced, the ward manager proudly pointed to a locked cupboard which contained all of the residents' spectacles and hearing aids. When asked why they were locked away, the ward manager looked at the author in complete disbelief and informed her that all the residents had terminal dementia and that they would only lose them.

The author received a similar look when she asked about any training needs the ward manager had identified in her staff group. The ward manager thought they should certainly have training in lifting. She had attended a training course on validation therapy which she thought was much better than reality orientation as it meant that nurses did not have to upset the residents by telling them where they were!

In the author's experience, the majority of units for people with dementia fall into this sort of category. This scenario is called here the 'Kippers and Curtains Culture'. In certain parts of Britain, this phrase is used to describe the sort of person who pretends to be well off by having nice curtains up at their windows whereas they are in dire straits financially and have to have kippers for supper every night. In other parts of the country, the phrase 'Big hat and no knickers' has a similar meaning. However, that particular phrase also has overtones of a rather liberal morality which is not appropriate in this context. Indeed, in the 'Kippers and Curtains Culture', any expression of sexuality on the part of residents would almost certainly be oppressed in some form or other. In this type of scenario, care units have the superficial appearance of New Culture but the underlying value base is still Old Culture.

To receive positive reinforcement, staff on 'Kippers and Curtains' units ensure that the place is pretty to look at for visitors. Safety of residents and their property is paramount and dire consequences result on units where safety is compromised. The staff are usually adept at the language of caring and demonstrate 'New Culture' principles with the most socially confident residents. This is most apparent in the trained staff. In the scenario presented above, the particular ward manager was not particularly tuned into giving a good impression of what went on. Had she been, it might have been believed that they provided good psychological care. There would have been no evidence to the contrary.

For care staff working in these sorts of environments, being able to 'rest' from direct patient care when these duties have been achieved remains a positive reinforcement. Training courses in statutory aspects of care are often provided and more senior staff may go on courses on interpersonal aspects of dementia care. Complaints and untoward incidences are rare on such units.

Example three

In 1997, the author sat behind two nursing assistants from that same unit. It was lunch time on a Team Away-day following the annual Quality Assurance Dementia Care Mapping Evaluation. They were discussing the graphs that their evaluators had shown which demonstrated the massive decrease in Personal Detractors (episodes of poor quality care) over the past three years. They were reminiscing about the horrors that used to occur and were shaking their heads in disbelief. They were saying how such things as treating residents as objects or not including them in conversations simply would not occur on their unit now. The fact that they were saying this to each other and not to anyone in authority was particularly heartening. Of course, it could have all been a set up ...

This is New Culture care. Care staff still receive positive strokes for ensuring that the unit is an attractive and comfortable place to live. Providing direct interpersonal care that enhances the psychological and physical well-being of *all* residents is regarded as paramount and the consequences for doing this are positive. In the third example, the positive strokes given to staff for providing this took many forms. Training in statutory and interpersonal care occurs with all grades of staff. On this unit there are two members of staff who are trained in Dementia Care Mapping (Kitwood and Bredin, 1992), as well as the line managers for the unit.

The unit is formally assessed using Dementia Care Mapping through the quality assurance programme on an annual basis (see Brooker and Payne, 1994; Brooker et al, 1998). Other regular care audits include incidence and care of pressure sores, care plans and feedback from carers. The results of the audits are discussed in full at the annual Team Away-days which include the entire 24 hour team. Staff have a direct means of being able to influence change in care practices through these. Although the results of all maps and audits are confidential to the units they relate to, staff can compare their performance to the average. They can also compare their performance against previous maps and audits. From a management point of view the positives are always emphasized during feedback sessions. The criticisms for not 'doing well' came from the staff team itself.

The New Culture is very new and many examples of the Old Culture still remain. The most important people in determining the quality of life for people with dementia are those who are providing for direct care. In the example given above this is obviously the direct care staff. Staff can change and fit into a new culture very readily if the settling conditions are right. There were only five years between examples two and three but the change in practice in interpersonal care provided on that unit was radical. The majority of care staff are kind people. The author would have classed herself as a kind person as a nursing auxiliary in example one and all her nursing auxiliary colleagues were very kind to each other. However, history relates that 'kind people' can do all manner of unspeakable things to each other if they are either rewarded for doing the unspeakable thing or they fear the consequences of what will happen if they do not comply. This is particularly the case when the unspeakable things are condoned by a higher authority or expert (see Milgram, 1974). This is a well known and straightforward paradigm from behavioural psychology (see Rachlin, 1976) and the author believes it is absolutely key in changing and maintaining cultures of care.

Which staff behaviours gain reinforcement is central in determining the culture that exists within care units. This reinforcement is largely in the hands of those who manage and purchase services. The behaviour of managers and purchasers of services is also largely determined by what they get rewarded for. This has to be determined by wider societal issues.

If balancing the books or making a profit is the priority for the managers and purchasers it will also be a priority for direct care staff. If it is the only priority for the managers and purchasers then, in time, it will become the only priority of direct care staff. If the qualities of the New Culture are also a priority for management and purchasers then they will be a priority for direct care staff.

The future

The participation of consumers within services, listening and acting on their views, involving them in planning, consulting user groups of all types on all topics has been seen as absolutely central in the provision of health and social services during the 1990s. The 1990 NHS and Community Care Act required service providers to consult with service users about resources. This has been particularly difficult to achieve with service users with dementia because they are such a disempowered group in society. The disabilities in memory and language functioning mean that people with dementia cannot participate in discussions about service provision. Generally, the consumers in this area are seen as the relatives and carers. Within the climate of consumerism, organizations such as the Alzheimer's Disease Society and Age Concern have become a much more powerful platform for carers to speak from than could have been imagined ten years ago.

The New Culture of Dementia Care sits well with consumerism and service users' rights. In his 1997 book, *Dementia Reconsidered*, Kitwood writes:

'Among all the changes that have occurred, one fact stands out above all others. It is that men and women who have dementia have emerged from the places where they were hidden away: they have walked onto the stage of history, and begun to be regarded as persons in the full sense. Dementia, as a concept, is losing its terrifying associations with the raving lunatic in the old-time asylum. It is being perceived as an understandable and human condition.' (Kitwood, 1997, p. 133)

The baby-boomer generation, born in the late 1940s and early 1950s, has now come of age and is starting to hold political sway within the Western world. This is now the generation that has first hand experience of caring for a parent with dementia and all the distress this includes. It is fairly commonplace now to hear of a celebrity or politician who has first hand experience of caring for a parent with dementia. As this generation ages, these people are unlikely to settle for 'Kippers and Curtains' culture care for their partners and friends. Unlike the present generation of old people, this generation is much more likely to challenge authority figures and be more assertive over their rights (Gilleard, 1996). All this bodes well for the continuance of the New Culture.

The growth in consumerism and a concern with quality, audits and standards has led to a huge change in emphasis in care practice and research within the wider care arena, not just in dementia care (Gillies, 1997). Although there is now a plethora of vehicles and methodologies for improving quality of care, they are generally based on a set of common principles. Ellis and Whittington (1993, p. 34) identified the following as 'essential parameters':

- Concern for excellence and standards – a vision of excellence and the striving towards it has to be central to any quality assurance exercise.
- Specificity and explicitness – quality assurance is a practical and rational process which develops reliable and valid tools for analysing and reviewing the quality of care.
- Adoption of a cyclical model – the cycle of deciding on standards, measuring practice and reviewing practice and standards. If any of these stages is missed, then it is unlikely that sustainable improvements will occur.
- Commitment – at an individual and organizational level there should be recognition that quality assurance does not just happen without time, energy and management.

The two sides of the care equation that have emerged very strongly over the past decade have been cost of services and the quality of services – particularly the quality based upon the consumer viewpoint. Although the ideas set out in health economics and quality assurance are not new, the language certainly is. Building a quality assurance strategy in order to improve service quality is necessary if changes in service quality are to be anything other than piecemeal and ad hoc. There is a wealth of new terminology backed up by new journals and courses which have legitimized these as very serious concerns indeed. Within the field of dementia care there is an area of work which is certainly in need of quality improvements. With the New Culture in dementia care there is certainly a vision of excellence and an increasing commitment to make things better. With more sophisticated instruments for measuring outcomes of care for individuals and care environments, there are the tools to be specific and explicit in measurement. Excellence is within reach. Cinderella did eventually marry a prince after all.

References

Alzheimer's Disease Society (1997) Experience of Care in Residential and Nursing Homes: A Survey. London: Alzheimer's Disease Society.

Bender M, Norris A and Bauckham P (1987) Group Work with the Elderly. Bicester: Winslow.

Booth T, Bilson A and Fowell I (1990) Staff attitudes and caring practices in homes for the elderly. British Journal of Social Work, 20, 117–31.

Britton PG and Woods RT (1996) Introduction. In: RT Woods (ed.) Handbook of the Clinical Psychology of Ageing, pp. 1–19. Chichester: Wiley.

Brooker DJR (1994) Quality assurance – lessons learnt about putting it into practice. Psychologists' Special Interest Group in the Elderly (PSIGE) Newsletter, 48, 37–41.

Brooker DJR and Payne M (1994) Auditing outcome of care in inpatient and day patient settings using Dementia Care Mapping. Can it be done? A preliminary report. PSIGE Newsletter, 51, 18–22.

Brooker DJR, Snape M, Johnson E, Ward D and Payne M (1997) Single case evaluation of aromatherapy and massage on disturbed behaviour in severe dementia. British Journal of Clinical Psychology, 36, 287–96.

Brooker DJR and Dinshaw CJ (1998) A comparison of staff and patient feedback on psychogeriatric services. Quality in Health Care, 7, 70–6.

Brooker DJR, Foster N, Banner A, Payne M and Jackson L (1998) The efficacy of Dementia Care Mapping as an audit tool: Report of a three-year British NHS evaluation. Ageing and Mental Health, 2, 60–70.

Burleigh S and Armstrong C (1997) On the scent of a useful therapy. Journal of Dementia Care, 5(4), 21–3.

Coleman PG (1986) The Ageing Process and the Role of Reminiscence. Chichester: Wiley.

Davies S (1996) Neurological Assessment of the Older Person. In: RT Woods (ed.) Handbook of the Clinical Psychology of Ageing, pp. 441–74. Chichester: Wiley.

Department of Health, Central Health Monitoring Unit (1992) Health of Elderly People: an Epidemiological Overview. London: HMSO.

Ellis R and Whittington D (1993) Quality Assurance Handbook. London: Edward Arnold (Hodder).

Feil N (1982) Validation – the Feil Method. Cleveland: Edward Feil Productions.

Gilleard C (1996) Community care: psychological perspectives. In RT Woods (ed.) Handbook of the Clinical Psychology of Ageing, pp. 319–32. Chichester: Wiley.

Gillies A (1997) Improving the Quality of Patient Care. Chichester: Wiley.

Hausman C (1992) Dynamic psychotherapy with elderly demented patients. In: G Jones and BML Miesen (eds) Caregiving in Dementia Research and Applications, pp. 181–98. London: Routledge.

Health Advisory Service NHS (1982) The Rising Tide: Developing Services for Mental Illness in Old Age. London: HMSO.

Health Advisory Service (1997) Services for People Who Are Elderly: Addressing the Balance. London: The Stationary Office.

Holden UP and Woods RT (1988) Reality Orientation: Psychological Approaches to the Confused Elderly, 2nd edn. Edinburgh: Churchill Livingstone.

King's Fund (1986) Living Well into Old Age: Applying Principles of Good Practice to Services for People with Dementia. King Edward's Hospital Fund, Project Paper no 63, London.

Kitwood T (1995) Cultures of care: tradition and change. In: T Kitwood and S Benson (eds) The New Culture of Dementia Care, pp. 7–11. London: Hawker.

Kitwood T (1997) Dementia Reconsidered: The Person Comes First. Buckingham: Open University Press.

Kitwood T and Benson S (eds) (1995) The New Culture of Dementia Care. London: Hawker Publications.

Kitwood T and Bredin K (1992) Person to Person: A Guide to the Care of Those With Failing Mental Powers. Essex: Gale Publications.

Lane DA (1987) Utility, decision and quality of life. Journal of Chronic Disability, 40, 585–91.

Little A and Doherty B (1996) Going beyond cognitive assessment. In RT Woods (ed.) Handbook of the Clinical Psychology of Ageing, pp. 475–506. Chichester: Wiley.

Milgram S (1974) Obedience to Authority. New York: Harper & Row.

Muijen M And Shepherd G (1997) Mental health services. In: The NHS Confederation, 1997/98 NHS Handbook, 12th edn. Kent: JMH Publishing.

National Health Service and Community Care Act (1990). London: HMSO.

Rachlin H (1976) Introduction to Modern Behaviourism, 2nd edn. New York: Freeman & Company.

Stirling E (1996) Social Role Valorisation: Making a difference to the lives of older people? In RT Woods (ed.) Handbook of the Clinical Psychology of Ageing, pp. 389–422. Chichester: Wiley.

Stokes G and Goudie F (1990) Working with Dementia. London: Winslow Press.

Threadgold M (1995) Touching the soul through the senses. Journal of Dementia Care, 3(4), 18–19.

Twining C (1988) Helping Older People: A Psychological Approach. Chichester: Wiley.

Wolfensberger W (1983) Social Role Valorisation: a proposed new term for the principle of normalisation. Mental Retardation, 21(6), 234–9.

Woods RT (1995) The beginnings of a new culture in care. In: T Kitwood and S Benson (eds) The New Culture of Dementia Care, pp. 19–23. London: Hawker.

Chapter 14
'I'm Not Very Religious, But ....'

PETER HUXHAM

'If we appoint you as whole-time chaplain to this hospital you will find that most patients with a church background will be visited by their own ministers or fellowship members. We would expect you to be chaplain to those patients who have no strong church allegiance.' This chapter has been written from experience gained during thirty-five years as an Anglican priest in parish and hospital ministry, much of it spent with people who would not regard themselves as church members. Parents, parishioners and patients are all thanked deeply for earthing and rooting this ministry to a level suited to their need.

'What is real?' asked the Rabbit one day ... 'Real isn't how you are made,' said the Skin Horse. 'It's a thing that happens to you. When a child loves you for a long, long time, not just to play with, but really loves you, then you become real.' (Williams, 1922). This simple story from the nursery illustrates the profound truth which underlines our whole life. It was put in another way by a prison governor who said 'relationships are the only things which change people'. This principle is widely accepted and practised in the rearing of children. The importance of bonding at an early age with both parents is now understood; so, too, is the role played by teachers, peer group, partners, work place and community as we acquire those skills necessary for our mental, physical and emotional growth and well-being. This principle is not so well understood or practised when the stage of life is reached when there is a gradual turning away from acquiring skills, possessions, status and friends towards losing them. For some, the first trauma is experienced when the children leave home or marry. For others, it is their retirement or the loss of a parent which can bring on severe physical illness and mental depression. Others, again, equally loving and dutiful, and well balanced, will experience grief and loss, yet be able to adapt more positively and even create a new life with the freedom which some losses can bestow.

194

All who have worked with older people will be familiar with the words 'I don't know how I did it, but God gave me strength' or ' I would never have got through without my faith. I don't know how people manage who haven't got a faith.' This is often said by a widow or widower who has heroically nursed a partner for months or years with the words 'I promised her she wouldn't go into a home' or by a patient whose life has been marked by tragedy and ill-health. This person might have suffered the death of her children and husband, and the loss of home, possessions, a limb, or breast or womb, and is now facing up to the end of life itself. Such people have seldom been religious: their lives have been too busy and too hard to have allowed them the luxury of going to church, but each one of them would have been worthy of the accolade 'salt of the earth'. What is it that equips people like these with such human qualities that they can cope with the major events of life and death while some who are more obviously religious, possibly attending church regularly, may be sad and insecure people, using their religion as a means of denial and unable to comprehend a God who might not answer their prayers for healing in an immediate and obvious way?

Amongst health care professionals, it is fashionable to find the answer by distinguishing between a person's spiritual needs and their religious needs. 'Spirituality is common to all, and that is not always synonymous with religion' (Gordon, 1997). 'Spirituality is often viewed as being synonymous with religion and a belief in God. Yet to adopt such a narrow definition is to exclude a multitude of people – atheist, agnostic, humanist – who may not share such beliefs but who nevertheless have a spirituality which is real' (McSherry, 1996). 'Perhaps it may help to see spirituality as a search for meaning, and religion as a particular expression of that' (Peberdy, 1993). Most people sum it up quite simply in the frequently used words, 'I don't have to go to church to be a good Christian!'

Helping another human being to cope with reality should be the aim of each person and the end result of both personal spirituality and religion, until 'enjoying relationships becomes more important than owning things, communication more satisfying than wealth, contemplation more relevant than accumulation' (Gordon, 1997). The majority of people in the community, in hospital or in residential care will be those who say 'I'm not very religious, but ....' In what follows, there lie those 'insights from elders' which inspired this book, and which are now explored further.

Send for Evelyn

'Send for Evelyn' was the regular cry whenever anyone was ill or dying in the family. Evelyn was a mother and a state registered nurse. When she set off to nurse an ailing relative, she took her young son with her, so that he acquired, without even realizing it, a familiarity with illness, dying and death, which remained of inestimable value in adult life, both personally and professionally. Such familiarity is now rare. There are many who reach middle age without ever having sat with the dying or seen a dead body. All too sadly, their first real contact with death may be when they lose a partner, which, nowadays, can often precede the death of a parent. Children who might have been able to visit a dying grandparent and take part in the funeral surrounded by other grieving friends and relatives, and thus sense that death is both momentous and yet normal, are unwisely protected from this experience of real life, while being allowed to watch all manner of violence and death on television. The child who grows up in a family where the elderly are cared for at home, or frequently visited while in care, will unknowingly absorb the assumption that the old are given respect, care and affection, while in return they willingly give their time to sharing their story and life experiences. Even if these become repetitive and tiresome, they do impart a sense of history and belonging to the youngest generation. As they say such things as 'I've had a wonderful life, but I'm tired now. I do wish the Good Lord would take me. I'm ready to go', so they create an atmosphere of trustful looking forward without any trace of fear, tinged only with the natural sadness of saying good-bye. This is a far better preparation for life and for death than the modern attitude which regards death as unmentionable and any proximity to it as something from which people need to be protected.

In the excellent series of publications by Counsel and Care, Rabbi Julia Neuberger (1996) complains that she did not see a dead body until she was well into her twenties. 'It is not talked about in any way, its inevitability, its desirability, and, most importantly, its meaning.' Whereas, 'older people often think, and when allowed to..., talk about death. They have usually seen more of it at first hand as contemporaries have passed away.... Their talking and thinking often yields wisdom the young would be wise to heed.' (Smith, 1996. See also Kübler-Ross, 1970).

The young child who crept into the bedroom where his great, great, great aunt lay dying with a jar of sweets beside her and tried to steal one, only to flee in guilty terror as she screamed out, learned an early lesson which he has never forgotten. The dying can often hear and understand even when they appear to be unconscious or cannot respond. Similarly, the child who went to sleep in his grandmother's room and was surprised to wake up in a large double bed between parents who had obviously been crying, discovered that it was all right for grown men to cry and that, at such times, all those who are left need warmth and togetherness. On another occasion, a young boy was allowed to carry the cross which led his grandfather's coffin into church. Being involved, being given a task, being allowed to cry together at these earlier experiences of death is a much better and much kinder preparation for life's later blows when one might have to face the death of a child or a partner. 'A caring family in which it is good to live and good to die' is the best possible preparation for an event 'which is not the end, nor merely a beginning, but the most important transition any of us will be asked to make' (Jewell, 1996 Pastoral Director, Methodist Homes for the Aged). People who have not been allowed to experience these perfectly normal events of human life will not feel comfortable within themselves when faced with a dying person whom they cannot avoid, and sad to say, they will be very poorly equipped to help the person who is dying to feel comfortable, cherished or understood.

'I do wish the Good Lord would take me'

Every doctor, nurse, minister of religion or carer will be familiar with this wish. It is usually a sincere expression of a person's willingness to let go of this life in a positive way, having achieved their purposes. It is usually accompanied by a sense of weariness, not of life itself, but of the effort to keep going. It is seldom accompanied by any fear of death, but naturally with some apprehension about being alone, or losing control and dignity. Very few people ask the direct question 'Am I dying?' Those who are dying, usually know. When such a wish to go is expressed, it should never be breezily dismissed with a cheery: 'Now, we don't want to think like that, Mother, you'll be up and running about this time next week'. How much better to acknowledge the remark by simply saying 'Yes, I'm sure you do. What do you look forward to most of all?' Most will then go on to talk about a wish to see loved ones again. Even if the listener has no belief in the after-life, he would not be insincere if he replied 'wouldn't that be lovely, what would you talk about?' In such simple ways as these, patients feel affirmed in their wishes and know that it is 'safe' to talk about such things. All who are involved in care of the elderly should read Charles Causley's poems 'Ward 14' and 'Ten types of hospital visitor' (Causley, 1992).

Relatives are often far less at ease with the concept of death than the elderly person. Chaplains are all too familiar with situations where they have befriended relatives in the corridors or waiting rooms over several days, but when they ask gently 'Would you like me to visit your mother?', there comes the firm reply 'Oh, no, we don't want her frightened'. It is, of course, the relatives who are frightened and are, perhaps unknowingly, infecting the one they love most with a sense of fear, whereas an unspoken assumption that things are as they are, can help all to accept the reality of the situation. Keeping up a pretence is exhausting for everyone, especially the patient, and puts up a barrier between people when they are most needing to be close and warm and open to one another.

The medical profession and the Churches must accept some blame for having encouraged such fears in the past. The vicar who began his visit to a parishioner in a nursing home with the question 'Are you prepared to meet your Maker?' only succeeded in startling the lady who promptly rang for Matron to enquire if there was something she had not been told. Later she confided 'I am quite prepared to meet my Maker but it was a bit of a shock to be asked that when we were hardly acquainted'.

Julia Neuberger (1996) emphasizes that the wish to die at peace with oneself is something people talk about as their most cherished hope, but that staff who have not been trained to do otherwise regard it as their duty to avert death rather than welcome it, while making the patient comfortable in the process.

> 'It is difficult to transform a whole culture of embedded reticence. It is hard enough to make a deliberate speech reform: to reform a silence is a tall order. Is it possible to bring into the open topics which persons prefer to keep silent?' (Douglas 1995 quoted by Neuberger p 24).

Neuberger continues

> 'Over 70% of people die in institutions ... we have witnessed a shift in authority and control over death from family and neighbours towards medical personnel, funeral directors and local authorities .... One consequence of medical advance is that the dying process can be far longer and more drawn-out. The energies of relatives are drained by the demands of care and lack of control over the process –. Today the notion of control is critical in the concept of a 'good' death.
>
> Yet the process of dying can itself be a very life-enhancing experience, though it often is nothing of the kind, bringing with it tenderness, love, and in many cases some kind of spirituality. If we are to work on the idea that dying can be life enhancing, then we have, older and younger people together, to work at the idea of dying well, and think what it means for the way we live'. (Neuberger, 1996 p 8)

'Then the old devil went and died on me!'

It was said in the tone of someone whose husband had gone off with another woman. She was really cross. When asked to explain what had happened, she replied 'Well, it was like this: we had our Sunday lunch and Bert took his fork and spade and went down the garden as usual. Then after a while, he came back in and said he had come over queer. I said, "You go straight upstairs and lie down and I'll bring you up a nice cup of tea". I made him a nice cup of tea and took it upstairs and blow me, the old devil had gone and died on me.'

Anger in the face of bereavement is a perfectly natural and healthy reaction and is only to be expected. It usually comes after the initial stages of denial and shock, but it can be instant as many doctors and nurses know. To be told: 'you are no flaming good' after having genuinely done one's best for the departed is hurtful. To be told forcibly: 'go away and *don't* talk to me about God', having been called to administer the Last

Rites, might seem offensive or blasphemous. But no offence is intended. The abuse is not personal: it comes from the immediate stab of pain felt by the bereaved, and it is not really addressed to a person but to the situation. The experienced carer realizes this, absorbs the initial onslaught and stays around to be with the bereaved when they come to themselves and are full of apologies. 'I'm sorry, Vicar, I don't know what came over me.' The priest does. It is the basic human reaction to an attack on all that is held most dear. A true story which illustrates this perfectly is told by Robert Llewelyn (1982) in his book, *With Pity, not with Blame*. It concerns a young father whose little girl had been very ill in hospital. One day, the news is much better and on his way he buys her a large chocolate cake. On his arrival he is met by the Ward Sister who breaks the news that there has been a sudden relapse and his daughter has died. The father turned on his heel, went straight to the chapel where he had so often prayed for his child, and threw the chocolate cake at the crucifix above the altar. Bereavement groups and student nurses are sometimes shocked at such uninhibited expression of anger, but anyone acquainted with the Psalms and the Book of Job will know that the prayer of anger is a valid prayer. Who has not winced at 'blessed be he that taketh thy children and dasheth them against the stones' (Psalm 137.9)? The God who absorbed such raw and primitive instincts in the Old Testament is the same God who placed himself upon the cross in the New Testament for the very purpose of taking all that might be thrown at him. Chocolate cake does not hurt anything like as much as the cruel nails nor as much as the death of a child.

The image of gentle Jesus meek and mild has done great disservice to those who need a religion which can cope with the darkest emotions and most despairing situations that it is possible for people to suffer. Properly understood, which it will be if properly taught, Christianity is one of the few religions that exists to accept and eventually transfigure pain, loss, failure, shame, sin and guilt, not by denouncing them but by absorbing them. The young father in the story expressed a valid prayer which signified a real, if stormy, relationship with God. Those who all too glibly talk about such things as 'being God's will' might feel that they are being more religious. They are in fact depicting an understanding of God which cannot satisfy a human being's deepest needs.

The person who is able to or allowed to express the normal stages of grief will eventually come quite naturally to the final stage of acceptance. Those who are unable to express grief at the appropriate time can often suffer serious physical or mental illness later on. 'Rose' held up wonderfully when her truck driver son had a heart attack and died in mid-life. Neighbours marvelled at the good ham tea she laid on after the funeral. 'Worked hard all her life, and still working', they said with approbation. On the anniversary of his death, she took to her bed and died within the week. The shock which had not been able to come out, had gone in, with fatal results.

Many an older woman has told, with tears in her eyes, 'the last thing I remember about my (stillborn) baby is seeing the midwife wrap him up and take him away. Can you find out what happened to him?' Very often the priest can. The local cemetery has records of stillbirth burials. The accepted wisdom of the time was that if a mother did not see her dead child, she would not love it or miss it so much. Kindly meant, it was unwittingly cruel. Nowadays, parents who lose a child through miscarriage, termination or stillbirth are asked about their wishes. Where appropriate, the child is held in its parents' arms, photographs and hand prints can be taken, and a suitable funeral or memorial service arranged according to their wishes. These choices were not offered to many women who now want to tie up these loose ends before they themselves go to join the child they never knew. Even in old age, a simple service, with the lighting of candles, and bereavement cards and an entry in the Book of Remembrance can help to ease the deep-down pain and anger which was not addressed at the time.

'Is it a sin?'

As the chaplain came on to a ladies' surgical ward, there was all the hubbub of visiting time, husbands, children, bunches of flowers, baskets of fruit, far too many visitors staying for far too long! Then, out of the corner of his eye, he saw her sitting all alone and looking quite blank; the one patient with no visitors. Kneeling down beside her, he made the usual remarks to engage in conversation, but with no apparent response; she still stared blankly ahead. Wondering what tactic to use next, he was hit between the eyes by the direct question: 'Is it a sin to commit suicide?' He responded with the usual questions: 'are you in a lot of pain?' 'No.' 'Have the doctors given you some bad news?' 'No.' Wondering what to say next, the patient delivered her next blow; 'well, come along, you haven't answered my question!' He knew he had not! Making up his theology on the hoof, he replied boldly, 'it won't hurt God if you commit suicide, but it will hurt your family. Is that what you want to do?' The subsequent conversation made it abundantly clear that that was precisely what she wanted to do. Why should an apparently mild old lady want to think about suicide when she was not terminally ill, was not in pain, and was not suffering from clinical depression? It turned out that she was in pain but the pain was in her heart, the pain of exclusion. There was trouble in the family. One daughter was going through a divorce but had not confided in her mother. The daughter had probably felt that she could not trouble her mother while she was ill, but the old lady thought that if people were not telling her the truth, if her daughter could no longer confide in her or seek her comfort and advice, then she might as well be out of it altogether. She was no more use as a mother. It is in such ways that genuine misunderstandings can lead to unnecessary distress.

Anxious relatives sometimes say, 'surely they can do something? You wouldn't let an animal suffer like that'. There is truth in that. While the human spirit is surprisingly noble in adversity, the suffering of unnecessary pain over long periods of time is exhausting and degrading. The wisest doctors bring in the pain-control specialist or refer their patient to the palliative care team. If they do not do so, the patient or the relatives should persist in asking for a referral. If this were done as a matter of course, there would be fewer requests for carers to 'do something' and less discussion about euthanasia. There will, however, be those who calmly and rationally decide for themselves that enough is enough. Two instances come to mind where highly intelligent women of deep religious conviction prepared themselves to leave this life and place themselves in the hands of God, past all taking back. Both were regular communicants, neither of them ever mentioned the subject, and certainly neither of them had lost their faith. It was only some time afterwards that the nature of their death was revealed and it did not appear sinful. Far from being acts of despair and rebellion against God, which has been the traditional teaching of the Church, these women had used their God given powers of reason and their spiritual training to make what was, for them, their greatest act of faith in a loving God. Their trust was surely not misplaced.

While there is much debate about euthanasia in medical and religious circles, there is little discussion about suicide. The 1998 NHS Green Paper, Our Healthier Nation, lists suicide with cancer, heart disease and accidents as one of the four areas targeted in the hope that suicide rates can be reduced by one sixth by the year 2010.

As recently as 1961 a person could be imprisoned for attempting suicide. The rulings forbidding burial in consecrated ground and demanding the forfeiture of the suicide's goods were not relaxed until near the end of the last century (Hinton, 1967). This stern attitude stems from the Church's interpretation of the Commandment 'Thou shalt not kill' (Exodus 20.13) and the fact that the best known suicide in the Bible is Judas the betrayer (Matthew 26.25).

It is now almost routine for the coroner to add the words 'while the balance of the mind was disturbed'. This verdict eases the way and consoles the relatives but it is hardly helpful for those who are of sound mind and yet still choose how and when to die. Nevertheless the Church has interpreted the biblical prohibition to allow for judicial killing and for the 'just war'.

Durkheim (1897) wrote of the concept of altruistic suicide, and gave as an example the captain going down with his ship. The Japanese kamikaze pilot (Inoguchi, 1959) wrote in his diary of the rigorous training and practice being worthwhile 'if we can die beautifully and for a cause'. Jesus's own words 'greater love than this hath no man, than that he lay down his life for his friends' (John 15.13) still move the heart at each Remembrance Day. Christianity has exalted the martyr and taught self-sacrifice but is confused and uncertain about suicide. Since 'suicidal thoughts are far from rare following bereavement, and, not infrequently, suicide does take place' (Hinton, 1967), it is clear that further research and theological exploration is required.

A personal view is that planning our departure from this life should be as morally neutral as planning to bring a life into the world. The consequence of taking one's own life, just like the consequence of begetting a life, will have far reaching effects which could be for either good or ill. Is society prepared to let each individual accept this responsibility?

Living Wills or Advance Statements/Directives have nothing to do with euthanasia or with assisted suicide, but are valuable tools which enable people to ensure that their wishes are known with regard to the treatment they would want in certain circumstances, and in specifying those circumstances in which they would not want to receive invasive surgery, resuscitation, or prolonged feeding when life had ceased to be something which could be lived. It goes without saying that such Living Wills or Advance Statements/Directives need to be drawn up with the help of an independent adviser, while one is in sound mind and in reasonable health (Morgan, 1995).

'Scratch my feet'

'Scratch my feet', said the dying man as he lay naked upon his bed. The chaplain had had the privilege of building up a relationship over many months with a particular patient who was 'not very religious, but ...' They shared an equally perverse sense of humour, so would sometimes talk, sometimes hardly say anything. If the chemotherapy was at a very bad stage he would swear at his spiritual guide to tell him forcibly to go away. Every Sunday, while he was in hospital, Holy Communion was shared. Now he had gone home to die.

Before Jesus shared The Last Supper with his disciples, he had girded himself with a towel and knelt to wash the disciples' feet and wipe them with the towel he was wearing. No washing of feet at the Maundy Thursday Liturgy ever meant more than fulfilling that simple mundane task requested by someone who was to die the next day. The chaplain had come prepared with Pyx, Holy Oil and Purple Stole ready to administer the Last Rites, but in this instance he found himself grateful, once again, for a patient who brought him down to reality. Fortunately, in the months before, there had been time to make the necessary spiritual and business arrangements. A broken marriage had been repaired, and particular interest taken in making a new will to give maximum benefit to his family by taking full advantage of all possible tax allowances. The zest for this task gave him the will to live for an extra month! So when the end came there was a sense of accomplishment rather than defeat. Business, personal, religious and spiritual needs had been met along the way; now it was time for the physical to take over – 'Scratch my feet, will you?'

In an incarnational religion the physical becomes sacramental, so the carer who gives the injection, cleans the mouth, wipes the bottom with sensitivity and an empathy for the patient's feelings, as well as with professional and hygienic expertise, is ministering to the Body of Christ, whether he or she realizes it or not.

One retired nursing sister in her nineties had been enormously distressed at soiling her bed, a common enough occurrence after bowel surgery. A task which she had done countless times for others seemed unbearable when required for herself. Later, when she had recovered, she was able to confide: 'Father, you know how distressed I was in hospital! Well, a wonderful thing has happened. During my meditation God showed me that Jesus must have been incontinent upon the cross. I've checked it up in a reference book and it's true. It's the inevitable consequence of death by crucifixion. If he accepted it, I must too, mustn't I?'

These two examples show how very different people were able to come to terms with some of the indignities people dread, and how they were able to bring into their situation an element of control, when losing control was what they feared most of all. It was relatively easy to minister to patients such as these because all along, there had been openness and honesty. Family and friends, doctors and nurses, had worked together with the patient, thus giving the person proper autonomy. 'The dying person does also have responsibilities as well as rights. ...Reasonable people do not take their leave (or emigrate) without preparation.' 'The patient needs to know that somebody is still cool, calm and collected and can take control if necessary.' (Webster, 1996). It is at this point that the chaplain is sent for. The patient is dying, medical staff have done all that can be done, and the family feel helpless and frightened in the face of a situation which is totally new to them. Far from frightening the patient, the presence of a chaplain can bring unrealized peace to fraught family members. It is not so much a matter of what the chaplain says or does, but the fact that he or she is there with them, is familiar with what is happening and not in any way afraid, anxious or pressing. The simple question 'Would you like me to give him a blessing?' is always answered in the affirmative and opens the way to prayers at the bedside in a more natural way than the all too clerical 'Shall we pray?' A tangible calm can be bestowed on the patient, family and nursing staff by simply recalling Christ's promise to be present whenever two or three are gathered in His Name, by saying the 23rd psalm and inviting the family to join in the Our Father, by repeating Christ's words 'Well done thou good and faithful servant, enter thou into the joy of thy Lord' or 'I promise you this, to-day you will be with me in paradise' 'I go to prepare a place for you ... and I will come again to receive you unto myself, so that where I am there may you be also'. After such prayers, it is not uncommon for the patient to die peacefully within a few minutes as if he or she had been waiting for their Nunc Dimittis, the permission to let go. The experienced chaplain has long ago committed such texts to memory so as to be able to respond spontaneously without needing to seek out Prayer Books and Bibles.

'Living dangerously'

'Living dangerously' is not the first description which comes to mind when thinking about life in residential care! But it was the phrase used by an enlightened manager of a local authority home for the elderly long before this approach became accepted. The resident under discussion was a widower who was used to going to the local for a pint or two each evening. Some of the older staff tried to dissuade him. 'Now you are living here, don't go out after dark. It's not safe.' '!!!' 'Now, now, Mr Smith, no need for bad language.' But why should Mr Smith lose his social life, having lost his wife and home? Fortunately the new manager had a different approach. 'There is only one rule in this house: we all change our underwear every day.' The house smelt sweeter and the residents began to live dangerously. It was to this home that a close neighbour came to live at 99 years of age, having spent a lifetime caring for her parents, brothers and sisters, as each in turn took to bed and eventually died. At 99 she was at last free to live her own life, and how she enjoyed it! For her 100th birthday, the home put on a party which outdid many a wedding reception. When the young reporter from the local paper asked if she would share her recipe for longevity with his readers, she replied mischievously: 'I think it must be due to never having had sex.'

Some residents would like to make love. It was always sad when a married couple had to kiss good night on the landing and then go off to different ends of the building because there was no provision for double rooms.

A blind theological student was sent on placement to a parish which had 500 places for elderly people within ten minutes walk of the parish church. Some were in the McCarthy & Stone range of retirement flats, some charitable trusts, some local authority and the rest private nursing homes. He was a mature student and wished to specialize in work with the elderly. His first assignment was to spend the morning at a local authority home. When he returned to the vicarage at lunch time, he was asked how he had got on; he replied 'Oh, I've had a great time!' 'Really?' asked the surprised vicar. 'Oh, yes, they told me all about their love life. It's being blind, you see they feel safe with me.' That was an important lesson. They felt safe with him. They could see that he did not, as yet, have a dog collar around his neck, and sensing that he could not easily identify them again, they felt confident enough to speak honestly.

Among the publications issued by Counsel and Care, the one entitled The Fullness of Time (Regan and Smith, 1997) gives examples of good practice discovered during the study of 14 residential homes, local authority, Roman Catholic, Jewish, Protestant, and secular in different part of the UK. In his Foreword, Lord Coggan writes:

> 'The aim of those who run the Homes of our country, and of those who live in those Homes, must be the full development of the person.'

The report asks what help residents should expect if they want to go to a concert, attend church or visit old friends. Significantly, many were experiencing and achieving much more than people would have thought they were capable of. 'Caring for older people is a much more difficult and resource intensive task than our society generally acknowledges.'

The Department of Health report, Homes Are For Living In (1989), lists six rights: privacy, dignity, independence, civil rights, choice, fulfilment and security. Autonomy might be a better concept than independence. Interestingly, it was a Church Army home which included 'the right to have your sexual and emotional needs accepted and respected'.

'92 percent of residential homes have at least an occasional religious service' (Myers, 1989) but sadly 'many in-house services are pretty poor affairs with ill-prepared clergy, no proper music and little or no staff support'. Some clergy are too busy to commit themselves to a regular visit. This robs the residents of the regularity which characterizes much religious observance. In an unpublished report (Butler, 1996) forty residents in Methodist Homes for the Aged were asked about the religious services provided. Over half said they were only 'quite helpful' or that their value depended on the person leading them. There is no excuse for irregularity, unpreparedness or shoddiness. Volunteers can usually be found, sometimes amongst the residents, to play a keyboard, provide flowers, support the singing, give a hand with finding hymns, presented in large print, prepare a table with clean cloth, candles and cross. Liturgy has its advantages since the familiarity of prayers, hymns and responses reaches even those with severely failing memories. This was borne out at worship in the chapel of an old-fashioned psychiatric hospital. Patients who, outwardly took no part in the service except by turning up voluntarily week by week, would rise unprompted and come forward to receive Holy Communion with devotion in their eyes when the priest gave the familiar bidding 'Behold the Lamb of God ... draw near with faith ...'

Far too often one hears the sad comment, 'I've gone to church all my life but now that I can't get out any more the vicar never comes to visit me.' The rural vicar might have seven parishes, but the total population may be less than two thousand, and church members fewer than a hundred and fifty in total. It is obvious that the clergy need extra training in this respect if the increasing numbers of housebound former worshippers are going to be allowed to continue to develop as part of the worship-ping community. Some useful guidelines can be obtained from the Christian Council on Ageing (Butler, 1996).

'I hate it, I hate it, I hate it'

This was the anguished cry of a priest discussing worship for the aged. Many clergy have felt the same at the prospect of yet another service in a day room. There is the embarrassment of switching off the television when some would prefer the current soap opera to a service; the effort to be heard above the noises from the kitchen or the cleaners; the interruptions from staff, residents and visitors; the near impossibility of creating an atmosphere of worship. All these add up to the feelings of uselessness and inadequacy which are, of course, the precise components of the cross which that particular congregation has to carry. How can the weight of that cross be eased for the participants as well as for the clergy?

There is a hint towards the answer in The Fullness of Time (Regan and Smith, 1997): 'We emphatically do not wish to suggest that people suffering from any degree of dementia are incapable of experience at the deepest level or lacking in spirituality – but it takes time.' It not only takes time, it takes training, and until recently none was available. The outlook is now changing. During 1998 the College of Health Care Chaplains dedicated its annual Mental Health Conference to the subject, with signifi-cant papers on 'Ways of meeting the spiritual needs of people with dementia' (Moffitt, 1996) and 'The spirituality of the dying' (Stanworth, 1998). In September 1998 the Christian Council on Ageing and Methodist Homes launched the Age Awareness Project. Their resources include a seminal book, *Spirituality and Ageing* (Jewell, 1999), ten practical booklets for churches and community groups, and a training module for ministers and clergy. With training there will come the confidence to plan and conduct appropriate worship in consultation with the worshippers and their carers. 'The dementia sufferer needs The Other for personhood to be maintained' (Kitwood and Bredin, 1992).

This chapter has not dwelt on the need for reticence in religious matters and for sensitivity towards the consciences of agnostics, humanists and atheists. Dennis Potter's parody of a service on the wards in *The Singing Detective* should prevent us from inflicting religion on those who do not want it. A straightforward apology to those who are unable to leave the room usually earns a tolerant reply: 'you carry on, dear, if it helps you'. Members of other faiths may feel doubly isolated if they are ignored or not asked what they would like to observe. In schools, provision is being made for multicultural celebrations to be acknowledged. It will take some years yet before the same happens in residential homes.

References

Butler M (1996) Worship in Residential Care. Derby: Christian Council on Ageing.

Causley C (1992) Collected Poems. London: Macmillan.

Department of Health (1989) Homes Are For Living In. London: HMSO.

Douglas M (1995) Cited in Neuberger (1996).

Durkheim E (1897) Suicide: a study in sociology translated by JA Spaulding and G Simpson (ed) (1952): London: Routledge & Kegan Paul.

Gordon T (1997) Clearing the dark corners of the mental attic. Professional Social Work, January 1997. pp. 10–11.

Hinton J (1967) Dying. London: Penguin.

Inoguchi R (1959) The Divine Wind: Japan's Kamikaze Force In World War II. London: Hutchinson.

Jewell A (1996) In: J Neuberger (ed) The End or Merely the Beginning. London: Counsel and Care.

Jewell A (1999) Spirituality and Ageing. London: Jessica Kingsley.

Kitwood T and Bredin K (1992) Towards a theory of dementia care, personhood and wellbeing. Ageing and Society. Journal of British Society of Gerontology, 12, pp. 269–287.

Kübler-Ross E (1970) On Death and Dying, p. 6. London: Tavistock.

Llewelyn R (1982) With Pity, not with Blame. London: DLT.

McSherry W (1996) Raising the spirits. Nursing Times, 92 (3) p. 48.

Moffitt L (1996) Helping to recreate a personal sacred space. Journal of Dementia Care, 4(3) pp. 19–21.

Morgan D (ed.) (1995) Advance Statements about Medical Treatment. London: BMA.

Myers B (1989) Religious Services in Retirement Homes. London: Marc Europe.

Neuberger J (1996) The End or Merely the Beginning. London: Counsel and Care.

NHS (1998) Our Healthier Nation. Green Paper, Cm 3852. London: The Stationery Office.

Peberdy A (1993) Spiritual care of dying people. In: D Dickenson and M Johnson (eds) Death, Dying and Bereavement pp. 219–223. London: Sage.

Regan D and Smith J (1997) The Fullness of Time. London: Counsel and Care.

Smith J (1996) Introduction. In: J Neuberger (ed) The End or Merely the Beginning. London: Counsel and Care.

Stanworth R (1998) The spirituality of the dying. Paper delivered at the College of Health Care Chaplains Conference, Bawtry Hall 1998.

Webster S (1996) Breaking Bad News. In: J Neuberger (ed) The End or Merely the Beginning. London: Counsel and Care.

Williams M (1922) The Velveteen Rabbit. London: Heinemann.

Index